THE MALE BODY AT WAR

THE MALE BODY
AT WAR

American Masculinity during World War II

Christina S. Jarvis

NORTHERN

ILLINOIS

UNIVERSITY

PRESS

DeKalb

© 2004, 2010 by Northern Illinois University Press

Published by the Northern Illinois University Press, DeKalb, Illinois   60115

1st printing in paperback, 2010

ISBN: 978-0-87580-638-9 (paperback : alk. paper)

All Rights Reserved

Design by Julia Fauci

Library of Congress Cataloging-in-Publication Data

Jarvis, Christina S.

The male body at war : American masculinity during World War II / Christina S. Jarvis

    p.   cm.

Includes bibliographical references and index.

ISBN 0-87580-322-9 (alk. paper)

1. Men—United States—History—20th century. 2. Masculinity—United States—

History—20th century. 3. Men in popular culture—United States—History—

20th century. 4. War and society—United States—History—20th century. 5. World War,

1939–1945—Social aspects—United States. 6. Body, Human—Social aspects—United

States. I. Title.

HQ1090.3 .J368 2004

305.31'0973'0904 22

2003061040

For Tom and Christopher, with love and appreciation

CONTENTS

LIST OF FIGURES

ACKNOWLEDGMENTS

While researching and writing this book I was fortunate to receive support from many individuals and institutions. At Penn State University, where I completed the dissertation on which this book is based, the English Department, the Research and Graduate Studies Office, and the Institute for Arts and Humanistic Studies provided me with generous research and travel grants. I also benefited enormously from an American Association of University Women dissertation fellowship, which offered me a year of uninterrupted writing time at a crucial stage of the project. Various administrators and programs at SUNY Fredonia have likewise contributed financially to this study, and I am grateful to Paul Schwartz, Dean of Arts and Humanities, and Maggie Bryan-Peterson, Director of Grants Administration, for underwriting my illustration and permission expenses. Tremendous thanks also go to Fredonia's Scholarly Incentives Program for providing me with release time and to the Mary Louise White Foundation for manuscript preparation support.

Many scholars, archivists, and individuals were helpful while I was conducting my research, and I owe extraordinary debts to the following people and institutions: Professor Kurt Piehler and the Rutgers World War II Oral History Project; military history archivist Richard Boylan and the staff at the Still Picture Branch of the National Archives and Records Administration; Michael Rhode of the Otis Historical Archives at the National

Museum of Health and Medicine, Armed Forces Institute of Pathology; William Keough and Pamela Cheney at the U.S. Army Military History Institute; and Carol Leadenham of the Hoover Institution Archives. I am also greatly indebted to the 138 World War II veterans who participated in my survey; they not only gave me valuable firsthand insights into wartime gender roles and body-related issues but also broadened my understanding of the war's impact on American culture and memory.

Additional thanks go to the following companies, agencies, and archives that have graciously allowed me to reproduce their materials: Munich's Central Institute for Art History, E.W. Scripps Company, Fleischmann's Yeast, the Florida Department of Citrus, the General Services Administration, the Hoover Institution Archives, the Museum of the City of New York, the National Archives and Records Administration, Packard Motor Car Company, Revere Copper Products, Incorporated, and the Wichita Art Museum. I am also grateful to Donald Anderson, editor of *War, Literature, and the Arts: An International Journal of the Humanities* for permission to reprint brief excerpts from my essay "The Vietnamization of World War II in *Slaughterhouse-Five* and *Gravity's Rainbow*" in my conclusion.

This project has benefited greatly from the careful guidance and constructive suggestions of former professors and colleagues at both Penn State and SUNY Fredonia. First and foremost, Susan Squier deserves a special measure of gratitude for her constant encouragement, superb mentoring, and inspiration; I cannot imagine what this book or my career would have looked like without her generous and continuing support. My other committee members, Deborah Clarke, Susan Jeffords, Jeffrey Nealon, Londa Schiebinger, and Evan Watkins, likewise offered valuable suggestions and thought-provoking engagements with this study, and I would like to thank them for sharing their knowledge and wisdom with me. My dissertation group also read and commented on various chapters, and I am grateful to Lisa Roney, Holly Henry, Harvey Quamen, and Julie Vedder for their sage advice and enthusiasm. While I am indebted to all my wonderful colleagues in the English Department at SUNY Fredonia for their assistance and encouragement, particular thanks go to Karen Mills-Courts, Ted Steinberg, and Scott Johnston for their editing help and thoughtful suggestions, and to my department chairs, Joan Burke and James Shokoff, for their commitment to the project. Colleagues outside the English Department also contributed to this study in important ways: Joanne Foeller prepared the index; Elke Schneider assisted with translations; and Jan Conradi offered her design expertise and insights on war posters.

I am very grateful to Susan Bean and the staff at Northern Illinois University Press, who made the publication of this book possible. Special thanks goes to Martin Johnson for expressing an early interest in this project and for his invaluable suggestions for transforming the dissertation into a book manuscript. Kelly Parker was extremely helpful during the editing process. Two anonymous readers for NIU Press likewise offered astute readings and productive criticisms that assisted me tremendously in preparing the final draft. I also owe an enormous debt to the scholars whose work on war, gender, and the body enabled me to think about this book in the first place.

Finally, I wish to thank my family and friends, whose love and support extend well beyond the boundaries of this project. While it would be impossible to recount my numerous debts to my parents, Patricia and Joseph Jarvis, I would like to acknowledge some of their specific contributions to this book. They not only provided crucial financial, computer, editing, and research assistance along the way but also sparked my initial interests in American history and interdisciplinary work. In addition to their guidance with historical sources and comments on selected chapters, Michael and Anna Jarvis have consistently offered their wisdom and humor. For housing and feeding me during my many research trips to Maryland and Washington, D.C., and for their interest in all my scholarly endeavors, extraordinary thanks go to Sharon, Spencer, and Becky Annear. Danielle Conger and Althea Bernheim have contributed more than they will ever know toward the completion of this project, and I thank them for their friendship, encouragement, and intellectually and emotionally productive conversations. I am also grateful to friends and colleagues who have made Fredonia such a wonderful place to work and live, to my grandparents, Jessica and the late Emory Coleman, for sharing their memories of World War II, and to my son, Christopher, who has given my scholarship on war and gender new meaning. Last, first, and always, I thank Thomas Annear for his love and unflagging support of both me and my work. I literally could not have finished this book without his help.

LIST OF ABBREVIATIONS

ABMC	American Battle Monuments Commission
AGRS	American Graves Registration Service
ALMA	American Limb Manufacturers Association
ASHA	American Social Hygiene Association
BPR	Bureau of Public Relations
CCC	Civilian Conservation Corps
CWA	Civil Works Administration
FAP	Federal Art Project
FBI	Federal Bureau of Investigation
FSA	Federal Security Agency
GCT	General Classification Test
MAT	Mechanical Aptitude Test
MOS	Military Occupational Specialty
MP	Military Police
NARA	National Archives and Records Administration
NRC	National Research Council
ODHWS	Office of Defense Health and Welfare Service
OHA	Otis Historical Archives
OWI	Office of War Information
PWAP	Public Works of Art Project
RAF	Royal Air Force
RG	Record Group
SPD	Social Protection Division
SSN	Specification Serial Number
TRAP	Treasury Relief Art Program
USMHI	United States Military History Institute
USPHS	United States Public Health Service
VA	Veterans Administration
WAC	Women's Army Corps
WPA	Works Progress Administration
YMCA	Young Men's Christian Association

THE MALE BODY AT WAR

INTRODUCTION

On November 10, 1954, President Eisenhower, Vice President Nixon, and many of the country's highest-ranking military officials dedicated the U.S. Marine Corps War Memorial at the edge of Arlington National Cemetery. Based on Joe Rosenthal's famous 1945 photograph of the second flag raising at Iwo Jima, the sculpture captured the collective effort, triumph, and patriotism that the original image and its facsimiles for the 7th War Bonds tour embodied. As the dedication program explained, however, this time Felix de Weldon's towering bronze sculpture offered "heroic proportions, proportions which could do ample justice to the magnificence of the scene which had inspired it."[1] Standing 78 feet high and employing 32-feet-tall figures, the monument did indeed provide the epic dimensions that the memorial foundation members had desired. Yet de Weldon did not rely on scale alone to suggest the servicemen's heroism. Although based on careful clay models of the six men in Rosenthal's photo, the sculpture transformed the men's physiques, offering more visible muscles that bulge through their uniforms. The lead figure, for example, crouches in a more compact and forceful position as he plants the flagpole into the ground, emphasizing his biceps and highlighting the strength of his upper body. The straining neck muscles, more chiseled faces, and generally enhanced muscular features of the other figures conjure up the type of masculine toughness that John Wayne personified in the 1949 classic combat film *Sands of Iwo Jima.*

While preserving one of the epic moments of World War II, Rosenthal's photograph, the Marine Corps memorial, and films like Republic Pictures' *Sands of Iwo Jima* endured as symbols of American power and military might in the postwar imagination. The fact that American strength was represented in these heroic male figures also speaks to the belief that the United States had developed "a sense of itself as a *masculine* nation" in the wake of World War II (Faludi 16). Indeed, America had emerged from the war as an economic, technological, and military superpower and continued to act with "masculine" toughness, force, and confidence on the global stage. The flag-raising figures, along with other heroic representations of World War II servicemen, also offered American men a "template for postwar manhood" (Faludi 16)—a masculine ideal that continues to resonate in U.S. culture. Although icons of American masculinity have shifted and changed over the past six decades, World War II models and images of manhood remain strong in cultural memory. The image of marines on Mt. Suribachi, for example, continued to offer symbolic resonance as Americans compared Thomas Franklin's enormously popular September 11, 2001, photograph of three firemen raising the flag amidst the ruins of the World Trade Center to Rosenthal's famous image. While invoking ideas of courage and patriotism, the allusion to the 1945 flag raising also lent World War II heroism to another set of men in uniform and confirmed the power of that mid-twentieth-century masculine ideal.

From where exactly did this World War II masculine ideal emerge? Did it emanate from a U.S. and Allied victory during the war, or were there other driving cultural forces involved? How did we shift from the troubled representations of masculinity in depression-era America to the hypermasculinized images of the war and postwar period? Moreover, how were extreme wartime masculine ideals maintained in the face of hundreds of thousands of wounded and damaged masculinities? How exactly *was* masculinity represented during the war? And what role did actual male bodies play in the construction of wartime and postwar masculinities?

This study attempts to answer these questions by exploring the impact of the Second World War on American male bodies and cultural constructions of masculinity. While E. Anthony Rotundo has shown that definitions of American manhood have historically been linked to various ideals such as public usefulness, landownership, personal achievement, and competitiveness, since the late nineteenth century and the rise of the physical culture movement, the body itself has been important to definitions of masculinity. According to Rotundo, since the late nineteenth century the body has become "a vital component of manhood," as "strength, appearance, and athletic skill" have served as crucial ways of measuring masculinity (6). Because of the body's centrality to definitions of manhood, this study examines both symbolic representations of male bodies and the embodied experiences of American men during wartime. Ultimately, I argue that during World War II the American military, government, and other institutions shaped the male body both figuratively and physically in an effort to communicate impressions of national strength to U.S. citizens and to other nations. Over time, a powerful male "body politic" emerged, as federal, business, and military officials, as well as portions of the American populace, utilized powerful, hypermasculinized male bodies in public images to reflect the United States' rising status as a world power.

These wartime and postwar reconfigurations of masculinity simultaneously demanded the physical transformations of American male bodies—especially those of the 16 million men who served in the armed forces during the war. Although the diet, physical fitness, and overall health of American servicemen greatly improved during the war, the war's transformations of male bodies were not always positive or innocuous. Combat and training accidents maimed bodies in countless ways, producing hundreds of thousands of wounded bodies and masculinities in need of physical and psychological rehabilitation. Thousands more became corpses, often leading to an additional kind of national service, as those bodies were interred and honored in national and local forms of commemoration. Often, however, the war's impact on the male body was more subtle and various. In addition to being shot at, American male bodies were physically examined, classified, categorized, disciplined, clothed in particular uniforms, sexualized via venereal disease screenings, and subject to numerous other processes by the military and other institutions. Servicemen's bodies were racially marked by the military's Jim Crow policies, which segregated units and disproportionately assigned tasks on the basis of skin color. Moreover, representations of particular male bodies—young, well-muscled, white—were privileged as the U.S. symbolically rebuilt its body politic and prepared for war. Establishing the dominant model of American masculinity as white and able-bodied also helped create a range of alternate, marginalized masculinities that departed from this norm.

By combining a cultural studies approach with extensive archival research documenting representations of male bodies and servicemen's experiences, this volume attempts to create a broad (though certainly not complete) picture of personal and cultural narratives of male embodiment during and shortly after the Second World War. Because approximately two-thirds of American men aged 18 to 34 served in the armed forces during the war (Patterson 13), the chapters that follow focus primarily on servicemen's bodies and the cultural institutions that shaped them. Consideration of the war's impact on servicemen's bodies through training, wounding, and combat also compels us to see how the war shaped broader cultural discourses about body-related issues, gender roles, and national identity. Not only did physical inspections of American male bodies, for example, have important repercussions for the more than 16 million men who were classified, categorized, and sexualized via these military screenings, but the statistical data that emerged from these inspections also influenced plans for rating children's fitness, revamping physical education programs, monitoring the health of war workers, and strengthening the bodies of Americans on a national scale.

In adopting a cultural studies approach, this study necessarily incorporates a wide range of methods and materials. Popular cultural materials such as posters, novels, films, magazine articles, and advertisements provide insights into 1940s gender roles and symbolic uses of the male body. Private materials—soldiers' memoirs, letters, and interview statements—offer servicemen's perceptions of their own bodies, masculinity, and health. Reports, correspondence, brochures, and circulars among military and government documents reveal the military's "management" of male bodies, which took place through medical inspections, physical training programs, and screenings for venereal disease and potential homosexuality. Additionally, 138 responses from World War II veterans to a survey specifically tailored to this project provide further insights into servicemen's wartime health and body-related issues. These diverse sources combine with numerous secondary sources to establish a foundation, a type of cultural "grid," linking technoscientific documents and popular materials with other historical narratives, from which to explore American wartime embodiment and masculinities from multiple perspectives. In creating this cultural grid, I analyze mass-produced posters, periodicals with high wartime circulation such as *Life* (3.8 million), *Collier's* (2.8 million), and *Time* (1.1 million),[2] and best-selling war novels, as well as rarer visual images, more specialized journals, and non-canonical literature to explore a broad range of depictions of male bodies.

Although this study draws from many diverse fields, including body studies, American history, World War II scholarship, gender studies, art history, sociology, and film criticism, my selections and analysis of materials have been largely influenced by my own grounding in literary studies. Print sources are privileged over other popular culture subjects such as film and music in part because several excellent studies of these topics already exist[3] and because I have been trained to be a close reader of texts. As my bibliography suggests, I have crossed disciplinary boundaries throughout my research to consider the visual and experiential aspects of male embodiment as I construct narratives about wartime masculinity. Ultimately, however, my arguments and choice of particular topics have been shaped primarily by the sources themselves. Having begun this study with numerous questions and the decision to examine different types of bodies produced by war (i.e., wounded, dead, classified, etc.), specific topics emerged from my survey findings, which were refined during years of archival and secondary research. Many initial questions concerning the long-term impact of servicemen's wartime cigarette smoking, post-traumatic stress disorder, the acquisition of tattoos, and other topics, for example, remain uninvestigated because survey responses and other documents failed to yield adequate or interesting information. It is my hope that future scholarship will explore these topics as our understanding of the Second World War's impact on American male bodies grows.

Because the field of body studies has increasingly complicated the term "body" by investing it with multiple meanings and contexts, it is no longer safe to assume that the terms "body" and "male body" are self-evident. My approach to studying the body stems from (though is not necessarily limited to) what might be called a social constructionist or sociocultural position. Drawing on the later genealogical work of Michel Foucault and a long line of other body theorists, I view human bodies as historically and culturally located entities shaped not only by institutions such as schools, the military, and the media, but also by the fields that study them.[4] In short, bodies exist in complex fields of cultural discourses and practices, and to understand them, we need to examine the ways in which institutions enculturate bodies through the creation of regulatory medical and social norms as well as through disciplinary techniques. Whether we turn to nineteenth-century corrective corsets or to the modern phenomena of bodybuilding or plastic surgery, we can see that bodies have long been considered pliable entities, subject to correction to prevailing cultural norms. When I use the term "male body" then, I am not referring to a universal biological entity but rather to a body that has been culturally encoded as "male" through a complex process of social, personal, and medical gender construction.[5] This does not mean that anatomical elements such as genitalia, sex hormones, and facial hair do not play an important role in determining what counts as a male body; on the contrary, these body parts and substances are defining elements in medical and social constructions of gender. However, if we view the body historically and cross-culturally, we find that the male body is not reducible to any singular set of characteristics and that what constitutes maleness has changed over time.[6]

To say that the body is produced within specific historical and cultural contexts, however, is not to claim that the human body is a tabula rasa or neutral medium passively awaiting cultural inscription. Elizabeth Grosz cautions that "the specific modes of materiality of the 'page'/body must be taken into account" as we analyze these cultural messages: "one and the same message, inscribed on a male or female body, does not always or even usually mean the same thing or result in the same text" (156). Examinations of specific corporeal materialities and their bearings on cultural inscription, of course, are not just limited to sexual difference; a specific tattoo might have different meanings depending on whether it appears on an African American, Latino, or Irish American male. Likewise, the presence of facial makeup communicates different impressions when worn by a twenty-five-year-old woman or a six-year-old girl and might be further complicated by the ethnic, religious, or national background of the female. Thus while bodies are socially mediated and coded through language and discursive practices, they still possess unique physiological makeups and individual corporeal histories. For the purposes of this study, this means that as I examine the cultural institutions and wartime practices that shaped large numbers of American servicemen's bodies generally, I will also consider factors such as age, class, race, ethnicity, sexual preference, and physical ability that affected these processes in significant ways.

In telling the story of military male embodiment during World War II, this study necessarily draws on other histories and theories of American masculinity. Like many other gender scholars, I view gender identity as a fluid process, performatively constituted over time through repeated gestures, activities, and signs in relation to cultural ideals about "male" and "female" identities.[7] My particular approach to analyzing wartime models of manhood draws on R. W. Connell's idea that masculinities are defined both collectively and in terms of "relations of hierarchy" (*Men* 10).[8] As Connell explains, masculine identities not only take shape in individual lives but also are "defined collectively in culture, and are sustained in institutions" (*Men* 11). While these masculine identities are largely constructed in terms of cultural oppositions between "male" and "female," masculinities also are defined in relation to one another. According to Connell, a culturally dominant or "hegemonic" model of masculinity generally exists alongside "subordinated" and "marginalized" patterns of masculinity (*Men* 30). Although the characteristics of hegemonic masculinity change over time and are always culturally specific, in twentieth-century American culture hegemonic masculinity has generally been associated with the values and representations of white, Protestant, able-bodied, heterosexual men. Subordinated and marginalized masculinities, meanwhile, have frequently included gay masculinities and male identities "produced in exploited or oppressed groups such as ethnic minorities" (Connell, *Men* 30).

Placing the male body at the center of analysis, this book examines the creation and maintenance of a hegemonic militarized masculinity that emerged in and across U.S. institutions and that was articulated in relation to masculine constructions of the German and Japanese enemies and those of "native" others as America engaged in global war. In addition to analyzing masculine identities marginalized in terms of race, ethnicity, and sexual identity, I also explore specific wartime "abject" masculinities produced through wounding and death. These explorations, I hope, will help fill a critical gap in scholarship about American masculinity, which has left World War II masculinities largely unexamined. Important studies have focused on pre–World War II American masculinity in the early republic, in the late nineteenth century, in the Spanish-American War, and in turn-of-the-century "civilization" endeavors, and many others have examined the postwar period, analyzing gender and the Vietnam conflict, cold war rhetoric and manly ideals, post-1960s white male identities, and representations of male bodies in the 1980s and 1990s.[9] Even Michael Kimmel's comprehensive study *American Manhood* neglects World War II masculinity, offering chapters on manhood between the wars and postwar ideals without addressing the Second World War itself.

The following chapters offer several different views of the male body during World War II. Chapter one examines symbolic representations of American male bodies and the ways in which they were used to communicate messages about national identity during the war. Beginning with the depression era and early efforts to rebuild the American body politic, it chronicles the profound shift in the public images of male bodies that occurred as the United States mobilized for war. The second chapter investigates the physical effects that this mobilization precipitated by exploring the military classification and control of male bodies and the broader effects these processes had on certain aspects of American culture. Next, I analyze the multiple meanings generated by wounded bodies and particular types of wounds in popular wartime discourses. In addition to their obvious impact on the morale of persons fighting abroad and those working on the home front, representations of injured male bodies offered important sites for redefining and reinscribing cultural definitions of masculinity—especially as America sought to restabilize gender roles radically configured by the war. Focusing primarily on the Pacific theater, where the war took on more overtly racist dimensions, chapter four explores the intersections of wartime discourses of race and masculinity and the particular ways these intertwined discourses were played out on the body. While highlighting the ways that white U.S. masculinity was often defined in relation to foreign, racialized "others," I also consider particular shortcomings of America's pluralistic, ethnically diverse wartime self-representations. The final chapter examines representations of dead American male bodies and their effects—from the realities of the battlefront to the symbolic evocations in the media, civic ceremonies, and monuments. The study concludes with a brief meditation on the legacy of World War II models of masculinity and the forceful victory culture that the war produced.

As the United States maintains its position as an economic, military, and technological superpower and continues to wage foreign wars at the start of the twenty-first century, it seems crucial that we examine the gendered terms in which this form of American national identity was first constructed during and after World War II. I hope that this study will contribute to this understanding as well as remind us of war's corporeal costs and implications.

ONE — **BUILDING THE BODY POLITIC**

FROM THE DEPRESSION TO WORLD WAR II

Muscles will win this war.

—Charles Atlas, qtd. in

Yank, June 6, 1942

Of the countless possible pairings of Great Depression and World War II images of the male body, perhaps none is as striking as Will Barnet's Federal Art Project (FAP) lithograph "Idle Hands" (fig. 1) and McClelland Barclay's navy recruitment poster "Man the Guns" (fig. 2). Produced a mere six years apart, the two images of American masculinity represent remarkably different though closely linked eras. Barnet's print depicts an unemployed man, hunched over with his head resting on his arms. The title, coupled with Barnet's careful shading and strong lines, forces the viewer to gaze at the worker's sinewy, elongated hands. Like many of Barnet's other FAP pieces, "Idle Hands" calls attention to the general despair of the depression as well as to the particular crisis in masculinity that the 1930s precipitated. With approximately one-quarter of the male workforce unemployed and millions of others reduced to part-time and federal relief work, the depression created millions of idle hands and raised numerous doubts about manhood in America. As masculinity studies scholar Michael Kimmel notes, "Never before had American men experienced such a massive and system-wide shock to their ability to prove manhood by providing for their families" (*Manhood* 192). Indeed, the male body in "Idle Hands" provides a fitting representation of masculinity in a nation crippled by the depression.

The Barclay poster, by contrast, offers a picture of American masculinity newly retooled for the United States' entry into World War II. The serviceman has replaced the worker as a key symbol of masculinity, and the strength, activity, and purposefulness of the figure in Barclay's image embody the characteristics of a nation involved in full-scale mobilization. The man's hands are no longer idle; instead, they hold a six-inch shell for the main gun on a destroyer. While the left hand grasps the end of the shell, the right arm cradles the tip, leaving the right hand free to create a clenched fist. The fist, like the rest of the sailor's muscled physique, suggests strength and power. But the man is no mere model in a 1940s muscle magazine; the forceful diagonal lines in the image emphasize that he is engaged in heroic activity, that he is doing his part to win the war. Unlike his depression counterpart, the sailor's manhood is not in question. As if the man's muscular upper body and his possession of the phallic shell were not enough, Barclay reminds us of his subject's unquestionable masculinity by placing the word "Man" in bold, red letters in the center of the poster. In Barclay's poster, a transformed symbolic male body emerges, suggesting that the process of shoring up damaged models of masculinity from the depression was at last fully under way.

Two poles in a wide spectrum of depression- and World War II–era images, the Barnet and Barclay pictures offer a glimpse into the symbolic transformation of male bodies that accompanied the very real rebuilding of American bodies, the armed forces, and the economy that occurred as the United States emerged from the depression and mobilized for war. Although several New Deal programs took important steps to reconstruct images of masculinity and to strengthen Americans' confidence in their nation during the depression itself, they did not produce the coherent and strongly gendered body politic that the rapid, full-scale mobilization of the war demanded. Militarily, the United States was ill prepared for its entry into war on December 8, 1941.[1] Having scrapped close to a million tons of warships as part of 1922 Washington Naval Armament Conference agreements, America failed to maintain even a "treaty strength" fleet and during the 1930s kept on average fewer than 100,000 men in the navy and just over 135,000 soldiers in the army (Dear 1177). As late as 1940, the army had only 269,023 men, the navy 160,997, and the marines a mere 28,345 (Dear 1177). These numbers were well below the anticipated force of 12 million men that the United States needed to engage in a global war, and despite the peacetime draft implemented in September 1940, the American military found itself short by more than 10.5 million men. In order to mobilize the necessary manpower and flex U.S. muscles abroad, it was crucial to reconstruct public images of masculinity on a national scale. While various New Deal programs such as the Civilian Conservation Corps (CCC) and the Works Progress Administration (WPA) offered some heroic images of male workers, a more sustained national imaging campaign was needed to help transform millions of still unemployed men and their thin physiques

1—Will Barnet's 1936 lithograph "Idle Hands" captures the despair millions of American men experienced when they lost their jobs and status as breadwinners during the depression. (Museum Purchase, Director's Discretionary Fund, Friends of the Wichita Art Museum, Inc., Wichita Art Museum, Wichita, Kansas)

2—The muscular sailor in McClelland Barclay's 1942 navy recruitment poster is one of many representations of powerful male bodies used to communicate impressions of national strength during the war. (Courtesy of the Hoover Institution Archives)

into muscular, able-bodied servicemen. For the United States, though, the problem of reconstructing the symbolic male body was not limited to individual citizens; the country had to take measures to reimagine and counter a body politic partly based on a disabled president.

The term "body politic" is not used here to suggest that the United States was or is represented in any singular embodied form the way the medieval body politic was figured in the idealized body of the monarch. Rather, the term is used as art historian Nicholas Mirzoeff uses it to propose that metaphorical representations of a nation through embodied images, whether in a monarchy, republic, or dictatorship, are always "site[s] of exchange . . . mediated by" visual signs (88). These spaces of exchange between people and nation are also in constant dialogue "with changing ideas of gender and cultural politics" (88). Thus, embodied symbols of the nation both reflect and influence prevailing gender, racial, and other cultural norms. Although both male and female bodies and symbols contributed to the newly strengthened national body politic of World War II, male bodies were particularly significant, as U.S. government agencies and the media utilized the human body symbolically in their representations of the nation. In keeping with centuries of artistic representation of heroic male bodies,[2] the symbolic muscular, youthful (often white) male body of the serviceman offered a more easily interpreted image of national strength and power than its female counterpart and was more in keeping with a nation engaged full-time in waging war.

Because the body politic has, since the late eighteenth century, failed to be located in any one centralized site, in investigating the rebuilding of the American body politic during the 1930s and 1940s, we must explore multiple places in which the nation was figured bodily: representations of male workers in New Deal artworks and in literature about the CCC; the media and government conspiracy to distance F.D.R.'s political body from his real, disabled body; the deployment of Uncle Sam images in cartoons and posters; and the general utilization of young, heroic male bodies in recruitment and other wartime posters and magazine advertisements. When analyzed concurrently, these subjects help provide coherence to a fragmented and changing body politic in the 1930s and early 1940s, which took shape across a wide cultural field. Upon examination of the ways in which the president, the symbolic head of state, and cultural icons like Uncle Sam were depicted in conjunction with idealized versions of "average" servicemen's bodies, a broader, ideologically inscribed American rhetoric of muscles and health emerges during the war and prewar period. Before turning to these topics, however, we must first examine the effects the depression had on the bodies and psyches of Americans as well as the particular challenges to masculinity that occurred in the 1930s. The Great Depression not only provided an important context and impetus for rebuilding the body politic during World War II but also ushered in important cultural and artistic programs and mass-production techniques that helped transform

Americans' relationships with public images. Moreover, many of the images of courageous workers depicted in New Deal artworks help establish figurative ideals that were later used in wartime representations of servicemen and other heroes.

UNMAKING MEN — 1930S CHALLENGES TO AMERICAN MASCULINITY

The devastating and long-lasting effects of the depression cannot be overstated. As journalist and depression historian Caroline Bird reminds us, "What is frequently overlooked and frequently forgotten is this: when the stock market crashed in October 1929, America stopped growing and did not really get moving again until the attack on Pearl Harbor . . . mobilized our resources" (xiv). The most obvious elements of this stagnation were the unemployment rates that remained high throughout most of the depression's 12 years. Just one year after the October 1929 crash, unemployment rates for non-agricultural workers had risen from 3.2 percent to 8.7 percent. By 1931 that figure climbed to 15.9 percent and rose steadily until 1933, when one in four members of the workforce was jobless (Badger 18). As grim as those statistics are, historian Anthony Badger argues that the realities of unemployment were probably worse: "The unemployment statistics were notoriously unreliable. It is quite likely that one third of those available for work were jobless" (18).

Most with jobs were not significantly better off than their unemployed counterparts; between 1929 and 1932, workers lost nearly a third of their real income, and "one economist estimated in January 1932 that half of those with jobs were working part-time" (Badger 19). It is hardly surprising, then, that an estimated one-third of the nation's families had an income below $1,200 per year and another third was right at subsistence level with an income of $2,000 per year (Badger 25). Even after a full four years of New Deal policies and federal relief, over a third of the nation was still "ill-housed, ill-clad, [and] ill-fed," as Roosevelt noted in his 1937 inaugural address. This one-third of the nation, the permanently poor, included much of America's black and elderly indigent populations. Often the last to be hired, blacks, women, and older workers were often the first to be laid off. An Urban League survey of 106 American cities reported "that the proportion of blacks unemployed was anywhere between 30 and 60 per cent greater than for whites" (Badger 25). In southern cities it was not uncommon for half of black workers to be unemployed with the other half relegated to racially marked jobs such as garbage collection, street cleaning, and domestic service. Despite these high unemployment statistics for blacks, many African Americans who grew up in the 1930s report that depression did not alter job prospects and economic conditions as radically for blacks as it did for whites. Recalling his memories of the period, Robin Langston notes that "it was the Depression because no white[s] and no blacks were working. The *whites* not working made it official" (qtd. in Terkel, *Hard* 90).

While these statistics begin to sketch out some of the depression's ruinous effects on the U.S. economy and standard of living,[3] they do not address the particular psychological impact that 1930s hardships had on many American men. Numerous stories of men's despair over losing their jobs are preserved in the letters and oral histories left behind. In a 1930 suicide note, for example, a Houston mechanic detailed his loss of self-worth caused by his unemployment: "This depression has got me licked. There is no work to be had. I can't accept charity and I am too proud to appeal to my kin or friends, and I am too honest to steal. So I see no other course. A land flowing with milk and honey and a first-class mechanic can't make an honest living" (qtd. in Badger 11).

Part of the rise in the national suicide rate during the first few years of the depression, this man's death also speaks to a powerful crisis in masculinity that the depression created. Michael Kimmel has argued that "for most men the Depression was emasculating both at work and at home. Unemployed men lost status with their wives and children and saw themselves as impotent patriarchs" (*Manhood* 199).[4] With 35 percent of the population (more than 46 million people) receiving some form of federal assistance at some point during the 1930s (Badger 190–91), millions of men were forced to swallow their pride (as the Houston mechanic could not do) and accept federal relief, eroding notions that they could still fit within the contemporary masculine ideal of the self-sufficient breadwinner. Former businessman Ben Isaacs recalls the humiliation he felt when he joined the relief rolls in Chicago: "Shame? You tellin' me? I would go stand on that relief line, I would look this way and that way and see if there's nobody around that knows me. I would bend my head low so nobody would recognize me. The only scar it left on me is my pride, my pride" (qtd. in Terkel, *Hard* 426). Often men's pride was hurt not just by the fact that they were receiving direct relief but also by the form in which it came. Local relief organizations continued to distribute food and goods directly to families rather than provide financial assistance. As one unemployed Pittsburgh man noted, this form of relief was frequently another affront to one's manhood: "Does a man's status change when he becomes unemployed, so that, while he was perfectly able to handle money when he had a job, he can't be trusted when he's out of work?" (qtd. in Badger 195). The depression operated on many fronts to erode a sense of masculinity based on the conception of the self-reliant breadwinner and patriarch.

To counter the many challenges mass unemployment posed to the breadwinner model of masculinity, men's magazines and other popular periodicals of the 1930s expanded their notions of manhood to include internal and external qualities that were not necessarily tied to men's status as wage earners.[5] Magazines such as *Collier's* and the *American Magazine* began to promote new forms of "modern masculinity" that "allowed men to understand themselves through their personality, their physical vitality, and their ability to enjoy leisure time" (Pendergast 163). Nevertheless, the impulse to equate manhood with successful breadwinning remained strong throughout the 1930s. In fact, many advertisements continued to prey upon men's fears about losing their breadwinner status in the same periodicals that promoted these new forms of a consumption-based masculinity. A 1934 Listerine advertisement, for example, capitalized on the anxieties of unemployed middle-class workers to promote its product. Featuring a photograph of a timid, downcast white-collar worker with his hat in one hand and his business card in the other, and the words "formerly with . . ." superimposed across his upper body, the ad focuses on *"The phrase that wrecks a* MILLION MEN.*"*6 With its bold type and suggestion of millions of "wrecked" men, the ad clearly taps into concerns about current unemployment statistics and the diminished economic prospects of most men. The text of the ad explains the worker's specific plight:

> He hands you a card half apologetically, half eagerly. You read across the bottom—"Formerly with." Then follows the name of a company that is a better company than the one he now represents. So with the company he represented before that one, and the one before that one. Down hill . . . pillar to post . . . same line of work . . . but down hill . . . and he doesn't know why.

Not surprisingly, the man's problem is halitosis, which is easily solved by using Listerine. While playing into consumer-based models of masculinity that focus on appearance and likability, the ad also relies on the ideal of the self-made man; it ultimately holds up the ideal of the "go-getting fellow, a stem-winding, whirlwind producer" who can still rise to the top—provided that he has pleasing breath, of course.

Other advertisements were more specific in targeting men's anxieties about their abilities to support their families. For instance, a 1938 magazine ad for the Fidelity Investment Association focused on the impact that a man's unemployment would have on his household. Featuring a photograph of a middle-aged white woman confronting her seated husband with the question "What would happen to us, John, if you lost your job?" the ad compels male viewers to reflect upon their status as the family providers.7 Shown only the back of the man's head, the reader is forced to meet the woman's worried stare and accusing posture as her husband contemplates the question that "husband and wife both dread to answer." Further elaborating on this query, the text of the ad asks "Where would they be, if the breadwinner were to lose his job?" While specifically gendering the role of the breadwinner as male, the ad also describes the man's "obligations" as family provider. He is expected to maintain the respect of his wife, to pay the regular bills, and, the ad suggests, to "have money enough to see [him] through the sunset years, to educate [his] children, to take advantage of business opportunities, to travel, [and] meet unforeseen emergencies." Although the ad promises that the Fidelity Investment Association will help men achieve these goals, the real onus is placed upon the male viewer and his ability to bring home and save part of a regular paycheck.

Although oral history accounts and letters reveal that the breadwinner ideal featured in these advertisements was held by many men outside of the ads' middle-class target audience, the ideal didn't always cut across racial lines. Recalling different expectations for black and white males during the depression, former teamster Clifford Burke notes that African American men actually had "one big advantage" in often having been denied the status and social and economic privileges many white male workers had received. Remarking on these differences, Burke states:

> Our wives, they could go to the store and get a bag of beans or a sack of flour and a piece of fat meat, and they could cook this. And we could eat it. Steak? A steak would kick in my stomach like a mule in a tin stable. Now you take the white fella, he couldn't do this. His wife would tell him: Look if you can't do any better than this, I'm gonna leave you. I seen it happen. He couldn't stand bringing home beans instead of steak and capon. . . . Why did these big wheels kill themselves? They weren't able to live up to the standards they were accustomed to, and they got ashamed in front of their women. (qtd. in Terkel, *Hard* 82–83)

Like many indigent whites and other minorities, Burke recognized that the culturally dominant model of masculinity based on the breadwinner ideal was not only racially inscribed but also firmly linked to middle-class income and social values. For many poor and working-class families, it simply was not feasible for the women to stay at home. The percentage of women working outside the home actually increased during the depression, and "fully 25 percent of American women labored for wages during the 1930s" (Nash 76). The percentage of black women working outside the home was twice that of whites, in part because of the limited wage-earning potential of black men.

In the wake of severe challenges to men's status as breadwinners, a few writers went so far as to view the United States as a "feminized" nation.[8] Even before the depression, some male employees had begun to see the workplace as a feminized sphere. Many women had entered the workplace en masse in the 1920s and 1930s, and jobs themselves were increasingly viewed as "feminized," requiring less sheer strength and unique "masculine" skills. According to labor studies scholar Stephen Meyer, "Removing the male traits of brawn and brain from workplace skills, Taylorism and Fordism redefined skill as the endurance of repetitive and monotonous tasks and their speedy and dexterous performance. For both craftsmen and laborers, their work became unmanly" (17). Written at the tail end of the depression, Roy Helton's 1940 *Harper's* article "The Inner Threat: Our Own Softness"[9] captures fears that America had become a soft, feminized nation.

Helton claims that America's greatest threat to survival was not the Nazi war machine, which had already taken a large portion of Western Europe, but rather "the feminizing influence on Western life that has mounted into dominance over every area" for the past "twenty-five years" (338). Due to advances in mass commercial culture and technology, Helton complains, "we live in a far daintier world than our fathers, but also a far less virile world" (338). Even the last domains of true manliness—fields like mining and industry—are threatened by technological advances: "The male economic function is taken over by Uranium 235, and there is nothing left for men to do but grow long hair or shake their fists at the planets. A Mr. Lipstick is the end product of our modern industrial romancing" (340). Despite claims that America has adopted a woman as its national symbol and that manhood is becoming obsolete, Helton is hopeful that the U.S. can stop this feminine influence before the nation has too much "comfort, and its sequel, degeneration" (339). The answer, according to Helton, is "to tie a male purpose to democracy" (342), to "harden" our young men and women "by work and weather to meet every possible storm" (343). Underlying much of Helton's article is a eugenics rhetoric, which places the body at the center of his plans for America to achieve "a more masculine purpose" (342).[10] Indeed, Helton calls for a "resolution to raise up on this continent the strongest, ablest, hardiest, and most intelligent race of men and women that ever inhabited the world" (343). Taking care to distance his vision of a newly strengthened, fit America from Hitler and his "machinelike" men, Helton nevertheless admires Germany's discipline and its emphasis on physical strength and hard bodies. For America to succeed in its upcoming war and for democracy to flourish in the postwar world, he suggests, the United States will need to reinvent its body politic and rebuild the individual bodies of its citizens.

Although disturbing to modern readers who know the outcome of Hitler's racial hygiene programs, Helton's emphasis on strengthening American bodies must be considered within the context of the depression's very real impact on the nation's health. Caroline Bird's description of the 12-year crisis as an "invisible scar" fittingly illustrates that the depression profoundly marked the bodies of many Americans; the scars, however, were far from invisible. While relatively few Americans actually starved to death, sickness and malnutrition increased dramatically, especially among the unemployed.[11] Unemployed families had an illness rate that was 66 percent greater than that of families with at least one full-time worker (McElvaine 18). Many unemployed workers were so malnourished that when they did receive work through New Deal programs or other sources, they had problems physically performing the same work they did before the depression. Nowhere is the story of American men's ill health during the 1930s more clearly told, though, than in the Selective Service's prewar and wartime rejection rates. Between November 1940 and August 1945, the army rejected close to 6.5 million men, or 35.8 percent of the men they examined for military service. The peacetime rates were even higher, when "total rejections for induction ran as high as 52.8 percent" (Foster et al. 16).[12] The regions hardest hit by the depression averaged more rejections than other geographical areas. Throughout the war, the South averaged a 50 percent rejection rate, while the Northwest, "referred to by draft boards as 'the health triangle,'" produced more I-A (fit for general service) men than any other region (Ralph Martin 2). The reasons for rejection were also telling signs of the general ill health of the nation's men. A leading cause for dismissal (17.7%) among peacetime draftees and volunteers was dental standards. Considering that these so-called "high" standards required registrants "to have six serviceable natural masticating teeth and six serviceable natural incisor teeth" or, in the place of natural teeth, "serviceable dentures," the health expectations for American men were by today's standards quite low (Foster et al. 21). These rejection figures reveal that the depression had an enormous toll on the bodies as well as the minds of American men and boys. Given the extreme challenges to public and private constructions of American masculinity during the 1930s, it is not surprising that F.D.R.'s New Deal programs attempted to repair damaged models of manhood as they sought more generally to provide national relief.

HEROIC WORKERS—THE CCC AND NEW DEAL ART

Part of Roosevelt's broader goals to restore economic and social stability, New Deal programs such as the Civil Works Administration (CWA, 1933–34), the WPA (1935–43), and the CCC (1933–42) sought to provide immediate relief for families by putting people back to work. Although they never supplied enough jobs to eliminate America's unemployment problems, these programs quickly put idle hands to use completing a wide range of public projects such as building parks, repairing roads, planting trees, and beautifying public spaces. The CWA, for example, employed 4 million people within two months of its November 1933 inception, and the WPA hired more than 8 million Americans during its eight-year life span (Nash 44). While providing immediate economic relief, the programs also worked to restore men's status as breadwinners. Because of the gendered nature of many programs' jobs, and restrictions that allowed only one family member to receive this relief work, the agencies primarily put men back to work. Employment in the CCC, in fact, was specifically limited to young men[13] between the ages of 17 and 25.[14]

Created on April 5, 1933, under Roosevelt's Executive Order 6101, the CCC employed more than 2.9 million single, jobless, primarily working-class young men during its nine years of existence. One of the New Deal's most popular programs, the CCC helped preserve America's natural resources as its enrollees transformed parts of the nation's landscape. Men in the CCC ultimately planted 2,356,000,000 trees, erected 66,000 miles of firewall, built 122,000 miles of minor roads, stocked streams and ponds with 1,000,000,000 fish, and constructed more than 300,000 permanent dams and 45,000 bridges (Merrill 196).[15] Moreover, the agency aided American families by requiring that CCC workers send home a minimum of $22 out of their $30 monthly wages. As historian Jeffrey Ryan Suzik has noted, though, the nation's 1,500 CCC camps were also important locations for building American manhood.

Unlike other New Deal work relief programs that restored men's status as breadwinners as a side effect of their larger mission, the CCC was explicitly constructed as a "man-building" agency. Promotional brochures, posters, official histories, and reports on the CCC frequently mentioned that one of the key goals of the program was to make its enrollees "feel like" and become men. Corps director James McEntee, in fact, titled his 1940 book on the agency *Now They Are Men* to suggest that the CCC played a pivotal role in helping enrollees achieve manhood. Further exploring this connection within his volume, McEntee explains that within the Corps's then-seven-year history, "two and a half million boys have had the opportunity to grow into men" (57). Indeed, throughout his descriptions of the conservation work done by the CCC, McEntee repeatedly turns to the "man-building" process that occurs during enrollees' six- to thirty-month stays in the camps. Describing the tree-planting program, McEntee writes, "When a CCC 'enrollee' (that is what the CCC boys are officially called) has planted 25,000 trees, he feels like a man" (18). Central to McEntee's definition of feeling "like a man" here, and throughout his volume, is the notion of performing useful, productive work. In his chapter on "Results," McEntee clarifies this connection between manhood and social usefulness: "The only way that boys grow to manhood is to undertake the work and responsibility of men. In the CCC they can feel like the work they are doing is important to the nation's welfare as the work of any man they know" (57). Given the program's official rhetoric and dominant cultural constructions of masculinity based on the breadwinner ideal, it is hardly surprising that former enrollees often reported that their work in the camp had "made a man" of them.

Program brochures and other forms of publicity likewise stressed the social usefulness of the unskilled and semi-skilled labor that CCC enrollees performed. The Federal Security Agency's (FSA) promotional booklet *The CCC at Work*,[16] for example, featured numerous photographs of the young men engaged in various types of manual labor. Often in their work uniforms but sometimes shirtless, the men in the photographs are shown swinging axes, carrying piping, and wielding picks and shovels as they engage in collective tasks such as road building, dam construction, and land terracing. To reinforce the social value of this manual work, one photo caption promises that "When this boy leaves the CCC he will know how to do something useful" (73), while another reminds readers that many CCC "projects have an important bearing on the community's health" (70). While primarily selling the program to working-class youths who wish to receive the "on the job training" (86) that the CCC provided, the booklet also elevates the nature of CCC enrollees' efforts by picturing men bravely fighting forest fires and rescuing families from floods.

The photographs of CCC enrollees also reinforce official claims that the program built able men by conditioning their bodies through work and calisthenics. Showing generally fit, lean men completing tasks requiring obvious physical strength, the photographs support McEntee's assertion that time in a CCC camp generally produced a "striking change in [an enrollee's] physical appearance" (58). Indeed, on average, youths gained 12 pounds and grew one-half inch in height during their stays largely due to the hard work, calisthenics, and nutritious meals that were part of camp life (Salmond 129). While testimonials from McEntee and former enrollees helped promote the program to Congress and future participants, reports of the physical transformation of the CCC man's body carried important symbolic resonance as well. In his introduction to McEntee's book, FSA administrator Paul McNutt claims that the CCC was a key institution for "build[ing] up the strength and vigor of society" (xii). After metaphorically describing the depression in terms of tubercular disease, McNutt notes that "the creation of the 'CCC' was one of the first strong measures taken by the government of the United States to combat the ills of the depression" (xii). The healing and preservation of society, McNutt suggests, stems from "building the health and character and skills of young men" (xii). Equating national strength and health with men's fitness and vigor, McNutt's comments point to the growing symbolic importance of the male body that would later become more widespread as America mobilized for war.

In offering both a literal and symbolic site of "man building," CCC camps endeavored to produce a particular type of working-class masculinity that fostered service to the nation. As McEntee outlined, the ultimate goal of the CCC in turning "idle boys" into "sturdy young men" was to produce "better husbands . . ., better workers, better neighbors, and better citizens" (69). During most of the agency's existence, this goal of producing "better" men meant instilling "respectable" masculine values associated with the middle-class breadwinner ideal. Jeffrey Suzik has noted, however, that after 1939 the CCC model of masculinity shifted from worker to soldier as America began its military preparedness programs.[17] Although carefully portrayed as a *civilian* agency during the antimilitarism and isolationism of the early and mid-1930s, the CCC, which employed some 225,000 World War I veterans[18] and used Reserve Army officers as camp commanders, cultivated a model of masculinity compatible with military service throughout its entire nine-year existence. Indeed, many "World War II officers prized CCC veterans as noncommissioned officers" (Bird 129) because of their training, work ethic, and prior national service.

At the heart of the "respectable" masculinity advocated by McEntee and others was a "good" work ethic. According to McEntee, becoming a good worker required more than developing physical strength and performing socially useful tasks; it meant becoming a disciplined, self-motivated worker. Like the "docile bodies" in Michel Foucault's *Discipline and Punish,* CCC enrollees were expected to develop self-discipline and self-correction to labor expectations. Explaining the Corps's role in this process, McEntee writes: "Still more important, the CCC can teach men how to work. It can drill the habit of work into them. It can teach them how to work when the boss is not around. It can teach them how to follow instructions on the job" (42). This "proper attitude toward work" (60), McEntee suggests, is almost more important "than the technical knowledge or mechanical proficiency" enrollees would learn during their time in the camps (60). Based on these and other statements by McEntee, it becomes clear that he saw the CCC as producing management-friendly workers.[19] Instilling this "proper" attitude meant shifting away from a "rough" masculine culture that advocated "opposition to employers" to a "respectable" model based on the "values of control, skill, autonomy, and independence" (Meyer 15, 16). This "proper" work ethic also lent itself to military service, which encouraged respect for command and independent completion of tasks.

Along with cultivating a good work ethic among enrollees, CCC officials sought to instill principles of "clean living" and discipline as they built "respectable" men. Often this involved the social disciplining of the men's bodies. According to McEntee and others, if CCC enrollees were to serve as symbols of America's potential, it was important that they be clean, well groomed, and disease free. In addition to an initial physical examination and regular monthly inspections of the enrollees' bodies for venereal disease, camp officials checked barracks to guarantee that the youths maintained sanitary conditions and displayed "proper habits of personal hygiene" (Holland and Hill 198). To ensure that the enrollees took proper care of their bodies, educational courses on health, safety, and first aid were offered at many camps. As former CCC member Blackie Gold recalls, the camps' emphasis on clean living was often so successful that enrollees themselves enforced Corps personal hygiene standards:

> In the days of the CCC's, if the fella wouldn't take a bath, we'd give 'im what we call a brushing. We'd take this fella, and we'd take a big scrub brush and we'd give 'em a bath, and we'd open up every pore, and these pores would get infected. That's all he needed was one bath. I imagine we gave a hundred of 'em. A guy would come in, he'd stink, ten guys would get him in the shower, and we'd take a GI brush. If a guy come in, he wanted to look like a hillbilly—no reflection on the boys from the South—but if he wanted to look like the backwoods, we'd cut his hair off. Yeah, we'd keep him clean. (qtd. in Terkel, *Hard* 58–59)

While it is impossible to estimate how many of these "brushings" went on in the CCC camps, Gold's story suggests that the carefully enforced hygiene regulations indeed had an important impact on former enrollees' bodily habits and deportment. Foreshadowing the mass military management of male bodies that would occur in World War II, the camps' clean living and discipline regulations even mandated that CCC enrollees wear a spruce-green military style uniform when they were not performing on-site labor.

In addition to shaping and regulating the bodies of enrollees, life in the camps was also designed to improve their manners and morals. Discussing visits to the homes of enrollees in their study of the CCC for the American Youth Commission, Frank Ernest Hill and Kenneth Holland note "that most CCC youth had little knowledge of social usage at the time of their joining the Corps. They were ignorant in such matters as appropriate dress on simple occasions, general conduct, speech, meeting people, and table etiquette" (210). To cultivate these "respectable" behaviors, some camps instituted courses in etiquette. Although these classes were never widespread or overenrolled, CCC administrators and educational officers were working on introducing a two-month course on "social training" as a regular part of camp life during the final years of the Corps's existence. Experimental educational programs at ten camps offered courses and individual guidance on such topics as table manners, courting, social dancing, and the art of conversing socially. Camp administrators also sought to eradicate enrollees' former "rough" recreational activities such as drinking, gambling, and "bumming around" by promoting participation in wholesome activities such as woodworking, sports, leathercraft, formal singing groups, and the camp newspaper. Indeed, brochures reinforced this idealized representation of camp recreation activities by including pictures of youths swimming, playing volleyball, attending religious services, and reading in the library.

Throughout Holland and Hill's and McEntee's writings on the CCC, proper social conduct, educational training, and wholesome recreational activities are inextricably linked to the notion of developing good citizens. While discussing the more than 85,000 CCC enrollees who became literate as a part of camp educational programs, McEntee notes that "their ability to participate as citizens in a democracy has been substantially improved" (51). While the connection between literacy and voting is logical in any discussion of democratic citizenship, other comments about enrollees' social deportment reveal that camp administrators often had a more specific model of respectable male citizenship in mind. Citing the necessity for additional courses in social training, Holland and Hill write, "It was not difficult to show that getting and keeping a job, successful courting and marrying, the proper raising of a family, and the future role of the youth as a citizen might all depend greatly upon phases of social knowledge and practice" (211). By linking citizenship with both "proper" social behavior and enrollees' status as future husbands and fathers, this comment once again highlights the Corps's efforts to produce respectable working-class men and to preserve the ideologically laden ideal of the male breadwinner.

By employing and training more than 2.9 million men, the CCC provided an important site for literally and symbolically rebuilding masculinities damaged by the depression. The Corps produced highly visible heroic and useful workers, and through its inculcation of "respectable" values, the CCC also preserved and extolled values associated with the ideal of the middle-class breadwinner. Moreover, official government discourses associating the "health and vigor" of the nation with the brawn and abilities of CCC enrollees endowed youthful male bodies with special metaphorical significance, opening the door for a more widespread use of symbolic male figures during World War II. More practically, CCC camps also became important training grounds for defense workers and soldiers as the U.S. began to mobilize for war. Although initially conceived of and publicized as a civilian organization, the CCC was quickly converted into an agency that served the nation's defense. In fact, Congress enacted legislation in June 1940 requiring the CCC to provide its enrollees with noncombatant training "essential to the operations of the Military and Naval Establishments" (qtd. in McEntee 64). Even without substantially modifying CCC programs, McEntee was able to boast in 1940 that "over 70 per cent of the jobs the CCC do are the same kinds that engineer troops perform in wartime" (67). With years of vocational training experience and proven military discipline, the CCC easily modified its focus to produce much sought after defense workers and soldiers. Once again, CCC camps offered a location for retooling national images of masculinity, as representations of toughened soldiers began to replace those of heroic workers.

The CCC was not the only New Deal agency that presented images of heroic workers and strong masculine bodies. Artists working for federally funded art projects such as the Public Works of Art Project (PWAP, 1933–34), the Treasury Relief Art Project (TRAP, 1935–43), the Section of Painting and Sculpture (1934–43), and the Works Progress Administration's Federal Art Project (WPA/FAP, 1935–43) also created images of brawny male workers as part of the programs' larger aim to uplift the American people's spirits. Unlike the explicit man-building focus of the CCC, the goals of New Deal art programs were considerably broader. In addition to employing thousands of artists in the visual, performing, and written arts and documenting the "American Scene," the programs sought to "democratize" art by bringing it to a wider audience through the creation of community art centers and public artworks.[20] With murals and posters appearing in schools, post offices, state capitols, government buildings, libraries, hospitals, prisons, and other tax-supported institutions, the American people entered into a new relationship with art—especially as they interacted with ideologically charged images.

Although it is impossible to characterize New Deal art in terms of any one style or content matter, public art as a whole was intended to supply the American people with optimism, patriotism, and a sense of common heritage and purpose (Park and Markowitz 31). To this end, several key themes emerged, as artists attempted to celebrate the dignity of the common man and woman, the practicality of the arts, New Deal programs, American history, social activism, and the "American Scene" (Bustard 22).[21] Whether presenting the past or present, farm or factory, city or countryside, artists frequently captured the heroism of everyday life, often through representations of Americans engaged in purposeful labor.

In order to depict the trades of local economies and to represent a wide variety of ordinary men and women, artists' images of purposeful labor took many forms such as mining, canning, fishing, milking, harvesting, repairing sewers, and building dams.[22] These representations of working Americans communicated a sense of hope and optimism and offered important messages about gender roles, democratic ideals, and the sexual division of labor. Art historian Barbara Melosh has observed that many New Deal artists used images of manhood and womanhood as tropes in a common political rhetoric. One recurring configuration, Melosh argues, "showed men and women side by side, working together or fighting for a common goal" (4). According to Melosh, this 1930s image of the "comradely ideal" can be viewed "as a revision of companionate marriage, one that deemphasized its privatism and instead made marriage a trope for citizenship" (4). Other images of men and women, such as depictions of the farm family, meanwhile, offered icons of "homespun democracy" (Melosh 4). Indeed, many New Deal murals and sculptures accentuated men's and women's combined efforts as they simultaneously stressed gender complementarity.

Given the particular crisis in masculinity that the widespread unemployment of the 1930s had precipitated, it is not surprising that most images of paid labor almost exclusively featured men. Although a few pieces did include representations of women working in traditionally feminine occupations such as teaching and nursing, most depictions of female labor focused on the domestic sphere. By showing an outdated sexual division of labor, the images helped calm anxieties over men's lost status as breadwinners while firmly gendering the workplace as a male domain. Often the male workplace in these New Deal artworks was one of heavy industry, as artists focused on the physically demanding labor of blue-collar workers. Like their counterparts in the CCC, these workers were often well muscled and generally depicted in a heroic manner.

Often compared stylistically to 1930s Soviet social realist images of workers, these heroic representations of brawny blue-collar workers were no doubt influenced by the growing labor movement in the U.S. and by Marxist theory. Ultimately, though, the images borrowed the iconography of the labor movement without many of its political intentions. Thanks to the conservative policies of Section, PWAP, and TRAP administrators, suggestions of labor unrest were not permitted. Instead of portraying class struggle or radical politics, artists largely focused on workers' physical strength, mastery, dignity, and cooperation with one another (Melosh 92). In Section art by Behn Shahn, Maurice Glickman, William Zorach, Michael Lensen, Sahl Swarz, K. William Gropper, and others, ordinary workers are endowed with a type of heroism as they labor productively and in full control of their environment.[23]

Covering the front entry of the Department of Interior Building in Washington, D.C., William Gropper's Section mural "Construction of the

3—Like many other New Deal artworks, K. William Gropper's 1939 Section of Painting and Sculpture mural "Construction of the Dam" endows workers with extraordinary heroism evident in their muscular physiques and awe-inspiring tasks. (Courtesy of the General Services Administration)

Dam" (fig. 3) provides a superb example of these artistic attempts to capture the heroism of industrial masculine labor. The grand scale of the triptych provides a certain epic quality to the scenes from the Tennessee Valley Authority construction project, but it is the brawny physiques and fearlessness of the workers that primarily convey their heroism. The strength and power of their bodies is revealed not only through the workers' broad shoulders and sturdy frames but also through the awe-inspiring tasks they perform. Five men in the far right panel forcefully ply their tools as they collectively bend and shape a set of steel reinforcement rods. In the center panel, a group of construction workers engages in a strenuous levering task, which compels some of the men to remove their shirts. Workers in the left panel, meanwhile, bravely attack the rock face with jackhammers and traverse sheer cliffs as they prepare the future side of the dam. Whether bending steel or moving rock, the workers reveal their abilities to tame the landscape through their physical prowess. Even the engineer and surveyor pictured in the corner of the center panel have muscular physiques. Physically completing the triangular configuration of men, the engineer and surveyor, it seems, could easily step in and perform this strenuous work as well.

Although heavy machinery and modern industrial processes are obviously involved in building the dam, Gropper emphasizes the human dimensions of the construction project. The three sets of workers in the foreground upstage the dam itself, which, like the concrete factory, serves as a backdrop for the men's labor. Notably absent, too, is the huge crane apparently moving the massive steel liner in the center panel. Reinforcing the idea of human control, the figure on top of the liner signals to the operator where to place the steel piece. Admist fears that mass production had contributed to unemployment and rendered certain masculine skills obsolete, Gropper's heroic representation of the dam workers effectively helped restore dignity and importance to physically demanding labor.[24] A cartoonist for the *New Masses,* Gropper held leftist political views that undoubtedly influenced his representations; the historically inaccurate image of black and white men laboring together reflected his political ideals rather than actual working conditions. Nevertheless, Gropper's mural fit within a larger body of New Deal art that sought to restore people's sense of hope as well as within a smaller body of work that specifically addressed the particular crisis in masculinity.

Although many New Deal public artworks shared common aims and themes, the sheer variety of projects and the local placement of murals and sculptures prevented 1930s images of male bodies from having the same widespread cultural effects that wartime representations would have. Lacking the coherent, more carefully controlled national imaging campaign that World War II posters and films created, New Deal art images offered important but local means for reconstructing images of masculinity during the depression. Notwithstanding, 1930s representations of heroic male workers in New Deal art and materials about the CCC played a key role in establishing the symbolic function and aesthetic ideals of male bodies and laid the foundation for the wartime efforts to rebuild American masculinity on a national scale.[25]

F.D.R.'S "TWO BODIES"

Perhaps the most significant rebuilding of the American body politic during the depression occurred in the creation of Roosevelt's individual body politic. Although scholars writing years after Roosevelt's death have commented on the parallels between a nation crippled by the depression and its leader's own damaged body, F.D.R. went to great lengths to ensure that the majority of American citizens did not learn of his permanent disability or of his later ill health. Throughout his 12 years as president, the true state of his health and disability was concealed from the American public, and his individual body politic was revamped time and again as Dr. New Deal became Commander in Chief.

In many respects, it is fitting to consider Roosevelt's body politic within earlier historical frameworks because he embodied American power in a manner never duplicated by any other president. Elected to four presidential terms in which he exercised executive power boldly, F.D.R. was somewhat of an institution in his own right, and he was often accused by his sharpest critics of possessing dictatorial or monarchical power. Although he shared authority with the other branches of government and clearly did not personify absolute rule as earlier European monarchs had, Roosevelt was for the American people the undisputed head of state. Given the immense power his person held, it is hardly surprising that the White House and the press promoted the fiction that F.D.R. had, like kings before him, two bodies—"a body natural, and a body politic" (Kantorowicz 7).

In his seminal study of political theology, *The King's Two Bodies*, Ernst Kantorowicz contends that, while medieval in origin, the notion of the king's two bodies was utilized in seventeenth- and eighteenth-century European monarchies and can be traced to Victorian English law in the form of an 1887 statute (4). As seen in the case of F.D.R., the premise on which mid-sixteenth-century English jurists defined "kingship and royal capacities" was remarkably similar to the one on which members of the press and government defined the president in 1930s and 1940s America:

> The King has in him two Bodies, *viz.*, a Body natural, and a Body politic. His Body natural (if it be considered in itself) is a Body mortal, subject to all Infirmities that come by Nature or Accident, to the Imbecility of Infancy or old Age, and to the like Defects that happen to the natural Bodies of other People. But his body politic is a Body that cannot be seen or handled, consisting of policy and Government, and constituted for the Direction of the People, and the Management of the public weal, and this Body is utterly void of Infancy, and old Age, and other natural Defects and Imbecilities, which the Body natural is subject to, and for this Cause, what the King does in his Body politic, cannot be invalidated or frustrated by any Disability in his natural Body. (Kantorowicz 7)

Like the king described in this passage, Franklin Roosevelt's image and power as president depended on the careful distancing between his actual disabled, often infirm body and his skillfully orchestrated body politic. In this denial of his natural body, F.D.R.'s body politic was achieved primarily through visual representations, which took the form of elaborate public performances, thoughtfully chosen photographs, and selected cartoons and illustrations.[26] Whereas monarchs of early centuries could easily distance their natural bodies from their bodies politic because few subjects saw them or their photographic likenesses in person, modern media technologies made it paradoxically both easier and more difficult to conceal Roosevelt's real corporeal status.

Prior to the summer of 1921, Franklin Roosevelt had, with the exception of a few childhood diseases and a bout of influenza in 1917, enjoyed good health for his day and was fairly active and athletic. Already having served as a Democratic state senator, assistant secretary of the navy to Josephus Daniels, and the Democratic vice presidential candidate in 1920, he was also well on his way to a promising political career. On August 10, 1921, however, an icy swim in the Bay of Fundy coupled with an earlier run with his sons changed everything. That night F.D.R. went to bed complaining of a chill. He did not realize it, but his trek up the stairs was the last time he would ever walk or stand on his own. After two weeks of high fevers, chills, and pains in his back and legs and several visits from doctors, F.D.R.'s worst fears were confirmed; he had poliomyelitis.

While the term "polio" hardly inspires fear or dread for those of us living in a post–polio vaccine world, in the early 1920s "poliomyelitis was frightening, even terrifying. It was present in everyone's consciousness as much as cancer, and sometimes even more than cancer" (Herzlich and Pierret 42). During the 1920s, roughly 25 percent of polio sufferers died in their first week of illness, and those who survived were almost certain to contract infantile paralysis. According to Claudine Herzlich and Janine Pierret's study of cultural perceptions of diseases, *Illness and Self in Society,* "poliomyelitis evoke[d] the image of an exclusion reminiscent, *mutatis mutandis,* of the exclusion that was meted out to great scourges of the past" (42). People saw the polio victim as a "diminished individual," as someone who is put "back into a world where he no longer has a place, [as] someone who is rejected or pitied" (Herzlich and Pierret 42). There was certainly a great stigma associated with the disease; as one F.D.R. biographer put it, "Nice families kept their disabled members at home in the back bedroom with the blinds drawn" (Grubin, "Grandest Job").

Given the specific shame attached to polio and the general stigma connected to ill health or disability for men at the time, the end of F.D.R.'s political career seemed almost certain.[27] With the help of his wife, Eleanor, and his trusted friend and political adviser, Louie Howe, however, Roosevelt quickly took steps to keep his political ambitions alive. On September 13, 1921, F.D.R. began his elaborate campaign to conceal his paralyzed legs from the press. Informing the media that F.D.R. would be boarding his train to New York at a different location, Howe created a diversion that allowed Roosevelt to be transported onto his train unseen. When the newspapermen finally reached the correct car, they found a smiling F.D.R. seated comfortably, smoking a cigarette and bragging of a voracious appetite. Later, at the Presbyterian Hospital in New York, Roosevelt's Harvard friend, Dr. George Draper, issued the following statement to reporters: "I cannot say how long Mr. Roosevelt will be kept in the hospital, but you can say definitely that he will not be crippled. No one need have any fear of permanent injury from this attack" (qtd. in Lorant 61). Thus began the denials of F.D.R.'s "natural" body and the creation of his body politic.

Roosevelt was fully aware of the social stigma attached to physical disabilities, and he knew that no man dependent on the use of a wheelchair or crutches would ever be elected to the White House. Despite visits to

Warms Springs, Georgia, experimental therapies, and vigorous exercise regimes, Roosevelt had not regained use of his legs, and so in 1926 he began to work with a physiotherapist to develop a more politically friendly method of "walking." At last shedding his crutches, which he called "political poison," Roosevelt would appear with a cane instead and would simulate walking by leaning on the strong arms of his sons Elliott and James as he moved his braced legs forward. Roosevelt and his sons tirelessly practiced this walk until it appeared that F.D.R. was moving of his own volition. Both Elliott and James developed steel-like arms and learned to chat and smile as they moved with their father so it would not seem like he was leaning on them. Because he only used the walk for short distances—from a chair to a podium or from a car to a building—and because a crowd frequently surrounded him as he moved, F.D.R. was able to convince the public that he was able-bodied.

Although Roosevelt's own denials of his handicap and his convincing walking performances were crucial to the political fiction of his able-bodiedness, it was the press that really created and maintained F.D.R.'s body politic. Whether out of admiration for the charming president or out of deference to his position, "there was an unspoken code of honor on the part of the White House photographers that the president was never to be photographed looking crippled" (Goodwin 586). In his 12 years as president, the press did not print a single photograph of F.D.R. in his wheelchair nor did they capture his disabled status on any newsreel. When he was photographed, Roosevelt was usually pictured from the waist up, seated in a chair or an open car. If he was shown standing, he was either behind a podium or placed with a group of people so his arm on a colleague's or son's arm was not noticeable. When overzealous members of the press attempted to violate the unwritten code preserving F.D.R.'s body politic "by sneaking a picture of the president looking helpless, one of the older photographers would 'accidentally' block the shot or generally knock the camera to the ground" (Goodwin 587). Thus, throughout the depression and most of World War II, the press used carefully staged photographs to assure a first crippled, then warring nation that Roosevelt, their head of state, embodied the strength, health, and physical ability necessary to guide the country.

Whereas Roosevelt's elaborate walking performances and public photographs transformed his real body into a more able one, political cartoons went beyond the confines of F.D.R.'s actual body to endow him with an even healthier, stronger body politic. Like press photographers, cartoonists and illustrators observed the unwritten code never to portray the president as infirm or disabled. Even after the 1936 Democratic National Convention when "Roosevelt lost his footing and toppled off the ramp leading to the rostrum . . . no cartoons were drawn, no word appeared in the paper" (Crispell and Gomez 83). Unlike press photographers, cartoonists possessed greater freedom to rebuild and reimagine F.D.R.'s body politic. Even before he was sworn into office, the *Philadelphia Record* ran a cartoon that endowed the president's body politic with strength and agility much more in keeping with F.D.R.'s younger, non-disabled body. In Jerry Doyle's March 3, 1933, cartoon, Roosevelt is shown taking out the trash of the previous administration while Herbert Hoover slinks off to the right. Roosevelt stands unaided and engages in a somewhat strenuous physical activity, lifting a heavy trashcan filled with Republican promises and garbage—supposedly synonymous entities. Reflecting his actual strong upper body (F.D.R.'s arms and chest had become quite developed from the swimming and exercises he did), the cartoon depicts Roosevelt with his shirtsleeves rolled, using his strong arms to pitch out the remnants of Hoover's policies. While he is certainly no tremendously muscled superhero, F.D.R.'s body politic as imaged in Doyle's drawing does indeed take on qualities of strength and athleticism.

Once in office, Roosevelt's body politic took on increasing vigor and heroism as he proved his leadership through his first Hundred Days and other New Deal legislation. Thus we see in H. M. Talburt's March 10, 1933, cartoon for the *New York World Telegram* (fig. 4) Roosevelt assuming the form of a burly lion tamer. The generously proportioned and sturdy legged Roosevelt, with whip in hand, charges at a ferocious lion allegorically representing the "financial crisis." Able-bodied and brave, this political embodiment of F.D.R. promises the American public strength, fearlessness, and action. This theme of F.D.R.'s heroism proceeding from physical strength appeared in numerous other cartoons that year. For example, Roosevelt undertakes the role of mounted policeman in Ding Darling's May 17 cartoon "And so, after all these years!" and the role of knight in Jerry Doyle's August 1 cartoon "His Greatest Fight Lies Ahead." In Darling's cartoon, F.D.R. appears as a real-life Dudley Do-Right, holding off the sinister, mustached banker with an outstretched right hand. In his other arm he protects a thankful damsel, who smilingly represents "public favor." Placed in an already popular heroic role, Roosevelt's body politic takes on the hero's genteel masculine virtues of strength, honor, courage, and attractiveness. Doyle's cartoon reinforces this message, portraying F.D.R. as an armored knight, sword and shield in hand, battling a dragon. His valor already proven by the slain alligator representing "fear," Roosevelt confidently faces the menacing dragon "deflation," while the shining light of "recovery" seems to predict his success. As these cartoons demonstrate, F.D.R.'s physical body was radically transformed in the process of creating his body politic. Given this symbolic transformation, it is hardly surprising that *Time* magazine described F.D.R. in terms of Herculean strength and heroism. In its coverage of the 1934 Man of the Year, *Time*'s writers exclaimed: "Franklin Roosevelt showed himself in the figure of Hercules striving to perform immense but modern labors, of a hero who in the U.S. tradition does all his labors on a neighborly basis."[28] Both visually and verbally, the press repeatedly distanced F.D.R.'s body politic from his disabled body, providing the weakened nation with a strong, courageous leader.

4—H. M. Talburt's portrayal of F.D.R. as a burly lion tamer is one of many 1930s images that help to endow the president's body politic with strength and heroism. (March 10, 1933, New York *World Telegram*, Scripps-Howard Newspapers)

Just as Roosevelt's body politic was created and maintained to inspire hope during the depression, it had to be revamped as America went to war. If Roosevelt could transcend his own damaged body, then perhaps America could overcome its economic crisis and military unpreparedness. Just as it was necessary to continue to conceal F.D.R.'s disabled status, it became increasingly important to hide his various maladies and illnesses. Although he suffered relatively few health problems during his first two terms, by the time Roosevelt signed America's Declaration of War on December 8, 1941, the strains of office were beginning to catch up with him. In addition to his chronic sinusitis, Roosevelt had developed severe hypertension with a blood pressure level of 188/105 and suffered "from bleeding hemorrhoids and severe anemia" (Crispell and Gomez 78). With America's entry into World War II, earlier rumors from the 1940 campaign about the president's ill health reemerged as the December 13, 1941, cover of *Liberty* magazine asked, "Is the president a well man today?" The White House responded as it had in the past with statements by doctors attesting to the president's good health. Roosevelt's personal physician, Ross McIntire, used the occasion of F.D.R.'s sixtieth birthday to counter *Liberty* magazine's claims by printing a statement about the president's excellent health and fitness regime in the February 2, 1942, issue of *Newsweek*. As the war progressed, though, F.D.R.'s health deteriorated, and America's early losses in the war took an especially hard toll on the president's overall disposition.

To preserve his healthy body politic and groom it for war, Roosevelt both emphasized and exploited his role as commander in chief. Since the 1940 election he had begun to highlight this aspect of office by making frequent inspections of defense plants and military bases. Throughout 1940 and 1941, "the press was given ample opportunity to picture the commander in chief watching army maneuvers and gazing fondly at aircraft carriers under construction" (Burns, *Lion* 435). As the war continued he was frequently photographed with his assistant General Watson and other uniformed military officials at his side. Even his personal physician, McIntire, was a naval officer. But it was the freedom afforded by his wartime role as commander in chief that played the most pivotal role in preserving F.D.R.'s body politic. As head of a nation engaged in war, Roosevelt could cite national security as the reason for his long absences from the White House, which were really due to poor health. This role also afforded him an excuse to remain close to Washington, D.C., when he was too ill to travel, allowing his wife to serve as "roving eye and ear" as she made important trips for him (Lorant 85). Moreover, under the guise of national security, Roosevelt used a long list of pseudonyms to conceal his 29 wartime visits to the Bethesda naval health facility. Though his role as commander in chief was responsible in part for his failing health, it helped maintain and redefine F.D.R.'s body politic.

Although events in late 1944 and early 1945 served to weaken Roosevelt's body politic, at the time of his death on April 12, 1945, most Americans were still unaware of his precarious health and the full extent of his disability.[29] Whether it was because they knew him primarily as a disembodied voice through his fireside radio chats or because almost all of the countless photographs of Roosevelt that decorated libraries, bus stops, barber shops, and homes revealed only his face and upper body, the F.D.R. the American public knew existed in a political rather than natural body. The legacy of this body politic has survived in F.D.R.'s 1997 presidential memorial. In Neil Estern's bronze statue, Roosevelt appears seated in a chair wearing his navy cape with his dog Fala at his feet. Although monument organizers considered commemorating F.D.R. in his wheelchair or with his leg braces on to praise his triumph over his disability, they ultimately decided to capture him as the American people at the time knew him—as an able-bodied leader.

Certainly the creation and preservation of Roosevelt's individual body politic during the 1930s and 1940s played an important part in the broader rebuilding of the national body politic as America rearmed for war; nonetheless, it constituted only one of many examples. While Roosevelt's individual body politic indeed suggested a healthy, respected leader, it was still linked to the actual body of a president who resembled a father figure more than a soldier. Further, unlike absolute monarchs before him, F.D.R. was not the sole embodiment of American power. The United States would need additional figures and embodied symbols to rebuild its body politic and reconstruct its public images of masculinity.

UNCLE SAM GETS A FACE-LIFT

As Nicholas Mirzoeff has suggested, the body politic is "always in dialogue with changing ideas about gender and cultural politics" (88). The embodied images that represent a nation not only influence but also are shaped by prevailing gender, racial, and other cultural ideals. Given the wartime emphasis on retooling American masculinity, it is hardly surprising that the principal embodied symbol of the United States during World War II was a man—the ever-present Uncle Sam. The fact that Uncle Sam served as a key allegorical figure during World War II is not in itself noteworthy; he has, after all, been one of America's primary national symbols since the early nineteenth century, when he was firmly established as the figure of the then-young republic. What is significant in terms of decoding the body politic during World War II is not only that Sam eclipsed female national symbols like Lady Liberty and Lady Columbia but also that he underwent a radical transformation in terms of appearance. With images of a newly hardened Uncle Sam, World War II ushered in a distinctly masculine national symbol, as the U.S. began to imagine itself more thoroughly within masculine terms.

An examination of U.S. posters from World War I reveals that earlier in the century Uncle Sam shared center stage with Lady Liberty and Lady Columbia in America's visual wartime experiences. Despite the fame and popularity of James Montgomery Flagg's 1917 Uncle Sam, drawn for the "I Want You" army recruitment posters, World War I offered a fairly egalitarian distribution of male and female allegorical figures. Indeed, it seems that Lady Columbia called men to service just as frequently as her male counterpart. In popular posters such as Kenyon Cox's 1917 work "The Sword Is Drawn" (fig. 5) and Francis Halstead's 1916 poster "Columbia Calls," a noble, robed Columbia with sword in hand joined with symbols such as an eagle and the flag to provide an unmistakable embodiment of America.

5—Kenyon Cox's 1917 navy recruitment poster featuring Lady Columbia is one of numerous World War I images offering a powerful female national symbol.

6—In contrast to images of Lady Columbia, many World War I representations of Lady Liberty, such as the one in this navy recruitment poster, emphasized Liberty's potential vulnerability and need for protection. (Joseph Christian Leyendecker, "America Calls—Enlist in the Navy," 1917, Museum of the City of New York)

Columbia's ubiquitous appearance in World War I imagery is only fitting, though, in a war that "could be called a war of rival imperialisms" (Riegel 9). A persistent national symbol since the early eighteenth century, Columbia in the late nineteenth century had begun to represent an increasingly imperial-minded America; she was an ideal symbol for a nation prepared to take on mighty empires. Lady Columbia, with her sword and implied strength, was also a fitting embodiment of a nation populated by the "new woman," who was about to gain the vote and greater access to the public sphere. Columbia's sister, Lady Liberty, however, was often emblematic of what America needed to protect.[30] In Joseph Leyendecker's "America Calls" (fig. 6), for example, Lady Liberty's survival is dependent on a young sailor as well as all future navy enlistees. In many ways, Lady Liberty functioned in a fairly classical manner for a female public symbol. She served as a reminder of the past, often embodying "feminine" virtues like chastity or representing "the motherly qualities of the nation" (Mosse, *Image* 8).[31]

Obviously, the reasons for employing masculine and feminine national symbols during World War I are complex, and representations of Uncle Sam, Lady Liberty, and Lady Columbia must be considered within a broader context of imperialist and republican imagery. However, I would suggest that the simultaneous usage of Uncle Sam and his female counterparts also reflected romantic constructions of masculinity that were associated with warfare during World War I. Amidst "the exuberance and crusading zeal that characterized the posters of the First World War" (Riegel 11), images of servicemen often offered a throwback to earlier notions of genteel masculinity, where honor and virtue were as much a sign of manhood as physical strength.[32] Herbert Andrew Paus's 1917 poster "The United States Army Builds Men," for example, featured one such soldier gazing at Europe on a large globe, confidently pondering his future wartime involvement. Behind the soldier three separate figures representing "crafts," "character," and "physique" personify aspects of a respectable manly ideal. While the symbols for "crafts" and "physique" seem to reflect contemporary norms, "character's" embodiment as an armored knight alludes to a medieval, chivalrous code. Like other images of serious and noble servicemen, Paus's soldier serves as an appropriate symbolic figure in a nation equally represented by both male and female figures, by "masculine" qualities like strength and "feminine" ones like virtue.

By World War II perceptions of and rhetoric about warfare had changed, and "most of the pretentious nobility and near-literary qualities in national posters were replaced by bolder and simpler images" (Gregory 7). Framed in binary and often more realistic terms, World War II was presented as a fierce battle of competing nationalisms and ideologies, which pitted the U.S. and democracy against the Axis powers and fascism. For the United States, a country waging war with the hypermasculinized German fatherland, clearly a female national symbol would not do—especially when foreign militarist leaders such as Hideki Tojo had called America "soft." The

7—Originally created as a World War I army recruitment poster, James Montgomery Flagg's famous 1917 "I Want You" portrait of Uncle Sam was reissued during the Second World War. (Courtesy of the National Archives and Records Administration, Still Picture Branch)

combination of shoring up damaged models of masculinity domestically and flexing U.S. muscles abroad, then, led to the dramatic eclipsing of female national symbols and a radical embodied transformation of Uncle Sam during World War II.[33] And while there are too many representations of Sam to track his entire imaging campaign, the representations generally depicted a younger, stronger, more virile national figure as America gained international power during the war.

Uncle Sam emerged as a strong presence early in the Second World War with a massive reprinting of Flagg's popular World War I poster "I Want You" (fig. 7), of which some 5 million copies were produced (Riegel 3). Modeled after the 1914 Alfred Leete poster of Lord Kitchener commanding Britons to enlist, Flagg's Uncle Sam certainly commands authority and has the dignity and wisdom of a founding father. However, he is not a fully embodied figure; we only see a portion of his upper body, and the emphasis is on his stern expression and pointing right hand. The simplicity and directness of the poster is in keeping with its function to remind viewers of their patriotic duty, but the Uncle Sam depicted therein does not offer a sufficient embodiment of the nation's increasing and desired strength.

With Tom Woodburn's 1940 poster "Defend Your Country" (fig. 8), however, a new Uncle Sam emerged, recently retooled for war. Certainly, Woodburn's Uncle Sam is a far cry from the burly sailor of Barclay's "Man the Guns" poster, but it marks an important shift in Sam's public imaging. Although Uncle Sam occasionally departed from his scarecrow physique during the first decades of the twentieth century, he remained for the most part a thin, elderly man with visible wrinkles in World War I representations.[34] Woodburn's Sam, by contrast, is ready to take action. He has thrown off his coat and hat and has rolled up his shirtsleeves; his open stance, unbuttoned shirt, and clenched fist indicate that he is ready to fight. The screaming eagle behind him reinforces his bellicosity; his muscular forearms let the viewer know that his blows will be hard. Although his hair, beard, and brows are still white, his face is less wrinkled and more energetic. Woodburn's Sam will not just call Americans to duty; he will take part in the war himself.

Uncle Sam's willingness to participate in combat is perhaps most clearly demonstrated in Ernest Hermlin Baker's poster "You've Got What It Takes Soldier" (fig. 9). Striking a pose reminiscent of Flagg's figure with right arm and forefinger extended, Baker's Uncle Sam offers a hardened, more vigorous national symbol. Instead of his top hat, coat, and tie, this Sam dons an army helmet, vest, and rifle. With his sleeves rolled up and his shirt open, this Uncle Sam seems prepared for soldiering. The most remarkable difference between Baker's figure and Flagg's earlier subject, though, is the body beneath the clothes. Baker's Sam has chiseled features; his face appears as if it could have been carved from stone. Likewise, his right forearm is cut by sharply defined muscles, suggesting that, although he is beyond draft age, this Uncle Sam could triumph on the battlefield. Other posters did, in fact,

8—Departing from the more static World War I representations of Uncle Sam, Lieu-tenant Colonel Tom Woodburn's 1940 army recruitment poster presents him as an ac-tive and fully embodied participant in the war. (Courtesy of the National Archives and Records Administration, Still Picture Branch)

take the additional steps to put Uncle Sam in the thick of fighting. In N. C. Wyeth's 1942 poster "Buy War Bonds," for example, a determined Uncle Sam stands in the middle of a billowing cloud, carrying a spear and an American flag seemingly filled with war supplies. Above him is the underside of a swarm of B-17 bombers; below him is a mass of infantry soldiers storming into battle.

When he wasn't on the battlefield or preparing for combat, Uncle Sam often took his new strength and vigor to the realm of industry and war production. McClelland Barclay's 1942 poster "Defend American Freedom," for instance, features another more youthful, stronger Uncle Sam donning a denim railroad worker's cap as he towers above an industrial plant. Again with coat off and shirtsleeves rolled, this Sam strikes a bodybuilder-like pose with both arms resting on his head, supposedly to hold his cap in place. The result, though, is a visual demonstration of Uncle Sam's strength and his ability to lend his physical prowess to industrial war work. This theme was repeated in the 1943 Pennsylvania Railroad advertisement "The Spirit of 1943!" which depicts an even younger Uncle Sam, rising out of the smoke of several factories. Straddling an industrial complex, he again rolls up his sleeves to reveal strong forearms and a tightly clenched right fist. The tanks and train streaming off the tracks demonstrate Sam's success in inspiring industrial production during a key phase of the war (Connery 72). Throughout the war, Sam continued to assist both troops and war workers, sometimes combining the tasks, as he does in James Montgomery Flagg's 1945 War Bonds poster. In the famous "Jap . . . You're Next!" poster, Uncle Sam is shown rolling up his sleeves and holding a large wrench in his left hand. Assuming a fighting stance, Sam seems ready to land a blow on any Japanese soldier who should cross his path. With the strength and forcefulness of Uncle Sam serving as the common thread, the poster effectively links war production, financial support of the war effort through bonds, and victory through combat.

The success of various government and private sector poster campaigns in establishing a stronger, more active Uncle Sam as the primary national figure is perhaps best measured by the American people's ability to recreate this version of Sam in their own visual imaginations.[35] The September 24, 1943, issue of *Yank* magazine provides one such example with its reproductions of the "mail murals" Private Frank Mack sent home to his wife. On one letter postmarked April 1943, Mack has drawn perhaps the youngest, most muscular Uncle Sam of all the wartime representations. Inside a boxing ring with his arms stretched out against the ropes, Mack's Uncle Sam relaxes after knocking out Japan (figured by Tojo) in the fight. Shirtless, Sam displays an extremely muscular upper body and, were it not for his beard and signature pants and hat, could easily pass for one of Barclay's ripped sailors. Mack's cartoon reflects his own conception of a newly rebuilt American body politic and the nation's increased confidence in the Pacific campaign. After being on the defensive for the first half of 1942, the United

9—Reflecting a larger trend during World War II, Ernest Hermlin Baker's 1943 Army Conservation Program poster portrays Uncle Sam in increasingly stronger and more youthful terms. (Courtesy of the National Archives and Records Administration, Still Picture Branch)

States finally began its counterattack against Japan with its initial victory at Guadalcanal in August 1942. It is hardly surprising that Mack would represent America with such a strong, virile figure at this point in the war.

While representations of Uncle Sam played a crucial role in reimaging the United States as a stronger, masculine nation, these images were only a small part of the literal and figurative rearming of America that took place during World War II. In order to understand more fully the particular physique of Mack's Uncle Sam and the broader use of muscled bodies during wartime visual campaigns, we must explore a range of bodily metaphors as well as the cultural contexts for these body ideals.

A RHETORIC OF MUSCLES—U.S. VERSUS NAZI IDEALS

As representations of Uncle Sam and selected New Deal imagery have highlighted, a muscular physique often symbolized strength, vitality, and heroism during the 1930s and 1940s. Indeed, throughout much of Western art history and even today, muscled bodies have been used this way to communicate those general ideals. This is not to say, however, that all muscular bodies are interchangeable or that muscles mean the same thing when they appear on different kinds of bodies (i.e., male, female, young, old, racially marked). In World War II there were tremendous differences in the ways individual countries employed representations of human figures—particularly male bodies—as they created their wartime bodies politic. Analyzing how the U.S. government and media constructed symbolic representations of male bodies in relation to Nazi ideals, for example, reveals several crucial differences in the ways in which images of muscles were utilized for propagandist ends. Already seen as a virile nation before the war, Nazi Germany and its hypermasculinized body politic offered the United States yet another reason to adopt powerful male bodies in its national self-representations. Nonetheless, the particular ideologies and gender politics of these two nations shaped the visual symbolism of their muscled bodies in unique ways. By comparing U.S. and Nazi bodily ideals and handlings of figures, we can see both their shared use of steeled male bodies as well as their key divergences in aesthetics and political ideologies.

Whereas representations of American male bodies during World War II have received scant attention, the fascist body of Nazi Germany has generated numerous studies.[36] In fact, scholars have pointed to National Socialist deployments of its armored male bodies as "the most emblematic of all representations of the body politic" (Mirzoeff 88). The fascist body of the Third Reich has received so much attention, no doubt, because Germany had an extraordinarily well unified state policy on art and controlled its figurative representations with extreme measures. The state sponsored and monitored the nation's sculpture, architecture, posters, art exhibits, and other artistic uses of public space and actually banned certain artists from producing art through Goebbels's invention, *Malverbot*—"the withholding of permission to paint" (Elliot 271). At the heart of Nazi art policy were the central ideas that art should be for the people and that it should represent the ideals of Germany's new age. This entailed creating new art as well as removing so-called degenerate art.[37] For Hitler and a party obsessed with racial hygiene, there was no better place to manifest these ideals than in the human figure—especially the male body.

In his July 18, 1937, speech at the opening of *Grosse Deutsche Kunstausstellung,* the Great German Art Exhibition, Hitler outlined his ideas about the function of art in his new world order. After denigrating the "primitive" modern art that had failed to understand or represent Germany's "New Age," Hitler praised the art in the exhibition for its ability to comprehend that "today's New Age is at work on a new type of Mankind" (qtd. in Willett 338). These artists and their works, Hitler contended, illustrated the idea that healthy and strong bodies conveyed both beauty and power. According to Hitler, these artists also comprehended that, at last, the German people had recognized their roots in the greatness of antiquity:

> Never was Mankind closer than now to Antiquity in its appearance and its sensibilities. Sport, contests and competition are hardening millions of youthful bodies, displaying them to us more and more in form and temper that they have neither manifested or thought to possess for perhaps a thousand years. A radiantly beautiful human type is growing up . . . This [is the] human type, which we saw appearing before the whole world last year at the Olympic Games in its proud, radiant physical power and fitness. (qtd. in Willett 338)

Given his long-standing admiration for Greek ideals of beauty, it is logical that Hitler saw a continuum between modern German bodies and those of their Greek predecessors, who also viewed physical imperfection as a source of shame. Nor is it surprising that the Nazi body politic came to be represented primarily in the form of classical, nude male sculptures and paintings.

The works of Joseph Thorak, creator of much of the Berlin stadium sculpture, and Arno Breker, the official state sculptor of the Third Reich, however, reveal that the idealized fascist body of the Nazi imagination developed out of the First World War as much as it stemmed from classical Greece. Whether in Thorak's "Comradery" (fig. 10) or in monumental sculptures like Breker's "The Party," there is evidence of Nazi attempts to "reconstitute the male body from the fragmentation of military and emotional defeat in the First World War" (Mirzoeff 88). These sculptures, like the ones before them at the 1936 Berlin games, embody strength and racial pride and represent a new, mechanized man—the ultimate man of steel—who will surely be victorious in the next war. In both Thorak's and Breker's work, muscular torsos invoke classical motifs of the breastplate; however, as art historian Bernd Nicolai points out, Thorak and Breker take this a step further, "fusing together the classical armour and the surface of the skin to create an amoured body" (336).

10—The two armored male figures in Joseph Thorak's 1936 sculpture "Comradery" are typical of the idealized male body in Germany during World War II. (Courtesy of Zentralinstitut für Kunstgeschichte)

Although they clearly communicated Germany's growing strength and military prowess to other nations (as in the case of the sculptures at the Berlin games), the steeled bodies' broader purpose was to seal up degeneration and dissent within the nation. As Hitler himself noted in his speech at the Great German Art Exhibition, the cleansing of art went hand in hand with the task of preventing "the hereditary transmission of . . . frightful defects in the future" (qtd. in Willett 338). Thus just as Germany needed to cleanse itself of those "prehistoric art stutterers," the Modernists too must rid themselves of the supposed subjects of Modernist works, "deformed cripples and cretins, women who look merely loathsome, men who resemble beasts rather than humans" (qtd. in Willett 338). Frequently, these "degenerate" elements of the nation, such as the Jews, Gypsies, and mentally ill, were described in terms of bodily metaphors; Nazi racial hygiene literature, for example, characterized Jews as "disease incarnate," as "parasites,"

or as "cancers" "in the body of the German *Volk*" (Proctor 195, 196). Because of the importance of these bodily metaphors and the general National Socialist emphasis on eugenics, a reimaging of the German nation and its future was best communicated through the body. Devoid of body hair and physical defects, Thorak's and Breker's male figures provided the perfect embodiment for a new, disciplined, racially cleansed Germany. In fact, though based on classical sculptural ideals, the figures have Nordic features, and Breker's statues adhere to contemporary appearance norms, sporting haircuts that "are generally fashionable" for the period (Nicolai 337). Moreover, with their machinelike bodies and terse expressions, the sculptures not only have eliminated any signs of weaknesses but also seemed to have cast off almost all human elements, leaving no room for fear or emotion. As Klaus Theweleit explains in *Male Fantasies, Volume 2*, this man of steel can "dam in" or "subdue any force that threatens to transform him back into the horribly disorganized jumble of flesh, hair, skin, bones, intestines, and feelings that calls itself human" (160). Free from these human elements, the man of steel is also free from any parasites or cancers that might ruin the body of the nation; in this sense, Breker's and Thorak's sculptures provide the ideal racial Nazi body politic.

In addition to racial hygiene principles, the sculptures of Thorak, Breker, and other artists manifested other important elements of the Nazi ideology. Although they bear Nordic features, the male bodies of Nazi art never seem to possess any real individual facial features; the sculptures seem anonymous and interchangeable. Historian George Mosse contends in *The Image of Man* that this anonymity is designed to reinforce the idea that the fascist man's body "belongs not to himself but to his people" (170). Thorak's "Comradery" figures express this concept; the two male nudes grasp hands in unity for the *Volk* and are seemingly indistinguishable. This ideal was represented in other Nazi artworks such as Albert Janesch's painting "Water Sport," which depicts four sets of men rowing in staggered crew shells. The bodies of the rowers move in unison, cultivating strength and discipline for the *Volk;* they strive not for individual glory but for honor for the nation.

Just as the fascist body was stripped of individual identity, so too was it dispossessed of sensuality despite its often nude state. Whereas the Nazis banned nude sunbathing and discouraged nudity in nonsymbolic art, the symbolic male body was almost always nude. According to Nazi art policy, the full beauty and perfection of the body was seen in the nude male figure. Moreover, the nude body "also pointed backward as the paradigm of a healthy world before the onset of modernity" (Mosse, *Image* 173). In order to preserve its proper morality, "the male body had to be prepared carefully before it could be offered for public scrutiny. Thus skin must be hairless, smooth, and bronzed. The body would thus be almost transparent; . . . it would lose any sexual appeal" (Mosse, *Image* 173). By abstracting the facial features and steeling the bodies, then, the muscled fascist body communicated strength and achievement but not narcissism; control and discipline yet docility in bending to the will of the state; and beauty but not sensuality.

In contrast to Germany, the United States had neither a centralized policy on art and public images nor a singular symbolic male body type to represent the nation and its ideals. Like Germany, though, America did place a special emphasis on emblematic male figures in its own efforts to rebuild the nation prior to and during the war. A careful examination of American wartime imagery suggests, however, that the United States deployed a wider rhetoric of muscles, which incorporated a broader range of bodies within its body politic. Before focusing on key differences between American and Nazi handlings of the muscled body, it is worth noting important similarities between the two nations' use of the steeled male figure.

Although the United States had been victorious in the First World War, it had the depression and its early World War II defeats to contend with as it revamped its body politic. Given the tremendous losses America suffered in territory and naval strength early in the war against Japan, it is not surprising that some advertisements and posters chose the Japanese as an implied audience to view America's newly steeled bodies. In an August 9, 1943, *Life* magazine advertisement for Florida Grapefruit Juice (fig. 11), for example, the copy urges the reader to "Ask a Jap what it feels like to be up against men who are fortified with 'Victory Vitamin C.'" As the viewer reads on, she or he finds that Tojo in particular is the person who has been invited to inspect America's men of steel:

> You bellowed it forth to the world, Mr. Tojo a year or so ago. *"Americans have grown soft."* Tell that to your Zero pilots today. Tell 'em if you dare! Or find a survivor from Guadalcanal and ask him what it feels like to meet a U.S. Marine! How well every Jap knows the truth today . . . for he's up against men with iron wills and nerves of steel—and bodies hard as nails.

The associations between servicemen's bodies and "iron," "steel," and "nails" are reinforced by the images of the men above the text. Shirtless or in undershirts, the men reveal their strength through carefully defined, muscled upper bodies. Like one of Thorak's figures, the center figure grits his teeth and grimaces in a tense, warlike expression, suggesting that he too has sealed off any weakness. But more than muscles and expression harden and "steel" his body. In the process of firing rounds off an anti-aircraft gun, the man's body image has been extended beyond his skin to encompass the gun he is firing. The image suggests that America too has its own mechanized men who will take part in the United States war machine.

This notion of man fusing with machine to create American steeled bodies is perhaps most evident in the navy and Coast Guard recruitment campaigns during World War II. Whether in Barclay's "Man the Guns" and "Dish it Out with the Navy" posters or in J. A. Wisinski's Coast Guard recruitment poster "Ready Then, Ready Now," we see excessively muscled

11—This Florida Grapefruit Juice advertisement provides an example of the steeled male bodies that helped comprise the American wartime body politic. (August 9, 1943, *Life*. By permission of the Florida Department of Citrus)

men loading shells into tremendous guns. The hardness of the shells and guns lend strength and impenetrability to the men's bodies, adding a phallic dimension to the men's physiques.[38] Although the men often work together to keep America's war machine running smoothly, it is important to note that they do not fade into an anonymous *Volk*. Even in the Coast Guard poster, which features five fairly abstracted contemporary figures, the presence of the three pirates in the upper left-hand corner invokes America's cult of individuality. Clearly not there for any logical or historically based reason (the Coast Guard's job would have been to stop plunderers, not recruit them into their own ranks), the pirates offer a symbol of America's first hero figures. Renegades of the sea and threats to the British navy during the eighteenth century, pirates became new American heroes precisely because they had no roots in the empire; they embodied America's rebelliousness, its maverick individualism. Further, whereas the Nazi male bodies forced the viewer "to acquiesce to its power" (Mirzoeff 91) and were stripped of any individual markings, symbolic American male figures often interacted with their viewers and retained distinct facial characteristics, despite their often tough expressions. The 1943 Office for Emergency Management poster "Give Us More of These!" (fig. 12), for instance, portrays a rugged sailor making direct eye contact with the viewer both to solicit financial support and to convey his determination.

Another crucial difference between American men of steel and their Nazi counterparts is that U.S. hardened bodies were not inscribed by racial hygiene theories.[39] As evidenced in the Florida Grapefruit Juice advertisement, the American muscled body symbolically directed its strength outward rather than inward, though the real audience for these images was American citizens on the home front. Although the American government and media felt the need to harden up bodily "softness" caused by the depression and to stop "internal weaknesses" caused by venereal disease, there were no official statements about or federal programs to control racial degeneration within. In fact, American World War II imagery often tried to emphasize the theme of "unity built on diversity" and sometimes even portrayed blacks and whites working together to win the war. Although most posters featuring African American heroes such as Dorie Miller and Joe Louis specifically targeted black communities, images of African Americans were still a significant part of the larger national body politic. The Zion Kosher Meat Products advertising campaign, for instance, "featured a black Uncle Sam" (Roeder 69), suggesting that symbolic male bodies were not exclusively white. Though black and white servicemen were never shown together because of U.S. policies on racial segregation, several posters, such as Alexander Liberman's famous 1943 poster "United We Win," did feature blacks and whites working together on the home front. Interracial cooperation was likewise presented in political cartoons like Alston's "Let's Go to Work, Brother" (fig. 13), where America was represented by the dual figures of Paul Bunyan and John Henry. In the cartoon, the two gigantic, well-muscled men tower above the

12—The individual facial features and virile chest hair of the sailor in this 1943 Office for Emergency Management poster illustrate some of the ways in which heroic American male bodies differed from their Nazi counterparts. (Courtesy of the National Archives and Records Administration, Still Picture Branch)

dwarfed leaders of the Axis nations as they literally stand on top of the globe, assuring American victory in the war. In selecting John Henry and Paul Bunyan as symbolic male bodies, the artist not only provides a racially diverse embodiment of American strength but also draws on American folklore and the mythos of the frontier to demonstrate that both blacks and whites contributed to the nation's greatness. Bunyan, the heroic figure of lumberjacking fame, unites with Henry, the railroad worker legendary for his incredible strength and feats laying track, to remind Americans of their past heroic achievements both on the frontier and in industry. Despite its normalizing whiteness, the American body politic accommodated racially diverse images, even if these images did not reflect the reality of wartime race relations.

Another critical difference between U.S. and Nazi symbolic male bodies is the presentation and aesthetics of the bodies themselves. Whereas the fascist body is almost always nude and exhibited in its entirety, the American symbolic male figure usually has only the upper half of his body bare and is frequently shown from the waist up. As posters and advertisements like "Man the Guns," "You've Got What It Takes," and "Just Ask a Jap" reveal through their croppings of bodies, the most visually important and most symbolic parts of the male body were the arms and chest. Even when full figures are portrayed in images like "Let's Go to Work, Brother," the significantly larger, unclothed upper body is clearly emphasized. These differences stem from the fact that representations of the American male body were not directly rooted in the classical Greek tradition, but in the more contemporary ideals of bodybuilding, 1930s representations of brawny workers, and, most especially, comic book superheroes.[40] The Nazis turned to classical Greek sculpture to communicate the beauty and perfection of the human form in an effort to reinforce racial hygiene theories. The aesthetics of American figures, however, were based on the bodily ideals evinced in comic books, which were predicated not on the natural perfection of the human body but on the realm of the superhuman. While they often assumed regular human form, superheroes could, with the aid of a magic word or swirling costume change, transform themselves and their bodies into superhumans with abilities and bodily characteristics that exceeded the realm of mortal powers.

This is not to suggest that the body ideals and aesthetics of comic books are completely without classical roots. Kenneth Dutton observes in *The Perfectible Body* that since the Roman empire "simplifying and stylising the features of the muscular upper body . . . [has] turned them into an instantly readable symbol of heroic strength and power" (51). American comic book heroes of the 1930s and 1940s like Superman (1938–) and Li'l Abner (1934–) took the artistic shorthand that conveyed heroism through a strong upper body to a new level by transforming the more realistic proportions of the past into "huge shoulders, bulging biceps and [an] impossibly narrow waist" (Dutton 210).[41] Although present in Barclay's figures, the members of the Coast Guard in "Ready Then, Ready Now," and Mack's Uncle Sam, the features are perhaps best illustrated in Price's public health posters for the Federal Security Agency.

13—An example of America's racially diverse wartime body politic, Alston's political cartoon utilizes two famous American folk heroes to suggest that cooperation between blacks and whites is needed in the war effort. (Courtesy of the National Archives and Records Administration, Still Picture Branch)

In the poster "Regular Check Ups Keep Him on the Job" (fig. 14), Price offers the quintessential representation of comic book body ideals. With a massive, bulging chest (not unlike Superman's), the male figure reveals a powerful, almost superhuman masculine body. He lacks the symmetrical proportions and bodily harmony of his Nazi countertypes, as well as their asexuality. His body and facial hair are signs of virility; his implied sexuality is part of—not a hindrance to—his idealized American manhood.

Because American wartime muscular ideals were rooted more directly in contemporary comic book norms than in classical ideals of male beauty, it was possible to disassociate muscles from the male body and still allow them to retain some of their symbolic meanings. A striking example of this phenomena is J. Howard Miller's famous War Production poster "We Can Do It!" which features Rosie the Riveter rolling up her right sleeve to divulge a muscled forearm and firm biceps. The woman's determined, serious expression and implied strength reveal that even America's female bodies have been transformed in the new body politic. In this respect, American artists utilized muscles differently

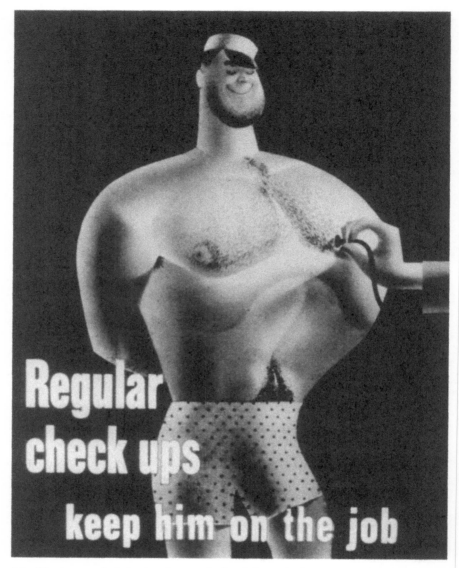

Regular
check ups
keep him on the job

14—The exaggerated chest and upper body of the male figure in Price's Public Health Service poster illustrate the influence of comic book aesthetics on the U.S. wartime body politic. (Courtesy of the National Archives and Records Administration, Still Picture Branch) than their Nazi counterparts; while Goebbels insisted that German women be depicted as strong and healthy, he specified that "the muscles of their arms and legs [were not to] be visible" (Mosse, "Beauty" 28).

Symbolic representations of female American bodies were allowed to take on some of the muscled form of male figures and were sometimes endowed with the heroism associated with those strong bodies. Introduced in 1941 and given her own comic book series in the summer of 1942, Wonder Woman entered the popular imagination with heroic physical features: "a strong, well-defined chin, and the slim, muscular body of an Olympic swimming champion" (Robbins 8). These features along with her sharp mind translated into heroic tasks as she endeavored "to save the world from the hatred and wars of men" (Hartmann 190). Despite the apparent hardening of female symbolic figures like Rosie and Wonder Woman, however, it is clear that these American women have not lost their femininity. As her carefully manicured nails, shaped eyebrows, and makeup suggest, Miller's Rosie possesses important cultural gender markings; she certainly would not be mistaken for a male war worker or one of Barclay's ripped sailors. Likewise, Wonder Woman still finds time between her adventures to apply makeup and pick out suitable earrings. Whether featuring women war workers, superheroes, or housewives, World War II imagery suggested that women could have muscles, strength, and heroism as long as their muscles were smaller than their male counterparts' and no gender boundaries had been crossed permanently. Thus the general trend toward constructing the U.S. as a masculine nation did not entail eschewing images of women; instead, typically "masculine" values were granted to female figures on a temporary basis as America reconstructed its wartime self-representations.

The Great Depression left many deep and long-lasting scars on the American body politic and presented significant challenges to the male breadwinner ideal. While efforts were taken to shore up damaged models of masculinity and strengthen the American body politic during the 1930s through the CCC, various New Deal art projects, and the creation of F.D.R.'s individual body politic, it was not until the United States entered World War II that a radical transformation took place. With the United States' full-scale mobilization for war came both a stronger, more youthful Uncle Sam and a broader rhetoric of muscles that placed comic book–inspired aesthetics at the heart of early 1940s bodily ideals. This transformation did not spring from any one central imaging campaign, but occurred instead through a variety of mediums—posters, comics, advertisements, propaganda booklets, and other art works—operating in tandem. The end result, though, was that wartime imagery primarily constructed the United States as a powerful, virile country as it embraced the serviceman as a key image of both masculinity and national identity. The serviceman's privileged position remained strong throughout the war, because the military classification and control of American male bodies had a broad cultural impact on discourses of health, sexuality, and physical fitness.

TWO— **CLASSIFIED BODIES**

SCREENING, SCULPTING, AND SEXUALIZING SERVICEMEN

The present national emergency gives to medicine what it has always asked for— namely, compulsory physical examinations. These examinations show the actual need for physical betterment of the nation.

—Col. Leonard Rowntree, *New York Times,* October 3, 1941

After being placed in Class I (available for military service) by one of 6,443 local draft boards, an American male between the ages of 18 and 36 was almost certain to receive an induction notice at some point during the war. The all-too-familiar telegram began:

> Greetings. Having submitted yourself to a local draft board composed of your neighbors for the purpose of determining your availability for training and service in the land or naval forces of the United States, you are hereby notified that you have now been selected for training and service therein. (qtd. in *This Fabulous Century* 170)

Upon receipt of this notice, the man advised his employer, said his good-byes, and, when the appointed hour arrived, boarded a bus to the army induction center. There, he stripped down to his underwear and waited in line with hundreds of other selectees for his medical examination. The selectee was then paraded before 11 doctors and a dental officer, who, following the MR 1-9, AR 40-100, or a set of later physical guidelines, processed men at their stations at a rate of 25 per hour. From his feet to his ears, he was poked, pricked, prodded, and measured. His height, weight, chest size, and other physical statistics were recorded, and blood and urine samples were taken for tests. He encountered ophthalmoscopes, stethoscopes, chest x-ray machines, and other diagnostic aids, which allowed the gaze of the doctors to penetrate beneath his skin. If the year was 1944 or later, his PULHES[1] rating or physical profile was determined, and he was classified physically in terms of fitness for combat duties. Regardless of the year, he would have been examined by a psychiatrist who asked him if "he liked girls" and screened for problems of the nervous system. After October 1944, he would have also taken an NSA (Neuropsychiatric Screening Adjunct) test, which placed him in one of seven groups according to disposition. Provided that his eyes, ears, limbs, genitals, and other body parts met the physical guidelines and that he was deemed mentally fit, the selectee would then be classified as I-A/I-A (H) (fit for general service) or I-B/I-A (L)[2] (fit for limited service), inducted, and passed on for further medical attention and classification.

After receiving various immunizations in the arm and buttocks and taking his induction oath, the new soldier would then be shipped to the reception center, where he would take his GCT (General Classification Test) and MAT (Mechanical Aptitude Test) and be interviewed by a psychologist to determine which MOS (Military Occupational Specialty) would be best for him. Once the classification officer reviewed the list of needed MOSs and considered the private's personality and GCT score/classification,[3] the new inductee's card would be marked with the appropriate SSN (Specification Serial Number). Based on this SSN, he would then be sent to the proper training center, where he would complete 13 weeks of basic training followed by unit and combined training. Despite this dizzying number of classifications and medical inspections the new soldier would have received, by this point, his period of military classifications and medical inspections would have only just begun.

During the Second World War, almost every American male between the ages of 18 and 64 registered for the Selective Service. Only those aged 45 or younger were liable for military service; the rest registered primarily to provide an inventory of men's occupations. At the end of the registration period in December 1945, 46,164,725 men in the continental United States had registered for the draft; only 1,533 had refused (Hershey, vol. 4: 200).[4] Out of these 46 million registrants, more than 18 million were examined at induction stations between November 1940 and August 1945 (Foster et al. 16). By October 1943, the armed forces had a strength of 10,425,916 men, and by the end of the war more than 10 million men had served in the army alone (Foster et al. 15). As these statistics suggest, World War II created a unique opportunity for the screening and management of American male bodies. The mobilization of this unprecedented armed force led not only to the advent of numerous new military classification systems but also to the creation of new discourses about bodies and the health of the nation. The mass screening of men and startling early rejection figures, for example, raised questions about the general physical fitness of America, while the military's privileged control of bodies allowed for invasive venereal disease suppression programs and medical experiments unthinkable in peacetime.

The military's classification and control of male bodies during World War II had profound effects on both individual servicemen and American culture. Three particular procedures reveal the remarkable ways that the military management of male bodies operated: initial medical inspections, physical training programs, and screenings for venereal disease and potential homosexuality. The intense focus on the male physique during the war made the male body a privileged site around which debates about the health of the nation unfolded. These debates raised interesting issues about the protection of servicemen's bodies and posed broader questions about who should be responsible for the health and maintenance of all citizens' bodies.

SORTING AND SCREENING

Despite mixed support from a public divided in their opinions over the United States' entry into the Second World War, Roosevelt pushed for and won the first peacetime draft in the nation's history. Introduced in the Senate on June 20, 1940, the Selective Training and Service bill became law on September 16, 1940. In the weeks following the bill's approval, Roosevelt issued executive orders outlining classification, selection, physical standards, financial backing for the bill, and procedures for induction (Hershey, vol. 1: 14). By October 16th, just one month after the Selective Service system went into effect, the nation was ready for Registration Day.

Under the terms of the first registration, all men between the ages of 21 and 36 were required to sign up for the draft. And on October 16, 1940, more than 17 million men poured into their local draft boards—hastily set-up stations in schoolhouses and other public buildings—to fill out their registration cards. The randomly numbered cards were then renumbered according to the order determined by the October 29th lottery. Based on the information given on those cards and in a separate questionnaire, local draft boards placed the men into four broad categories: Class I indicated men available for military service after examination; Class II consisted of men who were available for service but had been temporarily deferred for up to six months (Men whose jobs were in the defense industry or in areas related to the health and safety of the nation were placed in Class II.); Class III was comprised of men with dependents; and Class IV consisted of non-declarant aliens, conscientious objectors, men who had already completed military service, and those considered "mentally, physically, or morally unfit" (Hershey, vol. 1: 109). Once a man volunteered or was placed in Class I, his additional Selective Service classifications were based on the results of his physical examinations.

Whether an individual was examined by his local medical board or by the one at the induction center, the same basic physical standards were used.[5] An updated version of 1932 physical standards, the MR 1-9 guidelines issued in August 1940 were designed for selecting men who would be "physically and emotionally fit to withstand the rigors and hardships of combat in any part of the world" (Foster et al. ix).[6] Although they contained specifications for height, weight, and chest size, indicating a certain interest in physique and body build, the MR 1-9 standards were primarily concerned with the usefulness of male bodies—especially in terms of their military capacities. Thus the military standards attempted to screen out individuals that were not generally able-bodied or who had diseases or physical defects.

Although the idea of using physical standards in selecting inductees was not new (the army and navy had been using physical standards officially and unofficially since 1808), the guidelines used by the army and other services in World War II reflected important changes in thinking about the body and its role in military life. Drawing on a World War I innovation, the MR 1-9 standards disrupted earlier models, which declared men as either fit or unfit for military service by establishing the category I-B (fit for limited service). Although men in the I-B (later I-A [L]) category were not inducted until 1942 and comprised less than 10 percent of total inductions, they filled many important positions in an increasingly bureaucratized and service-oriented army. The classification I-B coupled with the later physical profiling system (1944) reinforced the idea that there existed a range of bodies and corporeal conditions that might be fit for military service. More importantly, though, the MR 1-9 standards reflected the idea that the military was interested in the concept of a "whole" body—a body of sound mental and physical health. Having spent almost $642 million in claims on neuropsychiatric cases stemming from involvement in World War I, the government and the military decided to ensure that inductees were psychologically fit by including a psychiatrist for the first time on all medical induction boards (Foster et al. 36). Psychiatrists examined selectees for existing nervous disorders and "personality defects," which might lead to a breakdown in combat, and for "moral defects" like homosexuality and other "sexual perversions."

Based on the individual's mental, moral, and physical fitness, he was classified as I-A, I-B, or IV-F (unacceptable for military service). The average I-A individual was 68.1 inches tall, weighed 152 pounds, had a chest size of 34 inches at expiration, and was generally free of disease, though after February 1943 he may have had a venereal disease provided he was receiving treatment and "no disabling complications existed" (Foster et al. 13). The I-B registrant was generally smaller in size, had certain defects such as poor vision, blindness in one eye, or missing digits, or perhaps possessed a nervous tic like stuttering. The IV-F individual, meanwhile, had failed to meet one or more of the physical or neuropsychiatric requirements for either class I-A or I-B.

With such a large number of American men being screened and sorted, military classification terms soon found their way into common parlance. Newspaper stories about the Selective Service system were filled with the terms, and "one's draft status became the topic of daily conversation and radio comedians' jokes" (Steele 2). The most well-known and highly discussed terms were I-A and IV-F, and these terms quickly found their way into popular songs and advertisements. Even before the attack at Pearl Harbor, for example, Betty Bonney's rendition of the song "He's 1-A in the Army and He's A-1 in My Heart" could be heard all over the country. Written by Red Evans and recorded on October 15, 1941, the song reveals both romantic patriotism and popular sentiments attached to the I-A classification.[7] With the clever play between the terms 1-A and A-1, the song valorizes the I-A man throughout the song as physically fit, brave, patriotic, and adored by his sweetheart. Not only has he "passed the toughest physical," earning a high rating on "Uncle Sammy's chart," but he has also overcome his inherent pacifism to serve his country in its time of need: "Now I've got a guy who never liked to fight, / But for Uncle Sam he'll fight all right." Although the I-A classification was intended to denote physical and mental fitness for general military service, it took on added meaning in popular discourse as it marked an idealized type of masculinity.

At the other end of the spectrum, the category IV-F also became a fashionable topic for songs and jokes. Ted Courtney's 1941 song "Four-F Charlie," for instance, became especially popular with servicemen and was "mentioned variously by *Yank, Life* and other magazines" (Palmer 81). Just as "He's a 1-A in the Army" equated the military classification with attributes beyond the physical requirements, so too did "Four-F Charlie." In Courtney's song, the IV-F man appears as "a complete physical wreck" who is "stout and always wheezing," as well as someone who is cowardly and impotent.[8] Because of his classification and his inability to serve in the armed forces, the song informs us, "Men won't sing of his wild daring / Girls won't praise his martial daring." Unable to prove his manhood on the battlefield, IV-F Charlie also lacks the ability to prove it in the bedroom: "And his blood is thin as water, / He can never be a father." Indeed, Courtney's lyrics equate the IV-F man with failed masculinity and failed humanity. Unable to be a blood donor and deemed profane, the IV-F man in Courtney's song seems barely fit to be a citizen.

While not everyone regarded the IV-F with such disdain, many Americans were concerned about the growing number of IV-Fs mentioned in articles based on Selective Service rejection statistics. General Lewis Hershey, director of the Selective Service, caught the public's attention with his report on the first 1 million men examined, which revealed that 400,000 men were deemed unfit for military service. The 40 percent rejection rate mentioned in the July report was soon topped by Hershey's October report, which stated that 50 percent of men examined after selection had been rejected because of their physical condition. The number of IV-Fs soon climbed to 1,098,098 by September 1941, reaching a total of 1,117,000 by December 8, 1941 (Hershey, vol. 1: 118). Despite the fact that these rejection statistics specifically measured the number of men found unsuitable for military service, many read the figures as a barometer for the nation's health. Leonard Rowntree, chief of the Selective Service Medical Division, was instrumental in creating an explicit link between rejection data and the overall health of the nation. In his October 1944 *Hygeia* article "Physical Fitness for America,"[9] Rowntree asserted that "the registrant presumably represents a cross section of the best manpower in the nation. The physical fitness of the total population may be inferred by comparison" (744).

Roosevelt's remarks on the subject, however, offered an especially powerful correlation between the rejection figures and the nation's collective health status. As reported in an October 3, 1941, *New York Times* article, Roosevelt stated that "he was worried about the health of the people of the United States as a result of the [rejection] figures" he had received (8).[10] According to the article, Roosevelt was so alarmed that he asked the military to double-check their findings. Dismissing claims that the rejection rates were high due to rigid physical requirements, Roosevelt pointed out that "the standards were somewhat lower than in normal times, not only for the Army but for the Navy" (8). Regardless of the reason for the startling rejection statistics, the figures called for debate about the status of the nation's health and invited solutions for improving overall fitness.

Whether one interpreted the data as a sign that the nation was deteriorating or improving physically, persons on both sides of the debate agreed that the draft revealed a great deal about the health of the nation. For example, in his July 13, 1941, *New York Times Magazine* article "What the Draft Reveals About Us,"[11] Cabel Phillips declared that the Selective Service reports provided an excellent index for gauging the nation's physical wellbeing. Phillips suggested, "An American Army is something more than a cross section of our manhood, it is a living mirror of what we, as a nation, are" (10). Whereas the majority of Americans seemed to believe that the country had declined in health and vigor, Phillips inferred that the army of 1941 revealed America to be "a sturdier, healthier and more enlightened people than we were a quarter century ago" (10). Citing the one-inch height gain and five-pound weight gain of the average recruit of 1941 as compared to his World War I counterpart, Phillips contended the advances in technology during the 1920s and 1930s had made America a healthier nation than it had been during World War I. Others following Phillips's lead cited Civil War and World War I rejection statistics, arguing that the slightly higher World War II rejection figures were no cause for alarm. In fact, they asserted, advances in medicine had minimized the effects of many diseases such as tuberculosis, which plagued many Americans shortly after the First World War.[12]

Despite Phillips's and others' claims that Selective Service reports should present no cause for alarm, the press and advertisers continued to advance the idea that the health of the nation was in need of repair. A Fleischmann's Yeast advertisement (fig. 15), for example, used the July rejection statistics to suggest that the diets of most Americans were to blame for the nation's poor health. Appearing on page 12 of the December 8, 1941, issue of

Newsweek, the ad features a sobering picture of four brand new, full dress military uniforms hanging in an otherwise empty closet. These unfilled uniforms remind viewers of America's unpreparedness for war while providing a visual referent for the military rejection statistics. As the text of the ad explains, these uniforms serve as reminders of the millions of "American men—*at the peak of youth*—[who] aren't quite good enough for the Army." These rejected men, "not the hopelessly crippled," the ad contends, are the ones responsible for making "the whole nation limp" because of their poor physical shape and diets. Fortunately for the army and the nation, though, these health problems are easily cured. As the ad suggests, if these servicemen and *"all* America" fulfill their nutritional needs by eating enriched bread and other nutritious foods, then we will "begin to see *more national fitness* than you could ever believe!" Although intended to make a patriotic statement while selling Fleischmann's Enriched Yeast, the ad establishes important links between military rejection statistics and poor national health, proposing a solution involving *all* Americans.

Despite the public outcry surrounding the release of various military rejection figures, the statistics were also viewed as an opportunity to monitor and subsequently improve the health of the American people. Responding to Roosevelt's early October remarks, Rowntree noted that the examinations presented a "golden opportunity" for medicine to attend to "the physical betterment of the nation" ("Reject" 8). Given the apparent productiveness of compulsory military physical examinations, many government and health officials advocated similar types of mass screenings to monitor the physical fitness of the entire nation. The move from military to civilian screening followed logically since the war required a full-scale national effort. Whether one was on the battlefield, in the factory, or at home or school, each American was expected to do his or her part in the war effort. Part of this duty, the FSA decided, was keeping one's body healthy and strong.

In addition to creating posters that reminded soldiers and civilians to take basic care of their bodies so that they might remain "on the job," the U.S. Public Health Service (USPHS), operating under the guidance of the FSA, began to monitor civilian health using procedures developed for the military. A central aspect of the USPHS's civilian screening program was the agency's campaign to promote the use of chest x-ray machines on persons working in the war industries. Discovered as an effective method of diagnosing the early stages of tuberculosis in 1926, the chest x-ray was included in army physical examinations from April 1939 onward. At first a required part of the officer's medical exam before commission, the chest x-ray was soon recommended in October 1940 for "all registrants in whom underweight, pallor, [and] abnormal chest findings . . . increased the likelihood of pulmonary tuberculosis" (Foster et al. 32). By early January 1941 the military suggested taking chest x-rays of all inductees, and by June 1941 chest x-rays were a mandatory part of all examinations. With advances in x-ray

Four
are unfilled...

Get this shocking fact:
Four out of ten American men
—at the peak of youth—aren't
quite good enough for the Army!

Fleischmann's *Enriched* **Hi-B₁ Yeast**

15—This Fleischmann's Yeast advertisement utilizes Selective Service rejection statistics to raise concerns about the overall fitness and health of the American people. (December 8, 1941, *Newsweek*. By permission of Fleischmann's Yeast)

technology sparked by military screenings such as new portable units and faster, smaller film radiographs, it became easier and more affordable to monitor the health of the civilian population as well. By 1944, USPHS employees began to take chest x-rays of "people working in war industries and war agencies" (Kevles 114).

Both the military and civilian chest x-ray campaigns presented the idea that frequent medical inspections with specialized medical equipment were necessary because health could not be determined solely by physical appearance. This concept gained currency in popular wartime advertisements and posters. The 1944 USPHS poster "You may look healthy, but what does your chest x-ray show?" for instance, juxtaposes seemingly healthy male and female war workers with a chest x-ray negative of someone suffering from tubercular infection. The question posed by the poster raises concern among its viewers, reminding them that only medical screenings and technologies can truly gauge their level of health. Less accusatory but similar in its support for x-rays as public health instruments, a Kodak advertisement appearing on page 43 of the February 22, 1942, issue of *Newsweek* highlights the ways in which mandatory x-ray screenings could serve as an important tool of national prophylaxis. Detailing the ways that "Kodak X-ray Film helps guard our armed forces against Tuberculosis," the ad features a photograph of a doctor comparing two chest x-rays, one showing "an inside view of a healthy soldier" and another from a rejected serviceman with "serious tuberculous infection." The photo's caption explains that this screening process not only keeps "unfit" men out of the military but also enables rejected servicemen to wage their own campaigns "against another enemy which can be conquered." Continuing this positive tone, the main text of the ad suggests that "even this war of frightfulness" has "its bright and hopeful side" because the mass screenings and x-rays of servicemen result in better national health. With the aid of Kodak technology, the future promises a "time when X-rays will make possible the examination of all our people." As both the USPHS poster and the Kodak ad reveal, the mass screening of male bodies during induction examinations established important models of collective prophylaxis that could be easily adapted for "preventing contagion across bodies, communities, and the nation" (Cartwright 152).

Whereas military screening and inspection techniques were most often adapted for use on the adult civilian population, some health professionals looked to the military for examples for monitoring children's health. Though no explicit references are made to the Selective Service's classification of bodies, Dr. Norman Wetzel's December 1942 *Journal of Health and Physical Education* article "The Simultaneous Screening and Assessment of School Children"[13] certainly appears to be caught up in the military's physical classification schema. After asserting that "some form of 'screening' is obviously imperative" for monitoring children's fitness, the article proceeds to describe a plan for the "active medical control" of children's health through a combined screening and physical classification system (576). According to Wetzel's system, each "selectee" would be assigned a letter/number rating after receiving a physical examination. Children would receive a letter to denote their "physique and development" and a number ranging from one (good) to five (poor) to denote their physical condition (577). Although Wetzel's classification schema offered a more complex system for sorting bodies than the military classification plan did, its basic facets were quite similar to military models. Both systems not only distinguished between fit and unfit bodies but also provided a barometer for monitoring the health of the nation. If put into widespread usage, the number of B-5s in Wetzel's scheme would certainly spark as much public concern as their IV-F adult counterparts.

While various forms of screening (military and otherwise) provided important vehicles for monitoring the physical wellness of the nation, they were nonetheless perceived as one part of the plan for improving national health. Thanks to notions that the body was a pliable, easily transformable entity, both the military and government developed programs for rehabilitating and resculpting bodies to fit physical requirements.[14] Given the success the military seemed to have in improving physique and overall fitness, it is hardly surprising that military training programs soon found their way into various debates over, and programs to improve, national health.

TRAINING AND FITNESS

Just as military physical examinations and classifications were frequently viewed as key wartime instruments for monitoring the pulse of the nation's health, military training programs were regarded as important vehicles for restoring physical vigor. Although servicemen could potentially lose their lives, limbs, sanity, or health through wartime involvement in the military, the various branches of the armed forces and their training programs were still viewed as places where men's bodies could be transformed into stronger, healthier entities. That idea certainly was the premise behind the navy recruitment poster "Healthy Bodies—Active Minds." A significant departure from its usual strategy of employing illustrations of burly men loading heavy guns, "Healthy Bodies—Active Minds" encourages men to join the navy by offering them physical and mental improvement. By including four sets of actual "before" and "after" posture photographs, the poster promises viewers physical development comparable to that shown in the pictures. The photos, taken before and after "six weeks of intensive supervised training" reveal not only drastically improved posture but also noticeable weight gain and increased muscle and chest size. As the poster informs us, the navy has "rebuilt" these men in both body and character, eliminating the softness of "easy going civilian life" while instilling military values and discipline.

While the navy poster was intended as a persuasive recruiting tool, the promises of improved physical fitness were quite legitimate. Naval cadets at Pre-Flight School at Chapel Hill, North Carolina, for example, gained on average at least five pounds and "lost an average of two inches around the waist" in 1942 (Physical Fitness Coaching School 9).[15] Men in all branches of the service commonly experienced remarkable physical transformations. Staff Sergeant Irwin Peters noted that he "gained 20 lbs. of muscle" during his basic training, while Technical Sergeant Frank Dauster reported that he "went from a skinny 150 to 175" (WWII Survey). Others like Lieutenant Robert King and Master Sergeant John Skinner felt that after basic training they were in "the best shape of [their] lives" (WWII Survey). For many new servicemen, basic training not only increased muscle tone and overall strength but also contributed to greater stamina and better cardiovascular fitness.[16] Not everyone, of course, experienced such dramatic physical changes; young servicemen already involved in sports or pre-military training witnessed only subtle transformations.

Even before they left basic training, many men noticed physical alterations in themselves and others. The army, in fact, encouraged its men to chart their own physical development by providing personal record books like *Soldiering for Uncle Sam,* in which men could record their measurements on five different dates to keep track of their height and weight as well as chest, bicep, waist, and calf sizes. Fictional accounts of wartime basic training likewise emphasized these physical transformations. In Leon Uris's *Battle Cry,* the narrator describes changes noticeable after only five weeks of boot camp:

> One day, five weeks after boot camp started, Danny Forrester had a strange sensation. He looked at L.Q., and Jones resembled someone he had met on a train. He took his mirror from his seabag and studied himself. There was a quarter inch of hair on his head. He rubbed it over and over again. And the feathermerchant, Ski, was looking filled out and hard. Not half so puny. "By God," he whispered, "we're becoming Marines." (55)

Popular advertisements also reinforced and played upon the notion that men's bodies were transformed through military training. A December 21, 1942, National Dairy Products advertisement on page 1 of *Time,* for instance, used a photograph of a man returning home after 13 weeks of basic training in the army for its central image. With his young daughter holding his uniform jacket as she gazes up at him, the man in the ad tries on his favorite civilian jacket. The now too-small sports coat looks ridiculous on the man, who flexes his biceps, showing off his new strength and vigor. The army has transformed him physically, making him (and millions of other soldiers) "huskier and healthier than he's ever been before." Like the Fleischmann's Yeast ad, the advertisement for dairy products promises readers "a finer, stronger America" if the nation adopts military training tactics— programs that incorporate "hard work," "regular hours," "*and good food.*"

Although the military strengthened the bodies of millions of servicemen as it prepared them for combat and other wartime duties, other steps had to be taken to rectify what the Committee on Physical Fitness deemed "the increasing softness of the American people" as a whole.[17] After reading Selective Service reports filled with startling rejection figures and studies showing America's lack of fitness in contrast to the "hardy specimens" of Axis wartime fitness programs, Roosevelt created the Committee on Physical Fitness in April 1943 and placed it under the jurisdiction of the FSA.[18] With an Olympic athlete as its chair and a large number of military members, the committee was charged with the broad duty of promoting health and fitness among all Americans and developing "a national program of physical fitness" ("CPF" 518). At its first meeting on June 16, 1943, the

committee outlined that its concept of physical fitness was closely connected to military ideals about the usefulness of bodies. As reports of the
committee's first meeting reveal, improved health was not seen as an end
in itself; instead, the goal was to promote "a fitness that will insure the ability to perform our tasks (whether military or civilian) efficiently and well
within the limitations of the human body" ("CPF" 518). Fit individuals
were expected to manifest "a high degree of health and vigor" and were encouraged to be "well disciplined individuals who reject soft living and take
pride in physical vigor" ("CPF" 518). Further, the committee advocated developing "in the mind of every individual a will to win" ("CPF" 518). These
goals and criteria for physical fitness demonstrated that the aims for civilian physical fitness were closely linked to military ideals and practices. Just
as the military's war machine depended on healthy, fit, well disciplined
bodies, civilian industrial machines relied on "strength, agility, stamina,
and endurance" of their workers to meet production needs ("CPF" 518).
Whether in the military or civilian population, individual fitness was increasingly defined in terms of possessing an aesthetically pleasing, useful,
disciplined body.

Although statements by Roosevelt, Leonard Rowntree, members of the
Committee on Physical Fitness, and other public figures called for the improved health and fitness of all Americans, certain groups of citizens were
targeted more than others. As one would expect, the Committee on Physical Fitness and other organizations working under the FSA emphasized the
health of war industry workers in efforts to minimize manpower hours lost
to sickness or injury. USPHS posters warned workers to be careful on the
job and encouraged them to maintain their overall fitness through good
posture, personal hygiene, physical fitness, and medical supervision.
Equally important was the health and fitness of schoolchildren. Because
they possessed bodies that seemed more malleable and because they were
already under state surveillance, schoolchildren were ideal subjects for
wartime physical fitness and training programs.

This focus on fitness and training programs for American schoolchildren
was not without precedent. During the late nineteenth and early twentieth
century, public figures such as Theodore Roosevelt and private organizations such as the Young Men's Christian Association (YMCA) and the Boy
Scouts advocated physical fitness regimes for middle-class boys as ways of
countering the "feminizing" effects of the American educational system
and the white-collar world.[19] Part of the broader muscular Christianity
movement, these groups viewed physical fitness as a means of fostering
masculine independence and instilling Christian values. Following the release of World War I rejection figures, however, the religious aspects of
these fitness crazes gave way to secular concerns as Americans worried
about preparedness and the strength of the nation. During the First World
War, individuals and organizations such as the National Association for
Universal Military Training began to recommend that American schools

adopt compulsory military physical training programs. In his February 4, 1917, *New York Times Magazine* article "Universal Training is Needed to Improve Country's Health," physician Lucien Howe outlined a program to stave off the "physical degeneration of the nation" by examining and training children (7). According to Howe's plan, common childhood defects like "spinal curvature, nearsightedness, and 'slouchiness'" could be corrected by "setting-up exercises of a military character," military discipline, and "training in alertness, quick response and efficient action" (7). Howe argued that these forms of training, coupled with military style quarantines, physical examinations, and, later, "the rigorous training of camp life" (7), would improve national health one generation at a time. While Howe's program was not adopted, World War I did generate national interest in physical education programs. Because of America's shorter and more limited involvement in the war, however, there were few military influences on physical education between the wars. As Marilyn Gibbs and Claudius Griffin explain, "A certain degree of apathy toward fitness returned with peacetime and the prosperity of the 1920s" (931).

Although the 1920s and 1930s witnessed some growth in school physical education programs, most curriculums emphasized leisure and recreational activities. Wartime programs incorporating military drill were soon replaced by a variety of activities and sports instruction, and it was "America's love affair with sports, games, and recreational activities" and *not* wartime concerns that led to the requirement of physical education programs in schools in 36 states by 1930 (Gibbs and Griffin 931). With the onset of the depression, though, schools were hit hard by budget cuts, and few new developments in fitness programs occurred. Unlike the CCC, which focused on building muscles along with vocational skills, schools still emphasized leisure time in their physical education programs, and the new curriculum did little to improve the "soft" bodies that would trouble government and health officials during World War II. Thus despite the construction of swimming pools, sports fields, parks, golf courses, and recreation centers through various New Deal work relief programs, overall interest in physical education waned during the 1930s (Gibbs and Griffin 932).

Following the attack at Pearl Harbor and the release of Selective Service rejection statistics, interest in physical education—especially within schools—increased dramatically, and school fitness programs once again received state, federal, and local attention. Concerned by reports of the nation's deteriorating health, many government and school officials hoped, as Lucien Howe had decades earlier, that better physical education programs would improve the nation's health one generation at a time. Members of the Selective Service system, the War Department, and the Committee on Physical Fitness, however, were a bit less idealistic in their goals for school fitness programs. More concerned with immediate issues of manpower, members of these groups looked to school physical education programs as places for producing fitter, better prepared men for the armed forces.

Leonard Rowntree, one of the most outspoken proponents of improved national fitness, cited school physical education programs as both the cause of and the solution to the growing number of IV-Fs. In his April 1943 presentation at the National War Fitness Conference, Rowntree contended that the poor fitness and health as revealed by military rejection rates was primarily due to a "failure in education" (372).[20] Calling for a revised curriculum with "a *more adequate physical fitness,*" Rowntree argued that peacetime education programs failed "to prepare men for the rigors of war" (372). What was needed, Rowntree suggested, was "an entirely new emphasis— emphasis directed to bodily development" (372). Rowntree's desire to revise education programs to accommodate military needs was shared by many others concerned with wartime manpower needs. Colonel Theodore Bank, director of the athletic branch of the War Department, for example, viewed school physical education programs as areas for improving boys' health to meet military requirements while providing basic premilitary conditioning. Bank stated:

> Many young men are entering the army today totally unprepared for military life. It takes weeks to bring them into the physical condition necessary for military training. *This means weeks of wasted time and effort which could be avoided, if every young man now in high school would engage in physical activities.* (qtd. in Rowntree 371)

Rowntree and Bank's view that school physical education programs should serve as an unofficial extension of military training programs received support from both the government and educators themselves. Considering the expected length of the war and 1943 estimates that 80 percent of boys 16 to 18 would "inevitably face service in the armed forces,"[21] military-influenced physical education programs seemed logical.

While no national mandatory premilitary fitness programs were instituted during World War II, a number of voluntary programs were established. The most famous of these programs, the High School Victory Corps, was a voluntary organization designed to prepare high school students for civilian and military war service. Created by the Office of Education, the program operated at state and local levels in 31 states. In addition to training students in "wartime citizenship" and skills needed for war industry work, the programs offered "pre-induction courses for the Army, such as fundamentals of electricity, shopwork, machines, radio code, Army clerical procedures, military drill" (Studebaker 483). Most importantly, from a physical educator's standpoint, the Victory Corps provided war fitness programs and premilitary physical training. The manual *Physical Fitness through Physical Education for the High School Victory Corps,* issued by the Office of Education and the Committee on Physical Fitness, in fact, incorporated the same basic fitness program issued by the War Department in its November 17, 1942, Training Circular #87. The Victory Corps's physical education program therefore stressed activities such as calisthenics, running, "grass exercises," and sports, as well as basic health and hygiene practices, to develop bodies fit for combat or military service. Complementing national and state programs, private organizations such as the YMCA developed special physical fitness programs in response to the war. Ranging from pre-military service classes such as a Boston YMCA's "Vigor for Victory Program" to "Boymandos" programs throughout the country, the YMCA provided multiple wartime fitness curriculums to prepare boys and men physically for combat duties and war work.[22]

Inspired by state and community fitness programs, many secondary schools and colleges revamped physical education programs to meet wartime needs as well. To assist with these program changes, the army, navy, Committee on Physical Fitness, and Office of Education conducted regional training institutes on physical fitness throughout the country between 1942 and 1944 to instruct teachers, administrators, and local representatives of community fitness programs. The Office of Education and the Committee on Physical Fitness also produced and distributed numerous premilitary training manuals and pamphlets so that schools could revamp programs on their own. As David Brace, principal specialist in physical fitness at the U.S. Office of Education, explained during an address at the National War and Peace Fitness Conference in April 1944, these institutes redefined physical fitness in terms of readiness for combat.[23] According to Brace, school programs were being encouraged to develop the skills "men entering the armed forces will be called upon" to have:

> to walk, climb, carry, lift, strike, run, jump, throw, swim; be calm in the face of confusion; alert and able to make quick responses; be able to hold cramped positions for long hours; have endurance for long continued efforts; be able to relax and recuperate rapidly; go long hours without sleep; render first aid; maintain personal cleanliness; face danger unflinchingly; obey commands willingly, live in crowded conditions without privacy; learn motor skills requiring close eye, hand, and body coordination; have a will to win; and be able to take punishment and come back smiling. (488)[24]

Cultivating the attributes and skills Brace outlined was a rather challenging task—especially for programs that had been geared toward developing fitness for leisure time. Nevertheless, members of the army and navy were quick to show instructors how existing sports and exercises could be modified to cultivate military fitness. After all, the armed forces themselves had been adapting selected sports and athletics into their training programs since the turn of the century.

At the navy's Pre-Flight Training School in Chapel Hill, navy fitness instructors started a coaching school to train high school and college physical education teachers as "ambassadors" for military "hardening and toughening," or what they called "the new regime of physical fitness" (Coaching

School 1–2). At the two-week programs, high school and college instructors participated in "indoctrination lectures," military drill, and fitness exercises and attended classes that explained how to set up appropriate athletic programs at their schools. The instructors received lessons in "football, swimming, military track, gym tumbling, basketball, soccer, rough-and-tumble wrestling and hand-to-hand combat" (Coaching School 8). During the lectures, naval fitness coaches encouraged school teachers to eliminate "recreational" sports such as softball, which did not provide enough physical conditioning, and to emphasize instead sports such as football and boxing, which did contain strong physical contact and competition. While calisthenics and conditioning exercises were deemed important for strengthening and hardening bodies, the major emphasis was on team sports. According to the navy instructors, team sports such as football and basketball would develop in boys "the will to win against all odds, the love of combat, willingness to sacrifice for an ideal, obedience, stamina, determination, aggressiveness, Spartan ruggedness and the desire to cooperate with others" (Coaching School 152). Apart from incorporating specific military exercises, testing methods, and physical standards, most high school and college programs adapted existing sports and athletic programs to fit new wartime fitness needs.

Not restricted to the domain of official training institutes and programs, the idea of adapting popular high school and college sports to premilitary physical training also found its way into advertisements. A November 1942 ad on page 504 of *Journal of Health and Physical Education* for Seal-O-San gymnasium floor finish, for example, featured a presumed correlation between athletic fitness and combat fitness. Appearing as the United States began its offensive phase of the war, the ad links sports skills with combat proficiency both visually and textually. In the top portion of the ad, two figures, a man in basketball attire and a soldier in combat gear, stand side by side, both in the midst of action. Both reach back with their right arms as they prepare to throw—the soldier a hand grenade, the athlete a basketball. The text accompanying the figures reinforces the parallels between sports and combat athleticism. Describing "rifled" passes and a "harder-hitting brand of basketball," the ad reminds viewers that the "sinew-toughening" sport will prepare and condition boys "for the 'bigger game' ahead." The constant play between the sports seasons and the "critical season" of the war along with references to "morale," "the will to win," "fighting minds and muscles," and "Victory" further reinforce the idea that athletic prowess and fitness will help both military and sports "squads" get their jobs done.

In addition to various school, community, and state physical education programs, young men could also engage in premilitary drill on their own. Boys could select one of the many preparation manuals published throughout the war, such as C. Ward Crampton's *Fighting Fitness: A Preliminary Training Guide* or Francois D'Eliscu's *How to Prepare for Military Fitness*. These books, "directed especially to the young men of seventeen" (Crampton ix), provided teens with military fitness tests and physical requirements as well as detailed lessons and exercises to prepare for almost any branch of the military. To supplement school fitness programs and skills learned in the Boy Scouts (readers were encouraged to go through the entire Boy Scout program), young men were to perform daily exercises and to engage in guerrilla war training activities such as "the Daniel Boone Escape Game" (Crampton 112). Like the Victory Corps's training manual, Crampton's text reproduced the War Department's Training Circular #87, so readers could achieve appropriate military fitness. Going beyond basic physical conditioning, however, both D'Eliscu's and Crampton's manuals also adapted basic sports movements and skills to specialized activities like grenade throwing, stalking, wartime wrestling, and night fighting. Further, the manuals contained appendices on military commands, terms, and formations. The only thing the manuals did not provide for young men interested in military training was a uniform.

Although schools and other organizations throughout the nation revamped wartime physical education programs to build the bodies and types of fitness prized by the military, some individuals felt this type of preparation was not sufficient. In his January 14, 1944, address to the Cleveland Boy Scout Council, Frank Knox, secretary of the navy, proposed a plan for a mandatory year of physical training for all boys at the age of 17 or 18. Following Knox's lead, E. B. Degroot, public relations director of the Boy Scouts, likewise called for compulsory military training. At the heart of these proposals was an early cold war mentality that America must be physically prepared for future conflicts. According to Degroot's justifications, "Never again must America be caught unready to go to war at the drop of the hat."[25] Despite Knox's and Degroot's proposals and other urgings for postwar strength, the military influence on school physical education programs did not last well beyond the war years. Nonetheless, from 1941 to 1945 military fitness ideals and physical standards had an enormous impact on national health and fitness debates and programs—especially those aimed at sculpting the bodies of America's youth.

SEX AND SURVEILLANCE—PROTECTING THE MEN PROTECTING AMERICA

In one of the many sex-related scenes of *From Here to Eternity* not included in the film version, the narrator describes "a queer investigation" in which military officers and police interrogate Prewitt and several other G company men about homosexual practices (Jones 396). After asking Prewitt if he has "ever been out with a queer" and receiving a negative response, the police lieutenant turns his investigation of suspected homosexual activity toward other men in the company (404). The policeman asks Prewitt if he has seen any of his company members with men "that looked like they might be queers" (406). Immediately following the description of the "queer inspection," the narrator recounts another scene dealing with sexuality, which offers a bit of the aftermath of the investigation:

> At the monthly Sex Hygiene Lecture and short arm inspection,[26] a week later, Capt Holmes made a short embarrassed speech about perversion and degeneracy, after the movies showing what syphilis and clap can do to you had been run off. The Chaplain, in his address on the importance of love in the sexual act and the necessity of sexual faithfulness and continence on the part of the male before marriage, did not mention [it] either. (409)

Although fictional, these scenes nicely capture the military's interest in monitoring the sexual behavior of its men during World War II as well as its assumptions that sexual experiences could be discerned from examining the bodies of servicemen. Whether in the investigator's inference that one could detect a "queer" by his looks or in the practice of inspecting men's genitalia for venereal disease through "short arm" inspections, we see a pattern of locating sexual identity and behavior in bodily signs. The scenes in *From Here to Eternity* also provide insight into military motives for physically and verbally investigating men's sexuality. As the lieutenant explains to Prewitt, "We're not trying to put the finger on any of you men. We're trying to protect you from these people" (404). Just as the military sought to protect American interests through the careful selection and training of servicemen, it also attempted to safeguard its men and the national body politic from "perverse" sexuality and sexual diseases by screening for homosexuality and venereal disease, with many of its screening methods relying on physical bodily markers for classifying sexual identity and behavior.

As Michel Foucault and other theorists have shown, homosexuality emerged as a distinct identity category or personality type within medical and scientific discourses during the nineteenth century. And since the late nineteenth century, various medical and social scientists have sought to locate the reasons for and forms of homosexual deviance in the body. It was not until World War II, however, that the American military began to outlaw homosexual persons rather than acts within its ranks.[27] In his study of gay men and women during the war, *Coming Out Under Fire*, Allan Bérubé observes that since the late eighteenth century the army and navy have banned the act of sodomy, making the act punishable by court martial and prison sentences. During World War II, the focus shifted from punishing the act of sodomy to "introducing into military policies and procedures the concept of the homosexual as a personality type unfit for military service and combat" (Bérubé 2). This shift in focus had important effects on later military policy, as it forced the military to develop new methods of diagnosis, surveillance, and interrogation.

While the army and navy had a long history of punishing the offense of sodomy under Article of War 93, no formal written procedures for screening out homosexuals during induction examinations existed until May

1941. Between 1921 and 1941, the army had some written guidelines for barring men with "feminine" bodily characteristics or men deemed "sexual perverts," but these standards were never actually implemented (Bérubé 12). With the addition of psychiatrists to World War II examining boards, however, screening procedures for eliminating homosexuals from potential I-A and I-B pools became a reality.

In War Department correspondence concerning the policy shift from punishing sodomy to banning homosexuals, military motives for increased surveillance of homosexuality become clear. Although officers disagreed over the cause of homosexuality and methods of punishment, they agreed that homosexuals must be banned to protect other servicemen. According to a September 9, 1942, memorandum written by officers of the Medical Corps stationed at Brooke General Hospital in Texas, homosexuality was "considered to be a definite mental abnormality," a form of "sexual psychopathy" without any cure.[28] The homosexual had to be banned from the army, the doctors explained, because "he constitutes a demoralizing element in any organization" and was a threat to the men "which sexually stimulate him." Further, the medical officers contended that "homosexuals often react to stimulating situations with emotional instability, panics and psychoneurotic symptoms." Thus, according to the officers' logic, homosexuals posed a threat to both other men's personal bodily space and to a unit's safety during combat.

In order to ensure that homosexuals were not admitted into the armed services, the War Department and Selective Service developed guidelines for psychiatrists to use during their mass screenings of inductees. While some homosexual IV-Fs could be weeded out on the basis of their Selective Service questionnaire responses, most had to be detected through physical and psychiatric examinations. During the early phases of screening, in late 1941, examining psychiatrists relied on a broad set of questions in their neuropsychiatric evaluations. They were instructed to ask men questions like "Are you married or single?" "Do you prefer the company or girls or fellows?" and "Do you like girls?"[29] and to observe the men's reactions as they gave their responses. After the United States entered the war and physical standards were placed under review, the Committee on Neuropsychiatry offered their own suggested revisions for the MR 1-9 standards. In these revisions, the earlier category of "sexual perversion" was further defined, and a set of diagnostic criteria was provided for screening out homosexuals. In the "Suggested Rearrangements of MR 1-9," Tracy Putnam defines "sexual perversions":

> Persons habitually or occasionally engaged in homosexual or other perverse practices are unsuitable for military service and should be excluded. Feminine bodily characteristics, effeminacy in dress or manner, or a patulous rectum, are not consistently found in such persons, but where present should lead to careful psychiatric examination. If a selectee admits or claims homosexuality or other perversion, or has a record as a pervert, he should be referred for special psychiatric and social examination. (16)[30]

In addition to providing certain possible physical signs of homosexuality, the revisions called for a more extensive and carefully outlined physical examination during psychiatric screening. In specifying that the "registrant will be examined stripped" (Putnam 2), the new guidelines for psychiatric exams "reflected a common belief among examiners that physical nakedness could reveal the 'naked truth' about the hidden aspects of a man's personality" (Bérubé 16). Thus examiners could locate homosexuality in physical characteristics like the "feminine" distribution of pubic hair and "feminine" fat deposits and could diagnose homosexuality through so-called effeminate gestures and mannerisms.[31] The assumption was that the homosexual was linked bodily or behaviorally to the feminine gender. Despite these "improved" screening methods, however, very few homosexuals were rejected on the basis of their induction examinations. After examining more than 18 million men throughout the course of the war, the military "had officially rejected only 4,000 to 5,000 as homosexual" (Bérubé 33).

Induction centers were not the only locations for inspecting and studying the bodies of homosexuals. Most reported or confessed homosexuals were sent to military hospitals, where they came under the watchful eyes of military psychiatrists. Eager to take advantage of the military's unique access to and control of men, military psychiatrists conducted numerous wartime studies on homosexuals to develop more reliable screening methods as well as insights into the homosexual as a distinct personality type. Over the course of the war, at least 15 such clinical studies involving more than 2,000 men were conducted, and the research was published in reputable scientific journals such as *The American Journal of Psychiatry, Psychosomatic Medicine,* and *The Psychiatric Quarterly.*[32] Like other doctors, military psychiatrists viewed the war as a unique opportunity to study men and medical issues not normally available to them in civilian life. As the psychiatrists noted, not only did "a greater proportion of homosexuals . . . come under the scrutiny of psychiatrists than ordinarily are observed in civilian life" (Greenspan 682), but also methods of study were more flexible and the "supervision more universal" (McNeel 500).

Because the military was interested in preventing future homosexuals from joining its ranks, many studies were aimed at producing additional diagnostic information and screening criteria.[33] One study specifically designed for and inspired by routine physical examinations was "the gag reflex test." As reported by psychiatrist Nicolai Gioscia, a military doctor's observation about the supposed lack of a gag reflex in admitted homosexuals led to the 1944 study[34] of "1,404 patients at a neuropsychiatric military hospital" (Gioscia 380). In addition to a physical exam and psychiatric evaluation, doctors gave soldiers a gag reflex test "by manipulating a tongue depressor around the uvula, soft palate, and pharyngeal vault" (380). The study found that individuals practicing fellatio generally did not have a normal gag reflex due to a conditioned control of the reflex during the sexual act. According to Gioscia, the findings of the study would be useful in detecting malingers who attempted to "obtain a discharge by professing homosexuality" and as an aid in screening out candidates for military service and civilian "positions where the sexual deviant must be eliminated" (380). While not all military psychiatrists shared Gioscia's views on homosexuals as threatening sexual deviants, there was a definite faction of military doctors that felt screening out suspected homosexuals benefited the nation as well as the military.

Another concern for military psychiatrists was the ability to distinguish between the "true" or "overt homosexual" and the "reclaimable offender." According to a January 10, 1943, War Department memorandum, not all men who committed homosexual acts qualified as "true homosexuals."[35] Given the stresses of war and the absence of "normal" sexual outlets, the memo suggested, some heterosexual men might be led astray. As the memo stated, "It is recognized that the Army will be serving during the period of the war in many parts of the world where the standards of morality may be at variance with our own and that there will be some men, who, through either alcoholic over-indulgence or curiosity, will submit to unnatural relations" (Lewis 1). To determine whether a man qualified as a "true" homosexual, all men suspected of engaging in homosexual practices were sent to psychiatrists for study and evaluation.

In their attempts to separate the "true" homosexual from the "reclaimable offender," military psychiatrists looked to both constitutional and environmental factors. Some doctors like Herbert Greenspan and John Campbell tried to develop a profile of "the homosexual [as] an exclusive personality type," which provided a sort of checklist of male homosexual characteristics (682). Claiming that homosexuality was a "congenital anomaly" present from birth, Greenspan and Campbell argued that an endocrine imbalance caused homosexuals to develop in a predictable fashion and to display certain feminine gestures and mannerisms. Thus, Greenspan and Campbell suggested, the "true" homosexual could be diagnosed by his "abnormal maternal attachment" (683), his "effeminate manner, appearance, temperament and interests" (684), and his "inclination towards the feminine in all possible spheres" (684). Although they urged readers not to view homosexuals as criminals or "detriments to society" (688) and actually suggested that homosexuals could serve effectively in the military in certain positions, Greenspan and Campbell's work served to reinforce existing stereotypes and methods for screening out homosexuals based on the observation of bodily signs.

While many doctors favored Greenspan and Campbell's ideas that homosexuality could be diagnosed through appearance, gestures, and mannerisms, others sought clues to a homosexual's identity through his statements regarding his sexual practices. In their psychiatric profiling of 200 male homosexuals, army doctors A. C. Cornsweet and M. F. Hayes concluded that the "true" homosexual or "oral pervert" could be diagnosed by the type of sexual pleasure he received (76). According to Cornsweet and

Hayes, the "true" homosexual's satisfaction was "purely oral," because he had become accustomed to the "active" role in fellatio.[36] Rather than experiencing sexual satisfaction throughout his body, the "confirmed fellator" felt pleasure solely in "the region of the lips, mouth and oropharynx" (76). Like Gioscia's findings, Cornsweet and Hayes's study was offered as a useful tool in "in distinguishing the true fellator from the malingerer who apes homosexuality but does not have the knowledge to describe the same localized sensations found in the true homosexual" (78).

Armed with diagnostic criteria and information about the "true" homosexual, military psychiatrists played key roles in deciding the fate of reported and self-proclaimed homosexuals. According to the January 3, 1944, War Department Circular #3, "The true or confirmed homosexual deemed not reclaimable" was to be given a blue discharge (without honor), while the "reclaimable" offender was to be "treated" and returned to duty under a different command.[37] Only offenders whose misconduct was "aggravated by independent offenses" were to be subject to court martial and punishment. In the end, discharge from the military largely depended on discharge boards and the members' attitudes toward homosexuality.

Just as the war led to new methods of screening and classifying men's bodies on the basis of health and fitness, it also led to new methods of inspecting men's bodies for supposed sexual deviance. Although these studies offered contradictory and often unscientific evidence, they were nonetheless viewed as valuable tools in the military's effort to protect both the servicemen and the community by diagnosing "sexual perverts." Common to many of the studies was an attempt to locate homosexuality in the body— whether through body build or secondary sex characteristics, or through bodily signs like gestures and mannerisms. By insisting that the "true" homosexual possessed visible "feminine" attributes, military officials were able to preserve the notion that the military was still largely a masculine domain, where a sculpted "masculine" body signaled heterosexuality. The military's policy of differentiating between the "true" homosexual and the "reclaimable offender," however, represents an acknowledgment that one's physique and appearance did not necessarily dictate one's sexual practices.

In addition to its ardent interest in studying homosexuality during the war, the military was also vigilant in its management of venereal infections. Through various venereal disease control and prevention programs, the military monitored not only the bodies and sex lives of servicemen but also the bodies of civilian women with whom they had sexual relations. According to official military rhetoric, these surveillance and management programs were aimed at protecting the health and productiveness of servicemen as well as the well-being and morality of the nation as a whole. While the servicemen themselves often viewed venereal disease prevention films and programs as "somewhere between ludicrous and dreadful" (Dauster, WWII Survey), the military, in conjunction with government and private agencies, poured a tremendous amount of resources into stamping out these "enemies within."[38]

Despite extensive and fairly successful efforts to control venereal disease during World War I, the U.S. government and military viewed the World War I venereal disease rate figures as numbers representing "unacceptable losses."[39] According to an Office of Defense Health and Welfare Services (ODHWS) report by Eliot Ness, "During the First World War, 7,000,000 man-days of service were lost to the United States because of venereal disease. A total of 338,746 men—the equivalent of twenty-three divisions—received treatment" (1).[40] Further, the report estimated, "The number of men infected with syphilis and gonorrhea exceeded those killed and wounded in action by 100,000" (Ness 1). Given the immense size of the armed force they would raise, the military could not afford to lose men to other enemies, "the bacterial Axis of spirochete and gonococci."[41]

Although World War II, like the First World War before it, brought the venereal disease problem to the nation's attention, important measures had been taken in the mid to late 1930s to raise awareness about VD rates, prevention, and treatment programs. Appointed to the office of surgeon general in 1936, Thomas Parran played a pivotal role in breaking the social taboo surrounding the discussion of VD. In addition to writing important articles on the topic for magazines like *Reader's Digest* and *Ladies Home Journal* in 1936 and 1937, Parran also organized a national venereal disease conference in December 1936 and pushed for the May 1938 National Venereal Disease Control Act, which provided federal funds to local, state, and national authorities to develop anti-venereal disease programs ("The Facts" 1). Further, his books *Shadow on the Land: Syphilis* (1937) and *Plain Words About Venereal Disease* (1941) attracted large audiences and linked VD control programs to the current war effort. Stressing the importance of a "clean" armed force, Parran warned the public that "weapons will avail us little unless our men are as good as our machines" (*Plain Words* 2).

Following Parran's lead, the army, the navy, the Public Health Service, the ODHWS, and the American Social Hygiene Association (ASHA) drew up the Eight-Point Agreement in September 1939, which provided "a broad, united attack on venereal disease by both the military authorities and civilian agencies in order to protect the health of men in uniform and the industrial worker" ("The Facts" 1). In addition to providing education, diagnosis, and treatment for military personnel and civilians, the agreement authorized the use of contact report forms and forced isolation for "recalcitrant infected persons . . . during the period of communicability" (2).[42] Thus even before the United States entered the war as a combatant, the military and the government had developed an extensive venereal control program in the name of national defense. This program was further supplemented with Public Law 163, or the May Act (actually passed on July 11, 1941), which made the practice of prostitution in areas near military posts, camps, or stations a federal offense. Under the May Act, military commanders could call on the FBI if local authorities failed to take proper "corrective measures." Thanks to the efforts of the Social Protection Division of the Office of Community War Services, however, the military only had to invoke the May Act in "areas adjacent to Camp Forrest, Tennessee, and Fort Bragg, North Carolina" (Ness 2). Created in March 1941, the Social Protection Division was charged with the task of monitoring and preventing the spread of venereal diseases and repressing prostitution in all defense areas—from camps to war industry plants.

At the heart of all these venereal disease control policies and programs was the idea that prostitutes and "loose" women were the primary instruments of contagion. Although changes in physical requirements in 1942 led to the army's limited induction of men with "uncomplicated cases of gonorrhea" and "adequately treated syphilis" (Foster et al. 28–29), the military maintained the official rhetoric that all VD cases originated in civilian populations. Whether in posters, pamphlets, or articles published in health journals or popular magazines, the military and federal authorities characterized venereal disease as a uniquely feminine threat to the whole, hard bodies created by the service. In the army's 1944 pamphlet "So You've Got a Furlough?" for example, soldiers are told they can protect themselves from VD "by having no sexual relations outside of marriage" and by avoiding "prostitutes, Pick-ups, Push-Overs and 'Easy Women.'" Further, the pamphlet explains, "prostitutes, practically without exception, are infected with Venereal Disease. They are not and cannot be made safe." The pamphlet cautions the serviceman to avoid prostitutes and these other "easy" women just as he "would avoid any other Booby Trap." To reinforce the danger of these "unsafe" vessels of disease, the brochure provides a visual reminder, offering an image of an apparently "loose" woman with the label "booby trap" stamped across her body.

This idea of likening prostitutes and other "easy" women to military threats like booby traps or enemy fire was also utilized in the Social Protection Division pamphlet "She Looked Clean But . . ." directed toward civilians.[43] After explaining that "The prostitute and the 'good-time' girl are usually carriers of disease and disablement" (1), the pamphlet proceeds to compare the damage the women have done to the injuries caused by Axis troops. Juxtaposing a picture of a prostitute with images of German and Japanese soldiers, the pamphlet informs readers, "For every man the enemy puts out of action—she puts out three" (1). As the pamphlet continues, it repeatedly reinforces the notion that prostitutes and "good-time girls" are "wounding" Americans—both in the military and in civilian life. These casualties, the booklet explains, damage the moral fiber of the nation and cost the government millions of dollars. The "$7,000 to $35,000 [cost] to train *one* man for the fighting forces" (7), the pamphlet suggests, becomes wasted tax dollars if that man is taken out of service by venereal infection. According to the booklet, the only solution is to suppress prostitution and to contain the threat of other "easy" women by keeping them away from bars, hotels, and other social establishments.

Artists designing posters for the army and navy likewise used military rhetoric and images to characterize prostitutes, V-girls, and other "loose women" as wartime enemies. Often juxtaposing images of supposedly promiscuous women with pictures of Axis leaders, the posters labeled the women as "another enemy to national defense" and urged servicemen to "know your enemy" when interacting with women of questionable morals. Drawing on World War I strategies, some posters personified syphilis and gonorrhea as voluptuous, often scantily clad women, and reminded viewers that both the diseases and their female carriers were "deadlier than the enemy." Although many military posters aimed at preventing venereal infection focused on a serviceman's contact with a single prostitute or V-girl, some posters emphasized the possible large-scale impact that venereal disease had on America's war effort. One poster reproduced for the Engineer branch of the army's Third Service Command, for example, featured an image of a nurse entering a venereal disease ward in a military hospital. Although the poster visually implies that the bedridden servicemen are part of Hitler's "army in America," it also subtly implicates the women with whom the men had sexual relations. With high heels, a short skirt, and a figure reminiscent of the prostitutes and V-girls in other venereal disease prevention posters, the nurse offers a strong sexual feminine presence, suggesting that Hitler's "American army" draws its strength from its female members. Other army posters, such as the locally posted "It Can Happen to You," however, made the presumed partnership between American prostitutes and the Axis more explicit. Also featuring bedridden men in the "venereal ward" of a military hospital, the poster shows a Japanese soldier placing his right arm on the shoulder of a voluptuous woman with the label "prostitute" superimposed over her short skirt. From the Japanese soldier's mouth a cartoon bubble issues forth, congratulating the prostitute: "You're a pal, babe. Keep up the good work."[44]

Characterizing venereal disease as a feminine threat associated with prostitutes and "pick-ups" gave the Social Protection Division and the military an easy scapegoat already associated with vice, allowing the organizations to shift the blame for rising venereal infection rates away from men and the military. Military policies and statements on VD frequently reversed traditional images of servicemen as the protectors of women and children, positioning them as the ones who needed to be protected from outside threats. In the October 1941 *American Journal of Public Health* article "What the Navy is Doing to Protect Its Personnel Against Venereal Disease," for example, F. R. Lang, a doctor and lieutenant in the Medical Corps, characterized enlisted men—especially the new recruits—as victims "of the wiles of prostitution" (1034). According to Lang, the "masculine world of strict military discipline" (1034) constitutes a safe space for sailors, but this space is constantly threatened by diseases that the serviceman can contract while off duty. He writes:

while on duty, the Navy man is surrounded with and protected by every known means of safeguarding his health, the cost of which represents a considerable investment, while conversely, when he leaves his ship or station on liberty he all too frequently is victimized by a depraved and sordid group of exploiters, who care nothing for his health. (1035)

Like Roosevelt and others who saw a correlation between the health of servicemen and the health of the nation, Lang viewed prostitution as a threat to the navy's efficiency and manpower supply, as well as to, "either directly or indirectly, the health and well-being of the entire nation" (1035). By damaging the bodies of servicemen and war workers, venereal diseases weakened both the body politic and the bodies that made up defense and industry forces.

Military sex hygiene pamphlets and private and government posters also portrayed male bodies as privileged sites for examination and protection. Taking Thomas Parran's previously mentioned plea as its motto, one USPHS poster urged America to "make our men as fit as our machines" with "regular physical check-ups" and blood tests for syphilis. Reminiscent of the steeled bodies of recruitment posters and wartime advertisements, the image in the USPHS poster likens the human body and its interior systems to a machine. Although the poster, distributed to war industry plants nationwide, was supposed to stress the bodily efficiency and productiveness that might be lost because of venereal infection, it also subtly employs the idea that hard, steeled bodies can dam out the soft, feminized threat of venereal disease. By including two small physician figures that seem to be monitoring the man, however, the poster implies that these steel bodies, like machines, can only be maintained with the aid of outside control and surveillance.

Other posters and pamphlets characterized the threat venereal disease posed to the male body as a danger to manhood itself. This idea was prevalent in the War Department's 1940 and 1941 "Sex Hygiene and Venereal Disease" pamphlet issued to men in the army and navy upon induction.[45] In the "Facts About Sex" section, the pamphlet establishes the idea that masculinity is rooted in the body—particularly the sex organs. It begins: "Manhood—Sex is what makes a man a strong two-fisted fellow. No little undeveloped boy can grow to splendid manhood without sex organs. They make a boy grow up with a vigorous body, and they give him grit and strength" (4). The discussion then proceeds to describe "male cells" that make "it possible for a man to become a father" and give "a man strength and bravery" (4). After equating healthy sex organs with strength and masculinity, the pamphlet proceeds to suggest that disease and/or overuse of these organs can "weaken a man." It claims, "Venereal disease may very seriously injure the sex organs, destroy a man's vigor, and ruin his manhood" (5). Not surprisingly, the booklet links venereal disease with the "loose" woman—"whether she takes money for her services or not" (6), positioning the feminine once again as a threat to the male body. This time, however, the danger is not described in moral terms but rather as a physical draining or corrosion of the male sex organs. The best and only definitive way to protect manhood, the pamphlet suggests, is through self-control and "a strong *will power*" (15).

Reinforcing the messages presented in the War Department pamphlet, army and navy posters equated venereal infection with a loss of masculinity. Some posters presented this message directly, urging men to "Keep Your Manhood & Virility" by "keeping away from the syph & clap." Others, meanwhile, emphasized the loss of manliness that accompanied the bodily destruction caused by syphilis. Private D. H. Silver's poster for the Third Air Force, for instance, featured an image of a blind ex-serviceman selling pencils to make its point about the loss of status and health. Pictured next to the phrase "Medal of Horror," the helpless and physically deteriorated ex-serviceman is clearly cast as a burden to society, not as an honorably wounded soldier. Following the military's cue, the ASHA portrayed venereal disease as a threat to manhood in its posters for the civilian population. In one poster, "The Glory of Manhood is Strength," the ASHA equated masculinity and strength with freedom from venereal disease by depicting a strong, muscled forearm ending in a fist. Next to the raised arm is the command to "KEEP CLEAN," which relies on the notion that "heritage of the cleanly is STRENGTH." The poster once again positions the male body as something to be preserved and protected for the sake of the nation's defense.[46]

While early military policies such as those outlined in the December 5, 1941, War Department Circular #249 advocated abstinence and self-control on the part of the serviceman, actual military practice and later policies reflected the idea that heterosexual activity, not abstinence, was seen as an essential part of masculinity.[47] In War Department letters and reports from a joint army and navy conference held on February 28, 1941, military officials admitted that "the perfectly natural desire of young men for the companionship of young women must be recognized" (2).[48] And while the conference focused on ways of providing "more wholesome feminine companionship" (2), army officers also brought up the fact that other members of the military favored regulating prostitution instead of repressing it. Proponents of regulated prostitution claimed that sexual activity was a normal part of "being a man" and that if brothels were put out of business, some servicemen might turn to homosexuality or other "unnatural" sexual outlets. Certainly among the servicemen themselves, there was a sense that sexual activity was part of being a "real" man and a soldier. As historians Beth Bailey and David Farber have noted, "Many high ranking military officers believed that 'any man who won't fuck, won't fight'" (121).

As the war progressed, the gap between official military policy and actual practices in dealing with venereal disease narrowed. Although the military never completely discarded its statements urging abstinence, the War Department did revise pamphlets and sex hygiene posters so that they focused more on prophylaxis and treatment. In fact, as former Pfc. Franklin Simon has noted, it was not uncommon for condoms to be "distributed when passes were given out" (WWII Survey). The most important change in military policy towards venereal disease, however, was the army's decision to stop penalizing men who were diagnosed with a venereal infection. After prompting from the surgeon general in January 1943, the army reviewed its policy of suspending the pay of individuals receiving treatment for venereal diseases, and on September 27, 1944, Congress repealed the earlier provision (Sternberg et al. 143–46). The bill also affected policies where, in some organizations, noncommissioned officers who acquired a venereal disease received a reduction in rank (Sternberg et al. 146). This radical change in army policy reflected both advancements in drug treatments for syphilis and gonorrhea and an acceptance of servicemen's sexual activity. According to the army's logic, removing penalties for men acquiring venereal diseases would check the spread of unreported disease. Many military officials feared, however, that abolishing penalties for venereal disease would give servicemen free rein to engage in reckless sexual activity.

Even before the army ceased penalizing servicemen who contracted venereal diseases, control programs reflected an acknowledgment that servicemen would inevitably engage in sexual activity. Shortly after the attack at Pearl Harbor, the army reorganized its Venereal Control Division and appointed venereal disease control officers to all its divisions. Control officers were charged with running education programs, maintaining prophylaxis facilities and distributing individual prophylaxis kits,[49] eliminating "civilian sources of infection," detecting and treating cases of VD, and collecting and analyzing data on venereal diseases acquired by men in units under their command (Sternberg et al. 154). Since the army held them directly responsible for VD rates in their command, control officers did whatever they felt necessary to prevent and control infection rates within their units. Often this entailed monthly "short arm" inspections and the direct monitoring of men's bodies. Sometimes, however, it meant sidestepping army policy by regulating prostitution and inspecting civilian women's bodies.

Although the May Act and the activities of the Social Protection Division closed many brothels in the United States and its territories, the act was ignored in Hawaii and other areas. As Bailey and Farber note in *The First Strange Place: The Alchemy of Race and Sex in World War II Hawaii,* many local and military authorities in Hawaii chose to ignore anti-prostitution laws and continued to regulate brothels by forcing prostitutes to have weekly gynecological exams and regular VD testing (99–101). In Honolulu, for example, the military failed to invoke the May Act, placed prophylaxis stations on Hotel Street—where most of the brothels were located—and posted signs in the waiting rooms of brothels "reminding men where to go and why they should" (Bailey and Farber 107). The Hotel Street prophylaxis stations were both well used and effective; by mid-1943, medical workers at these stations could treat 1,500 men each hour. Thanks to regulated brothels and a strong prophylaxis program, "The Hawaii military district had the lowest VD rates in the armed forces" (Bailey and Farber 107, 121).

Although the May Act applied only to the United States and its territories, venereal disease control officers were encouraged to suppress prostitution by cooperating with local authorities overseas. To the dismay of army and government officials, it became increasingly evident "that prostitution not only existed but in some oversea areas was being actively supported by U.S. Army commanding officers" (Sternberg et al. 173). In places like Naples and Sicily, army medical officers inspected brothels and drew up a list of "approved" ones, placing all others off limits. At the acceptable ones, the military set up prophylaxis stations and placed MPs there to ensure that the men used the condoms. Further, a Medical Department enlisted man inspected each soldier upon arrival, and local doctors checked prostitutes for disease under army supervision (Sternberg et al. 213–17). In the Philippines and other Asian territories, army personnel actually assisted in "the routine checking, examination, and treatment of hostesses and prostitutes" (Sternberg et al. 301). As their reports indicate, venereal disease control officers did not hesitate to extend their surveillance to bodies of civilian women in their efforts to lower VD rates in their units.

On the home front, state health boards assisted control officers. Invoking quarantine acts, which allowed them to isolate people with communicable diseases, state health boards created camps for women of "easy virtue." An April 1943 *Collier's* article by J. D. Ratcliff[50] reported on the first of these camps, the Leesville Quarantine Hospital, which was established under the direction of George Leiby in Louisiana. Funded by the FSA, the 120-bed barracks and hospital provided a mandatory treatment and education program for women mentioned in the military's venereal disease contact reporting forms. In addition to medical exams and drug treatment programs, the women received sewing lessons and other instruction and were required to meet with social workers, who aimed to reform the "wayward" women. Although the camp was officially called a hospital, the barracks was surrounded "by a charged-wire fence" and was "patrolled by state troopers" (Ratcliff 16). Like other threats to the health of servicemen, the women—"wasters of manpower"—were contained to preserve the safety of the nation. Following the success of the Leesville Quarantine Hospital, 30 abandoned CCC camps were renovated to create similar facilities near army camps. Unlike the internment camps for Japanese Americans, however, the camps for these women were designed to contain temporary threats to the nation; the women were allowed to leave once they had been cured and "reformed."

World War II created a unique opportunity for the screening and management of American male and female bodies. Selective Service classifications and the mobilization of an unprecedented armed force led not only to the advent of revised military classification systems but also to the creation of new discourses about bodies and the health of the nation. These discourses in turn led to the formation of new physical training and screening programs for war workers, schoolchildren, and other civilians, which were heavily influenced by military methods and ideals. In the name of national defense, the military, in cooperation with government and private organizations, also developed extensive programs and testing methods to eliminate "sexual perversions" and venereal disease from its ranks. These efforts, aimed at "protecting" servicemen, often resulted in the direct surveillance of military as well as civilian bodies. Military, ASHA, and Social Protection Division rhetoric excused these forms of surveillance and other proposals for national mandatory VD testing[51] as necessary means of preserving the nation's health and defense. Military screenings for homosexuality and wartime venereal disease prevention programs, however, often resulted in practices rarely tolerated outside of wartime, as individual liberties and bodily privacy were frequently impinged upon in the name of strengthening the nation's body politic.

In keeping with visual representations of the wartime body politic, the serviceman's body became a privileged site for developing and communicating ideas about national strength. Selection, training, and venereal disease suppression programs worked in tandem to create an armed force of America's healthiest men and to keep the nation's servicemen "as fit as our machines." While medical advances in treating diseases and an extensive prophylaxis program offered the military powerful tools for protecting its men from VD, the U.S. still had to contend with other wartime threats to servicemen's bodies and constructions of masculinity. Wounds from combat, accidents, and other diseases often offered more serious challenges to servicemen's bodies and masculine ideals, and even greater national efforts by the government, media, and medical profession were required to rehabilitate the war-wounded body.

PERSONAL, POPULAR, AND MEDICAL NARRATIVES

A wound was not simply damage to the body like a crumpled fender on a car. A wound was a process.

—Albert Cowdrey,

Fighting for Life

Between 1942 and 1945, popular American periodicals printed numerous stories about the "miracles" of modern military medicine. Readers not only learned about the wonders of the new sulfa drugs, penicillin, dried plasma, and whole blood transfusions but also encountered advertisements for E. R. Squibb & Sons and Johnson & Johnson that informed them "How the Army Cares for Your Boy if He Is Wounded." Medical reports and advertisements explained treatment and evacuation processes and provided readers with encouraging statistics about the army and navy's 97 percent success rate in saving the lives of those wounded in combat.[1] *Time*'s April 2, 1945, story about a Russian doctor's wartime surgical work transplanting testicles from dead bodies to living men then, appeared to be just another "miracle" of wartime medicine.

The article, "Virility Transplanted," detailed Dr. Anatole Frumkin's past reconstructive plastic surgery techniques for repairing genital wounds as well as his latest experiment in grafting testicles. The spectacular results of a transplant of a dead civilian's testicles to a Red Army colonel were described in the article: "The colonel's piping voice went down, his red beard sprouted anew, the fat around his hips disappeared, and he began to take an interest in women again" (55). Although these results were similar to ones that could "be achieved by regular hormone injections of pellets of slow-dissolving hormones implanted under the skin" (55) and were not guaranteed to last indefinitely, the essay nonetheless ended with the vision of potentially restored "normal" masculinity and corporeality. The medical report's hopeful ending countered its ominous beginning, which described German "castrator mines" and mentioned the fact that these "most inhumane of all war wounds" have "driven hundreds of men to suicide in World Wars I and II" (54).

Although it was one of many reports on the wonders of military medicine, the *Time* article was unique in its subject matter. For some Americans, it may have been their only wartime exposure to the fact that mines and artillery mutilated the genital area just as randomly and frequently as they targeted other parts of the body; they certainly would not have seen any images of American servicemen with genital wounds. As George Roeder has noted in *The Censored War*, "All photographs that depicted what appeared to be genital wounds ended up in the files of censored materials and remained there even after release of other images of painful wounds" (115). Even in the censored files, the wounds depicted in the photographs remained unnameable; official captions to the images frequently described the injuries as "abdominal wounds" (Roeder 115).

Indeed, the unnameability associated with photographs of genital wounds was in keeping with servicemen's wartime actions and attitudes. While in combat, infantrymen often crossed their legs under shell fire, and bomber crews would frequently sit on their helmets, exposing their heads, when they encountered flak. In the words of Keith Wheeler, a wounded war reporter for the *Chicago Daily Times*, there were simply "places where a man dreads being hit" (25). Later in his 1945 volume *We Are the Wounded*, Wheeler offered more emphatic comments about the particular horror of a wound in the groin: "Nothing much worse can happen to a man this side of death" (175). Wheeler's comments and the servicemen's actions reveal that, even in the face of death, men frequently privileged the safety of the penis over the rest of the body in order to maintain a sense of phallic masculinity.

As the *Time* article highlights, individual war wounds changed in meaning for various audiences. Whereas a genital wound might signal the end of a serviceman's "livable" embodied existence, for a plastic surgeon, it might represent an opportunity to advance medical science. Both responses, however, are linked to cultural definitions of masculinity predicated on the notion of the "whole" strong body. As chapter one revealed, idealized representations of male bodies were of physiologically intact, well-muscled, steeled entities that represented national strength. The inevitable presence of wounded bodies therefore posed potential threats to the wartime body politic as well as to America's postwar strength and its return to normalcy.

Elaine Scarry suggests in *The Body in Pain: The Making and Unmaking of the World* that the fluidity of the wound's referent forces us to interpret wounded bodies in relation to various signs and contexts (118). Each wound is unique in terms of its occurrence, context, and experiential dimensions, and each wound and wounded body holds varied meanings for different viewers. Despite the uniqueness of each wound, however, during the war there emerged a notion of the generalizable wounded body, which could be interpreted across a wide range of discourses and deployed in multiple contexts for propagandist and other ends. Personal, popular, and medical representations of wounded American male bodies during and immediately after World War II reveal a range of cultural responses to U.S. war injuries. In addition to their obvious impact on the morale of persons fighting abroad and of those working on the home front, the representations of wounded male bodies offered important sites for redefining and reinscribing cultural definitions of masculinity—especially as America sought to restabilize gender roles radically reconfigured by the war. The war-wounded male body and efforts to rehabilitate it highlight the centrality of servicemen's bodies in constructing national self-definitions as well as the performative nature of masculinity. Paradoxically, the injured male body became a vehicle through which the U.S. could demonstrate its strength by rehabilitating men through superior technology and by extolling men's own self-generated remasculinizations. Nevertheless, an examination of war-wounded bodies also reveals that war produces alternative or "abject" masculinities that exist alongside and in opposition to dominant cultural representations.

Although Scarry's notion of wound as referentless reminds us that we must consider wounds and wounded bodies within their unique contexts and interpret them in relation to cultural signs, it does not provide a vocabulary for considering the generalizable wounded body—the wounded body that still imparts meaning across a wide range of cultural discourses. Julia Kristeva's writings on abjection, however, offer a point of departure for analyzing the war-injured body. Her work provides a ground for theorizing the commonalties of various types of wounds as well as for rethinking the wounded body in relation to the "whole" body and dominant models of gender identity.

Drawing on the work of anthropologist Mary Douglas, Kristeva outlines her notion of the abject and its relation to bodily fluids in *Powers of Horror: An Essay on Abjection.*[2] According to Kristeva, the abject marks the boundaries of subjectivity; it registers the limits of the human universe, demarcating the realm in which humans stray into the territory of the animal, the nonhuman (12–13). Neither subject nor object, "the abject has only one quality of the object—that of being opposed to the *I*" of subjectivity (Kristeva 1). While Kristeva examines abjection to illustrate how subjectivity gets constituted through a process of exclusion (abjection) and to examine women's historical exclusion from the subject position, the concept of the abject has important implications for understanding the ways in which culture marks embodied subjectivities. Certain bodily fluids such as blood, saliva, urine, and feces, Kristeva argues, can be viewed as the abject because they traverse the boundary of the body. These fluids not only "collapse the border between [the] inside and outside" of bodies but also, through their culturally marked status as pollutants, threaten the body with illness or death—the end of subjectivity (Kristeva 53, 71). Ultimately, however, it is not the "lack of cleanliness or health that causes abjection but what disturbs identity, system, order" (Kristeva 4); the pollutant's potential for disrupting subjectivity depends on the degree to which it is prohibited by cultural demarcations of the clean and proper body (69–72).

In her own discussion of body fluids and Kristeva's writings on the abject, Elizabeth Grosz suggests that abjection of bodily fluids and waste has distinct meanings for sexed bodies. Whereas the female body has traditionally been constructed "as a leaking, uncontrollable, seeping liquid; as formless flow; as viscosity, entrapping, secreting" (203), the phallicized male body has been constructed as self-contained, impermeable, and sealed-up (Grosz 201). Therefore bodily fluids and the suggestion of permeability pose a particular threat to the male body. As Grosz explains, "Perhaps it is not after all flow in itself that a certain phallicized masculinity abhors but the idea that flow moves or can move in two-way or indeterminable directions that elicits horror, the possibility of being not only an active agent in the transmission of flow but also a passive receptacle" (201). Because they present a challenge to phallic impenetrability, Grosz contends, men's bodily fluids are generally not represented or are distanced from the body through rites of cleansing or by transforming fluids into solids (201). Through these efforts men can "demarcate their own bodies as clean and proper" (Grosz 201).

This prohibition against showing "leaky" male bodies partly explains why American soldiers did not shed any blood in print until a May 14, 1945, issue of *Life* ran a Robert Capa photo depicting a dying soldier next to a pool of his own blood or why Office of War Information (OWI) censorship policies kept images of crying servicemen conspicuously out of view (Roeder, *Censored War* 1, 124).[3] Despite these cultural prohibitions against representing men's bodily fluids, World War II forced its participants to deal with a tremendous amount of the abject. Through its production of corpses, filth, and injured bodies, combat undermined the notion of the impenetrable male body in multiple ways.

In addition to the corporeal damage caused by anti-personnel weapons, combat also exposed the limits of the phallic body through fear-inspired bodily wastes and fluids. Despite men's best efforts to "keep a tight asshole"[4] and to behave bravely under fire, fear often overcame the will to maintain the perception of a sealed-up body; in the face of terrifying combat, bodily wastes such as feces, urine, and vomit provided visible signs of that fear. According to the results of one World War II questionnaire, "Over one-quarter of the soldiers in one division admitted that they'd been so scared they vomited, and almost a quarter said that at terrifying moments they'd lost control of their bowels. Ten percent had urinated in their pants" (Fussell, *Wartime* 277). Although servicemen knew that such bodily manifestations of fear were common on the battlefield (and most likely occurred

more frequently than any study reported), a tremendous prohibition remained against acknowledging this loss of manhood. The dread of allowing
other men to view one's corporeal signs of cowardice was so great, veteran
and World War II scholar Paul Fussell reports, that men refused medical attention for fear of exposure. In *Wartime: Understanding and Behavior in the
Second World War,* Fussell describes one such incident: "During the Normandy invasion, a group of American soldiers came upon a paratrooper
sergeant caught by his chute in a tree. He had broken his leg, and shit and
pissed himself as well. He was so ashamed that he begged the soldiers not
to come near him, despite his need to be cut down and taken care of"
(278). While not explicitly thematized, the paratrooper's shame was probably linked both to the exposure of his fear and penetrability as well as to
cultural associations of fluids with the feminine and the infantile. The solution to preserving one's manhood, veteran Edward Wood points out, was to
"deny the juices in yourself" (65). As he explained, "There are enemies out
there, boy, to get you if you go soft . . . you'll get carved up if you aren't
hard as a rock on the killing grounds" (65).

Defining the limits of the self-contained, whole body, the untimely and
uncontrolled release of fluids during combat easily falls within the realm of
the abject. I would argue, however, that the damage inflicted on the body
through war wounds might also be understood in terms of abjection. While
not all individuals perceived their wounds as marking the limits of the
body or boundaries of subjectivity, many personal and popular descriptions
of war injuries construct the wound as "foreign" or "not self."

Popular novels such as James Bellah's *Ward Twenty* (1946) and Betsy Barton's *The Long Walk* (1948), for instance, feature characters who, when recalling their initial wounding or viewing their damaged body, see their
wounds as alien, "not self." In *Ward Twenty,* Pasquale Cancellare reflects on
the moments after his 1943 injury in Naples: "He saw what he was dragging after him as he tried to crawl away—saw with utter disbelief and sudden, white horror" (32).[5] Cancellare's reaction of terror in seeing the mass
of flesh from his buttocks is similar to Woody's daily experiences in *The
Long Walk.* Inspecting his neighbor in the ward for spinal injuries, Woody,
the novel's protagonist, contrasts Mac's muscular upper body and his with-
ered lower body: "Here, with his paralysis, the character of his body changed.
Below the place of his spinal wound the skin was dry and scaly. . . . The perfection of the man's chest and upper body was contradicted so acutely in the
weak helplessness of his hips and legs. The sight never failed to shock him"
(3). Reflecting further on the other men's bodies and his own, Woody concludes, "With their wound, the source of life had been split in two in
them. Still, drugged with shock, they had looked upon their motion-
less, senseless legs, as remotely as if they were those of a wax dummy"
(4). It would be a long time, Woody surmises, before the men would be
able "to reabsorb their paralyzed legs as their own" (4). Woody's reflections reveal that the men have drawn new boundaries for their embod-

ied subjectivities; the portions that can be controlled and read culturally as "masculine" get aligned with the notions of self while the wounded sections of their bodies remain abject.

Perceptions of the wounded body in terms of abjection likewise appeared in personal wartime narratives of injury and treatment. In *We Are the Wounded,* for example, Keith Wheeler reminds his readers that the war produced abjection not only through corpses and "filth and decay and violence" (12) but also in the bodies of the wounded. Wheeler's descriptions of being wounded as a state almost worse than death highlight the ways in which culturally invested notions of wholeness assist in designating the injured body as abject. While "whole" (not injured) himself, Wheeler felt pity for the dead and horror over what "it must be for each dead man to be aware of the repulsive trash his body had become" (13). After his injury, however, Wheeler notes that it was the wounded who in fact became "human debris" with their "bodies as badly wrecked, as shorn of dignity, as helpless as the dead" (13). According to Wheeler, the dead, who no longer owe "an obligation to the wasted wreckage of their bodies" (13), achieve a form of freedom in their disembodied subjectivity. The wounded, though, have to endure "the decay of themselves" and to "accept a sentence to live out a man's time chained to a body that was only half, or less than half of a man" (13). Wheeler's comments link the wounded body both to abject substances (waste, decay, filth) as well as to an abject masculinity. In Wheeler's framework, the "whole" male body is accorded the status of masculine subjectivity while the wounded body becomes "less than half a man." What Wheeler fails to realize is that the "whole" male body is not a natural source of masculinity. The abject wounded body is vital to conceptions of the "whole" body; "whole" masculinity defines itself by what it excludes or rejects—bodily fluids, waste, wounds.

ON BEING WOUNDED—SERVICEMEN'S PERSPECTIVES

In addition to the 292,131 U.S. battle deaths that occurred during the war (Wallechinsky 206), approximately 671,000 servicemen suffered nonfatal combat wounds.[6] Given the fact that more than 16 million American men served in the Second World War, these battle casualty rates may seem quite light—especially in comparison to the 11 nations that suffered higher death totals. However, considering that "fewer than 1 million, probably no more than 800,000, took part in any extended combat" and that combat soldiers comprised only 14 percent of overseas American troops, the chance of being injured in battle was quite high (Linderman 1). Participation in battle, however, was not the only way that American bodies were injured; millions of servicemen suffered bodily injury through training exercises, accidents, malingering, and from diseases. In fact, of the 994,241 army disability discharges issued between 1942 and 1945, "86% resulted from disease, 3% from nonbattle injuries, and 11% from wounds" (Reister 13).

Diseases in the Pacific theaters, such as dengue fever, malaria, dysentery, typhus (scrub), jungle rot, and "blue nail," could be particularly virulent and often left their victims with lifelong side effects.[7] In the end, bodily injuries from nonbattle causes greatly exceeded the number of combat injuries, and most servicemen suffered some type of wound or illness requiring medical attention. According to U.S. Census Bureau figures, during World War II the army recorded 17,919,000 hospital admissions while the navy and marines had 5,514,000 admissions (Census Bureau 1140).[8]

Despite the large number of men who received combat and nonbattle wounds, there are surprisingly few accounts of wounding and treatment by the servicemen themselves. While this silence no doubt stems from the pressures associated with hegemonic constructions of masculinity, the absence of personal narratives may also be due in part to the general inexpressibility of pain and the nature of wounding. Elaine Scarry has noted that pain and wounding resist "objectification in language" because the experiences cannot be confirmed and possess "no referential content" (4–5). Without a common vocabulary for expressing pain and wounding, servicemen would have had difficulties communicating their experiences to civilians and even to other servicemen who did not share their particular type or severity of wound. Even if pain and wounding did not resist expression in language, many servicemen probably had little desire to dwell on injury experiences. Because of social pressures urging veterans to obtain employment, further their education, and return to their former social roles in postwar America, few servicemen wanted to publicly dredge up the horrifying memories of war or to relive a process that threatened the masculine wholeness of their bodies. The narratives of war wounding and recovery which do exist—hospital interviews, questionnaire and oral history responses, and published nonfiction narratives—provide insights into servicemen's perspectives on their war wounds and the process of recovery. While the uniqueness of each serviceman's wound(s) and war experiences precludes any definitive descriptions, the narratives reveal certain commonalties and themes.

As Keith Wheeler's comments about genital wounds have shown, there were some parts of the body where men dreaded being hit more than others; well-known medical statistics about the particularly high mortality rate of abdominal, chest, and head wounds made those areas especially feared targets. Of these wounds, abdominal wounds had the highest mortality risk—"290 percent above average." Chest wounds were next lethal with an 85 percent above-average mortality rate, followed by head, face, and neck wounds, which had a mortality rate "about 30 percent above average" (Beebe and DeBakey 82). But men were not simply concerned with the location and type of bodily damage a wound might inflict. Particular methods of wounding were dreaded almost as much as injuries to specific body parts. Veteran Eugene Sledge recalls that death or wounding by bullets seemed "so clean and surgical" compared to other technologies of destruc-

tion (qtd. in Fussell, *Wartime* 278). Modern technological advances in artillery, mines, booby traps, and air and tank warfare, however, made bullet
wounds a relatively rare occurrence compared to earlier wars; in World War
II men were four times more likely to be wounded by "weapons other than
bullets" (Cowdrey 162). For ground troops, artillery barrage or shelling was
a particularly terrifying mode of wounding because of the horrific physical
and psychological damage it inflicted. Quoting veteran Vernon Scannell,
Fussell notes that the term "emasculating" was used to describe "the special
fear caused by shelling" (278). A destructive technology that could atomize
bodies from a great distance, shelling threatened both the wholeness of the
body and the masculinity of men who could not directly confront this enemy fire. With shelling there were no hand-to-hand confrontations or
other opportunities for soldiers to prove their fighting prowess.

Ironically enough, sometimes the urge to preserve the appearance of
masculinity and the wholeness of the body led to a desire to be wounded.
As Fussell explains, "To spare themselves the awful moment of psychological breakdown, with its appearance of cowardice, soldiers wanted to be
wounded: except for death, a severe wound was the only way out that did
not imply letting the side down" (*Wartime* 281). Such attitudes led to the
concept of the "million dollar wound"—an injury serious enough to get a
serviceman permanently out of combat but not so damaging that life or
limbs were lost. These attitudes also occasionally led to malingering or self-
inflicted wounds. While the incidence of malingering was so low that it did
not merit treatment in the army's *Medical Statistics in World War II,* it did
occur often enough to warrant discussion in wartime volumes on military
medicine. In his 1942 article "Malingering,"[9] Lieutenant Colonel Albert
Groves Hulett estimated that some 50 thousand cases (mostly psychoneurotic) of malingering were not detected by medical examiners during World
War I because of a reluctance to recognize "that all men are not possessed
of manhood" (528). Although Hulett's essay focuses primarily on types of
deceptions that Selective Service examinees might attempt, he also discusses the various bodily mutilations that soldiers might inflict on themselves to avoid combat or to obtain a discharge:

> Instances wherein a man has chopped-off fingers or an entire hand, a toe or
> even an entire foot, has had all his teeth extracted, punctured his own ear-
> drum or blinded one eye with acid or caustic alkali, has produced a rectal, oral
> or nasal ulceration by chemical or mechanical agents, has slashed a tendon in
> his arm or leg, or even deliberately fractured a limb, are on record. (523)

Obviously extreme examples, these instances of malingering reveal the extent to which some servicemen went to escape the possibility of more extensive bodily injury—damage over which they would have no control.

Just as there were shared attitudes toward particular types and modes of
wounding, there were certain conventions for describing wounds. A shared

feature of many narratives, for example, is the importance placed on the circumstances in which the wound was received. Almost all of the hospital interviews and nonfictional narratives I have encountered begin with the time, place, and immediate events leading up to the moment of wounding. Typical narratives might begin, "On January 10, 1945 at about 0930 hours, my tank was advancing toward the enemy in the Bastogne area, when an armored piercing shell hit us" or "I was wounded near Schleiden, Germany, on February 3rd."[10] This tendency to stress the context in which the wound occurred may be, in part, due to the context's superior ability to convey pain or distress. As Elaine Scarry has noted, many medical histories begin with a description of the accident (or moment of wounding) because they "more successfully convey the sheer fact of the patient's agony than those sentences that attempt to describe the person's pain directly" (15). Thus the corporal's description of the "armored piercing shell" and its fragments might convey the severity of his wound and the damage done to the tank better than accounts of his "flopping leg" and "a stinging sensation some-where in his body."[11] Further, the general context of the events leading up to the injury helps provide a point of reference often absent in the moment of wounding itself. Repeatedly in the hospital interviews, soldiers remarked that they did not know they had been hit until they noticed bodily signs such as blood or pain, or the actual wounded portion of the body. Service-men frequently made comments such as, "I don't remember any particular sensation on being hit," "I remember nothing whatever of the moment when I was hit," or "I did not realise [sic] at the moment it had hap-pened."[12] Indeed hospital interviews and nonfiction narratives reveal that the act of wounding is irreducible to any single moment. The spatial and temporal moment just before the wounding, however, becomes fixed in the soldier's mind, serving as a reference point for his entry into the abject, the land of the wounded. The concreteness of this moment stands in marked contrast to the fluidity in time and embodied existence that accompanies a serious wound.

The circumstances surrounding the injury also became important for ser-vicemen as they tried to understand and give meaning to their wounds.[13] Historian Gerald Linderman has noted that although the "conception of combat as a test of the individual" had lost some of its staying power since the Spanish-American War, during World War II the myth "that combat was the ultimate test of the soldier's courage and manhood" was still very much alive (8). Thus wounds incurred while fighting bravely, in the con-text of killing a large number of enemy soldiers or taking a key location, could bestow honor or sense of purpose to the wounded individual. The military system of awarding medals such as the Purple Heart to "the honor-ably wounded" reinforced this concept. In his discussion of the medal cere-mony for those wounded at Iwo Jima, Keith Wheeler explains, "You don't feel like a hero exactly, but you do feel that your hurts and time and cir-cumstances of your receiving them merit a certain amount of time and attention, maybe even sympathy and admiration" (214). Further, medals and the context of receiving a wound helped convey the experience to others; a civilian might better understand the horror and pain of a wound if it could be linked to a battle involving tremendous casualties such as Normandy, Tarawa, or Iwo Jima.

Not all wounds, though, were "honorable wounds," and these nonvalorous injuries often complicated the individual's struggle to assign meaning to a wound. In his discussion of a young private's attempts to make sense of his missing legs, Wheeler writes, "Chuck hadn't even the considerable moral satisfaction of having lost them in combat. He was a Second Division marine whose legs had been shattered in a training accident when a satchel charge exploded ahead of time and too near" (111). The randomness or lack of honorable circumstances of a wound could sometimes impart lifelong consequences. Edward Wood Jr.'s memoir *On Being Wounded* details the ways in which his September 7, 1944, injury in France "irrevocably changed [his] life" (ix). An infantry replacement in 1944, Wood longed to prove himself under fire in order to gain the respect of his new squad. On his first day in combat, however, he was hit during an artillery barrage while digging a foxhole. Reflecting on his wounds, Wood writes: "In my deepest self I still wondered about my combat experience—wounded in the butt and only a day at the front . . . I embarked on the terrible desperate search for a meaning to my wounding" (76, 83). Wood's efforts to understand his wounds lead to reflections about his perceived cowardice and, ultimately, to lifelong reflections about familial and cultural definitions of masculinity.

Wood's memoir, which describes his wound as a force in radically altering his embodied subjectivity, also exposes other aspects of wounding and abjection. Although Wood is troubled by the circumstances of his wound and its ability to mark the limits of his culturally intelligible masculinity, he also embraces "the land of the wounded" and the sense of community it affords. Wood finds in his abjection, in his separation from the confines of "whole," impenetrable masculinity, a liberating site of freedom and exchange. Detailing his treatment at the Battle Aid Station, Wood recalls:

> Here at the front, before there were forms and bureaucrats to describe and fasten me to some categories of wound and pain, I touched men who, for an instant, cared for me with greater compassion than I had ever experienced at any time or place in my life—men who lit my cigarette and held it in my fingers while I puffed, men who turned to me again and again, seeing if my paralyzed hand would yet move, if my bowels were free, my urine not pink with blood, murmuring to me gently, even crying. (18)

Wood recognizes in his treatment at the front and in subsequent hospitals "a softness so difficult for the American male to express—always there but held back, contained by some impenetrable shell, breaking open now and warming me after I was wounded" (19). Wood's description of the empathy and community is echoed in Wheeler's account of the treatment of the wounded at military hospitals. In addition to being tenderly cared for in the hospital, Wheeler asserts, the wounded are also "among their own kind, men who have shared his experiences, with whom he can live and talk on terms of mutual knowledge and understanding" (223). Wounds, in calling attention to the limits of the body and phallic masculinity, can also be interpreted in terms of flow and exchange rather than loss. The wound becomes a site of interaction both between a body and medical processes and between embodied individuals. In short, the wound troubles the concept of the "whole" phallic body by revealing that all bodies are in process, constantly engaged in loss, and provides the medium for individuals to break down barriers constructed by notions of phallic masculinity.

In fact, what emerges is an alternative, abject masculinity produced by war. Novelist James Jones and other World War II veterans point out that wounding and combat create a space for a more fluid masculinity—one that exists apart from yet in relation to dominant cultural constructions. In *The Thin Red Line,* Jones describes this alternative space that men enter after being wounded:

> They had crossed a strange line; they had become wounded men; and everybody realized, including themselves, dimly, that they were now different. . . . They had been initiated into a strange, insane, twilight fraternity where explanations would be forever impossible. Everybody understood this; as did they themselves, dimly. It did not need to be mentioned. . . . Tenderness was all that could be given (45).

As this passage reveals, not only are the wounded "initiated" into an alternative space where tenderness and exchange replace violence and sealed-up subjectivities, but *all* of the men are altered by combat. Through their contact with the dead, the wounded, and their own bodily fluids, the men of C-for-Charlie company enter combat's world of abject masculinity. Although still caught up with cultural definitions of masculinity, the men are free to explore alternative homosocial bonds and actions discouraged within cultural gender norms. Within the space of combat's abject masculinity, men can engage in homosexual activities without being labeled "queer," the uncontrolled release of bodily fluids becomes somewhat normalized, and men can express fear, tenderness, and other culturally inappropriate feelings. Thus despite its associations with honor and valor, combat produces a range of masculinities, which both reinforce and undermine cultural definitions.

"WHEN THE WOUNDED COME HOME"—POPULAR NARRATIVES

America's entry into World War II precipitated a dramatic rebuilding of the U.S. body politic—one based primarily on youthful, whole, well-muscled male bodies. These whole bodies communicated national strength as well as phallic impenetrability, reinforcing popular notions that masculinity was tied to a whole, strong body. America's entry into the war, however, also presented very real opportunities for these whole, strong bodies to be maimed and destroyed. Quite clearly the presence of wounded bodies offered the potential to destabilize America's newly rebuilt body politic. This may have been the case had the OWI and Hollywood's War Activities Committee not carefully shaped America's visual experience during the Second World War. Wartime censorship policies limited the release of pictures of war dead and presented the public with sanitized images of the war wounded.

In his study of wartime censorship policies, George Roeder outlines the ways in which the OWI and other government and nongovernment agencies controlled the public's exposure to war images. Following World War I censorship practices, "the government prohibited publication of any photographs of the American dead . . . for the first twenty-one months of American involvement in World War II" (Roeder, *Censored War* 8). Further, the OWI restricted the publication of "photographs of those maimed in combat" and of injuries incurred through training accidents, racial incidents, malingering, battle fatigue, and "friendly fire" (Roeder *Censored War* 3, 16, 24). During the first year of U.S. involvement, the American public saw very little evidence of the war's damaging effects on the bodies of American servicemen. This conspicuous absence of dead and wounded bodies in the media troubled Roosevelt's advisers, who feared that the American public would misperceive the scope and human cost of the war. An OWI memo explained the problem: "The public was getting the impression that 'soldiers fight, that some of them get hurt and ride smiling in aerial ambulances, but that none of them get badly shot or spill any blood'" (qtd. in Roeder, *Censored War* 10). Fearing that the public would be unprepared for the return of war wounded and that it had become complacent in its war efforts, the OWI and the War Department's Bureau of Public Relations (BPR) began to clear more images of wounded and dead American servicemen for publication. In fact, beginning in 1943, government posters and commercial advertisements began to incorporate representations of wounded servicemen in order to rekindle patriotism and to motivate persons on the home front.

Despite these more liberal censorship policies and the increased representation of wounded American bodies in posters, news stories, and advertisements, the true horrors of war were still concealed from the public. With few exceptions, images of wounded American servicemen showed bodies that were clean, decently clothed, and notably intact (Fussell, *Wartime* 269). Rather than presenting challenges to the newly strengthened wartime body politic, many of the images of the wounded actually reinforced it. As in the case of earlier wars, the wounds of American servicemen were often constructed as "badges of honor," as tangible marks of masculinity proven on the battlefield.[14] Nevertheless, this practice of presenting war wounds as heroic often depended on a certain erasure of the injuries themselves. For example, when *Life* ran its December 28, 1942, article and photo spread on wounded servicemen from the North African campaign, the actual wounds were conspicuously absent. Taken from the waist up, the photographs depict smiling servicemen seated or lying in their hospital beds while they hold up their Purple Hearts. A prime example of the photographs that gave the public a false sense of the war's toll on American bodies, the images depend entirely on context to communicate the servicemen's wounded status. Were it not for the hospital setting and the presence of the medals, the viewer might not know these men were injured. In this case, the actual wounds are displaced by the medals and captions below the pictures, which combine to bestow courage and honor upon the subjects. This strategy of concealment continued even after the OWI and other agencies liberalized their censorship policies. Advertisements such as *Newsweek*'s October 16, 1944, National Dairy Products ad "When the wounded come home" demonstrated that it was possible to represent the wounded without actually showing their injuries or any other threats to their masculinity. Featuring a photograph of a seated young serviceman receiving his lunch while he convalesces on the deck of a ship, the ad emphasizes the rapid recovery of the wounded due to advances in medicine and a sound dairy-rich diet. Were it not for the presence of a nurse in the photograph and the copy of the advertisement, the viewer would have no way of knowing that the apparently healthy, hearty serviceman had suffered any bodily damage. The image and text work together to shift the focus away from the injuries to the serviceman's renewed "strength and morale" (1).

As the war progressed and America suffered increasingly heavier casualties, popular representations of the wounded were less likely to conceal injuries completely from viewers. Working on the same principle of erasure, though, posters and advertisements often minimized the corporeal damage of the wound, stressing instead the heroic nature of the wounded serviceman. An advertisement for Packard Engines (fig. 16) appearing on page 80 of the June 26, 1944, issue of *Life,* for example, illustrates how depictions of injuries could be deployed to stir patriotism and endow veteran workers with heroism. Focusing on the wounding of Private Charles Turner, the ad juxtaposes a large illustration of Turner's injury with a smaller photograph of him at work in the Packard plant assembling aircraft engine parts. In the combat scene, a rugged, strong Turner wrestles with a Japanese soldier despite having a bayonet plunged into his leg. Although the bayonet pierces cleanly through his thigh, Turner sheds no blood and offers no indication that he is in pain. Further, the soldier in the upper left corner of the picture whose gun is carefully trained on the enemy attacker assures the viewer of the Japanese soldier's imminent demise. The advertisement's title and copy further reinforce Turner's wound as evidence of his courage and determination; the text informs readers that Turner's infantry company had been engaged in a grueling three-month campaign and that he went down in "one of the bitterest hand-to-hand encounters." Even after this "severe bayonet

16—Like many government posters, this Packard Engines advertisement characterizes its subject's wound as a mark of American courage, heroism, and determination. (June 26, 1944, *Life.* By permission of the Packard Motor Car Company)

wound," the copy notes, Turner is still engaged in "the fight" as part of America's war machine. More than just a testament to Turner's heroism, the advertisement employs Turner's wound, honorable discharge, and production work to shame other Americans who might not being doing "as much as [they] can." Nevertheless, the full extent of the wound's corporeal damage is again obscured; all physical and psychological injuries have been minimized.

War Production and War Bonds posters also utilized images of wounded soldiers to simultaneously valorize the wounded and shame people on the home front into contributing more to the war effort. Robert Sloan's popular 1943 poster "Doing All You Can, Brother?" (fig. 17), for instance, depicts a lieutenant, who, despite his head wound, has apparently remained at the front. Behind him a gray, desolate backdrop littered with debris, artillery, and military vehicles suggests the battle in which he has apparently incurred his wound. The wound itself is also implied; a small patch of blood seeps through his bandage, while other faint bloodstains soil his otherwise clean uniform. Like the anonymous 1943 poster "A Good Soldier Sticks to His Post," which depicts a soldier with a head wound at his machine gun post, Sloan's War Bonds poster utilizes the idea rather than the reality of wounding. In these posters as well as in the Packard advertisement, wounds pose little threat to the wholeness of the body, reinforcing rather than jeopardizing masculinity.

In addition to substantiating the recipient's courage, wounds were also deployed in posters and advertisements to denote the bravery and sacrifices of other men. A common theme in many posters depicting wounded bodies was the rescue or treatment of the wounded by a buddy or medical officer.[15] Whether in a plea for more weapons, better security, or recruitment, these posters used the presence of wounded soldiers to demonstrate the fearlessness of other soldiers as well as the valor of the wounded. In the General Electric Company's poster "Give Us More Weapons," for instance, a fierce and determined soldier helps his wounded buddy to safety so they both—one immediately and one after treatment—can return to battle. The wounded serviceman has, presumably, made the war a bit more personal for both parties, motivating the soldier assisting him to plead for more weapons in order to exact fierce and powerful revenge. Like most depictions of the war wounded, the General Electric poster shifts the focus away from the corporeal damage that has been inflicted on the serviceman to issues of bravery, determination, and revenge.

Although most wartime posters and advertisements minimized or obscured bodily damage, a select group of posters emphasized the vulnerability of the wounded. Recruitment posters for the Army Nurse Corps often utilized photographs of and testimonials by wounded servicemen to motivate women's enlistment. Instead of focusing on the bravery of the wounded soldiers or on their ability to remain in the fight despite their injuries, these posters highlighted the roles nurses played in restoring the men's health. With titles like "I'D HAVE BEEN A GONER . . .," "SHE STOOD BY ME

17—The accusing stare and direct address of this wounded soldier in Robert Sloan's 1943 War Bonds poster effectively shames citizens on the home front into contributing more to the war effort. (Courtesy of the Hoover Institution Archives)

FOR HOURS," and "SHE GAVE ME COURAGE . . .," the posters acknowledge both the extreme vulnerability of the wounded and the agency of the nurses. To reinforce testimonials of nurses' tireless and effective care, the posters relied on images of wounded still in need of further treatment. The image accompanying the poster "I'D HAVE BEEN A GONER," for instance, features a soldier in a hospital bed still very much dependent on blood transfusions, bed rest, and traction. And while the damage done to his body is suggested rather than explicitly shown, this wounded serviceman nonetheless offers a softer, more vulnerable version of masculinity.

Just as representations of wounded servicemen were deliberately controlled and deployed in posters and advertisements, they were also carefully utilized in wartime and postwar novels. As historians Susan Hartmann, David Gerber, and Timothy Shuker-Haines have shown, the injured veteran was an especially important figure in cultural narratives attempting to renegotiate postwar gender roles.[16] Although the Second World War offered men a proving ground to demonstrate their masculinity and to erase the emasculating forces of the depression, the war also provided women with increased opportunities and independence. The economic and sexual power women gained through paid work and greater participation in the public sphere represented a potential challenge to a social order predicated on the centrality of the male patriarch and breadwinner. Further, the war also produced hundreds of thousands of physically and emotionally injured men who represented damaged masculinity in one form or another. Thus the fate of the wounded veteran in cultural narratives took on special significance as America attempted to restore masculine power and normalcy within society and to sustain its new hypermasculinized construction of itself. Precisely because the wounded body exposed the limits of phallic impenetrability, its restoration to wholeness or its remasculinization became a key component in many postwar cultural narratives.

Because of the vast number of films and novels focusing on World War II veterans, it is impossible to offer a single reading of the wounded veteran's role in these cultural narratives.[17] Nevertheless, historians, gender studies scholars, and film critics tend to emphasize the role of women's narrative agency in shoring up "the ruins of masculinity" (Silverman 52). Indeed, as films such as *The Best Years of Our Lives* and *The Pride of the Marines* demonstrate, women's loving devotion and marriage had tremendous curative effects on injured veterans renegotiating their masculinity and place in postwar America.[18] This focus on women's agency, however, often leads to an erasure of men's own self-healing powers and to readings that obscure the consolidation of male power in postwar America. Despite struggles within postwar masculinity and the privileging of certain models of masculinity over others, men's dominant status as a whole remained unquestioned.

World War II novels such as *Broad Margin* and *The Flesh and Mary Duncan* and films like *The Men* complicate interpretations of the wounded veteran as a damaged model of manhood healed only or primarily through feminine powers. While female characters do play a role in the healing process, wounded veterans in these narratives experience a process of self-generating remasculinization, which is, in part, performed on female bodies. With their focus on the wounded veteran's literal and symbolic impotence, these works target key anxieties about the injured veteran's place in postwar society.

Published in 1945, A. R. Beverly-Giddings's *Broad Margin* details the homecoming and rehabilitation of Page Nugent, a young American fighter pilot, shot down and severely wounded while serving with the RAF. One of the first wounded veterans to return to the small, traditional community of Tidewater, Virginia, Nugent is immediately positioned as a representative figure for the wave of returning veterans to come. The people of Tidewater recognize the power veterans will have in shaping postwar America, and they look to Page to see the direction change will take. As Freddy Wynn, another serviceman, points out, "When, after the war, a couple of million Americans return from foreign lands all thinking as you do . . . there may be a change over here" (27). Thus in addition to Page's thoughts on politics and the economy taking on significance, his physical recovery and masculinity become central to a vision of America's future.

Despite Page's obvious heroism—enlisting with the RAF before the draft, fighting bravely, surviving multiple machine gun hits during his descent into the ocean—his badly wounded body calls his masculinity into question. Pale and weakened by his wounds and long convalescence, Page suffers a far greater wound than his exterior immediately reveals. The narrator explains that Page experiences an "unnatural stillness of his loins"; "the vital urge was missing and it left him as placid as the geldings in the paddock" (34). His wounds so strongly mark the limits of his masculinity and wholeness that Judy, his friend and neighbor, remarks, "He may never be a man again" (30). Because of his condition, the Beauly family discourages their daughter Melody from pursuing marriage to Page despite his good family name and estate. Page, in fact, also resists Melody's offers to help rehabilitate him, opting instead to heal himself before consenting to marry.

After "feminine" cures like bed rest and the care of his mother and housekeeper fail to aid his recovery, Page turns to the company of men. He cultivates friendships with Will Beauly, a farmer at heart, John Merrion, an ex-British officer, and Mordecai, a Natty Bumpo–esque loner who hunts and lives in a cabin by himself. Ultimately, however, it is Page's own return to the land and manual labor that rehabilitates him. Deferring marriage and a business job at the local plant, Page begins assisting his servant Abel with the farmwork, gradually increasing his hours and intensity over a period of several weeks. By the end of the novel, Page is rehabilitated both physically and emotionally; he possesses "new vigor" as well as a suntanned, strong body and "improved appearance" (202). Most importantly, though, Page is remasculinized as he regains his libido and desire for marriage. The novel concludes with Page and Melody's imminent marriage and a promise that despite his return to the corporate world, Page will remain close to the land. While *Broad Margin* deals with other important postwar issues, such as the future of race relations in the U.S., the novel offers a reassurance that any wartime damage to American masculinity is both temporary and mendable. Further, the novel reminds readers that although returning veterans will settle into domestic life and the business world, their masculinity is self-generating and easily rephallicized.

Monte Sohn's 1948 novel *The Flesh and Mary Duncan* provides a more complex and more violent tale of its protagonist's remasculinization. Set in the Chicago suburb of East Littleton and New York City, the novel details George Trapple's postwar homecoming, marriage, and rehabilitation. While Page Nugent's injuries and goals for recovery are described early in *Broad Margin,* Trapple's wounds remain a mystery to both his family and the reader for more than half of the novel. Although the reader discerns that George has suffered some terrible physical wound while in combat in North Africa, the injury itself remains conspicuously absent from the narrative. Instead of discussing his wound, the first half of the novel focuses on George's readjustment problems, his distance from his fiancée, Mary Duncan, and his generally odd behavior. Through dreams, flashbacks, and George's own confessions to Mary, the reader soon discovers why George's wounds are concealed from everyone; the physical wounds described in hastily written letters from North Africa are in fact symptoms of conversion hysteria. As George confesses in shame, "There never *was* any wound" (166).

Although not physically wounded himself, George is haunted by his contact with other wounded and dead bodies, and he becomes both ill and abject. While under the apparent influence of scopolamine, George narrates several traumatic combat experiences. In addition to witnessing a tank crew being burned alive, George mentions other horrifying interactions with the war injured. In one instance, he encounters a man propped up against an olive tree trying to light a cigarette. When he reaches the man, however, he discovers that "his guts were hanging out of his belly and he was trying to stuff them back" (168). The series of grim interactions culminates with George's narrative of his company's assault on a hill in Central Tunisia. The reader learns that George has been hit by a large, decapitated body during his ascent up the hill and that, while dragging a buddy to safety, he has fallen into a pit of decaying bodies. These events are so traumatic that even their retelling causes George to vomit and, ultimately, results in George's "paralyzed" arm. While not manifested physically, George's wound results in the same type of abjection that other injured servicemen experience. His contact with bodies that are not "all together" and that are "coming apart" forces George to witness the limits of his own subjectivity, to experience abjection. He not only reacts to these dead and wounded bodies through the expulsion of his own bodily fluids but also is compelled by his repressed fear and horror to experience his own loss through his "paralyzed" arm.

What results from George's "wounding" is a double loss of masculinity. His contact with other wounded bodies and his own injuries reveal the limits of his phallicized, whole body. This loss of wholeness is then compounded by the shame of being mistaken for a "real" wounded veteran. Out of a desire to forget his war experiences, George never discusses his "wound," allowing others to construct its meaning and imagine his scars. More so than Page, George offers a model of damaged manhood in serious need of rehabilitation. Like Page, he is physically impotent—unable to make love to Mary even after they are married—and socially impotent— unable to settle into his proper social role. Unlike Page, however, George has no wounds of honor, no scars to mark his heroism in combat. Thus George's rehabilitation is both a more difficult and more pressing cultural narrative of masculinity.

As the novel develops, George adopts a series of strategies for rephallicizing his body and restoring his masculinity. His first strategy is one of denial and disassociation, as he attempts to distance himself both from his own "damaged" body and from Mary's more fleshly one. This effort to separate himself from the body is, of course, linked to his desire to forget the horrifying corporeal events of the war. But it might also be read as an attempt to become a disembodied subject aligned with the "masculine" realm of reason and spirit. From his father's comments, we learn that George regards his own body with shame and horror. Jim Trapple mentions that George refuses to visit the doctor, to go swimming, or to dress in front of anyone and that he bathes "in a bathroom without lights, as though there was something even he didn't want to see" (181). George quickly extends his loathing of his own body, though, to all flesh—especially female bodies. George demonstrates this distaste for women's bodies by tearing the cover off a copy of *Life* magazine, "which showed the near nudity of a blonde female in diaper bathing suit" (16). The most forceful evidence of George's repugnance toward flesh, though, is found in his own comments. During one of his conversations with Mary, George explains:

> A body is an envelope . . . a bag, just a bag, only it's made of skin. You never know how terrible it is, not until you see it burst open and spilled right in front of you . . . And once you've seen it, you grow to hate it, not just because it is hateful, but because you know it hates you, and you know that it is going to be a permanent part of you, in your head and mind, and you're never going to lose it. (121)

As his comments reveal, George's loathing of the body stems precisely from its limits, from its penetrability and its lack of solidity and wholeness.[19] Because of the body's inevitable weakness, George reasons, it is better to remain within the realm of the mind and to construct the body as not-self.

This strategy of disassociation and continued horror of the flesh inevitably proves ineffective, and George must locate other ways of restoring his lost manhood and rephallicizing his body. Like Page, George realizes that work can provide a vehicle for remasculinization. As he throws himself into his radio advertising job, working long hours and climbing the corporate ladder, George discovers that "he was becoming useful again, important" (221). Paradoxically, it is through work in this "feminized" industry that George begins to recover his masculinity; in studying the patterns of female consumption and learning to manipulate women's desires, George discovers a type of phallic power. Although not yet cured of his physical impotence, George gains a type of sexual power through his position. The narrator remarks, "The advertising agent [is] a commercial Casanova, predestined to be promiscuous. The countless children he sires never bear his name" (194).

Although he begins his process of rephallicization at work, George completes it at home. In the novel's closing scene, George and Mary return from a company party, quarreling over George's jealous accusations of Mary's supposed sexual advances toward Mr. Thorne. After George offers to arrange a date between Mary and his boss, she slaps him, igniting George's rage and fury. In the disturbing moments that follow, George strikes Mary with "a hard blow on the face [that] sent her backward against the bureau" (267). Following this blow, George tears off Mary's nightgown, carries her to the bed, and then, after a seven-word apology, has sex with her. As the narrator and Mary explain, this burst of violence and penetration is enough to rehabilitate George. He is physically transformed—"Even in his sleep there was a strength and poise about him that was new" (269)—so much apparently that Mary proclaims, "Oh, Gio. You're well again. You're well" (269). At last, Mary's wish that George will "dominate both [their] lives" (161) has come true.

While Mary certainly plays a vital role in George's recovery, it is not her loving devotion or willingness to marry the impotent George that aids his rehabilitation. Instead it is Mary's ability to serve as an effective "other" to George's masculinity that helps rephallicize him. Having rejected abject models of flow and exchange, George attempts to seal up his own body— first denying his corporeality and then hardening it through violence and penetration. As George distances himself from Mary and gains masculine authority through work, he comes to see Mary as a potential object against which to define his masculinity. Shortly after we are told that George "was becoming useful again, important," we learn that he begins to regard his wife and female bodies in a new light: "Mary—the body that was Mary— was like some flower of precious rarity. It was his . . . whenever he should come into its total possession" (221). This vision of Mary as his possession, coupled with the violence that turns his own body into a type of weapon, ultimately assists his rephallicization. Just before he penetrates her, George is comforted and aroused by the vision of Mary "lying there, pitiably little, beautifully slight upon the bed" (268). And after intercourse, George discovers that Mary's body no longer holds fears for him "at all, except a new dread for its safety" (268). Thus Mary's body becomes a site on which to act out and reenact his masculinity. Not only does its penetrability and permeability serve as a foil for his own larger, more hardened body, but also it provides an object for protection, a motivation for George to display his manhood. In the end, *The Flesh and Mary Duncan* offers a vision of postwar normalcy achieved by damming up the softness and fluidity of the male body through penetration and violence acted upon the female body.

Fred Zinnemann's 1950 film *The Men* likewise offers a narrative about a wounded veteran's remasculinization that depends both upon violence and a process of self-regeneration. Unlike *The Flesh and Mary Duncan,* however, this violence is not played out on a female body, and the remasculinization is not achieved through a return to work. Instead, the central character, Ken Wiloceck (Marlon Brando), regains his sense of masculinity and normalcy through a rigorous routine of physical therapy and dangerous behavior as well as through advances in American technology. In many ways, Ken's rehabilitation is the most remarkable of the three central characters because his status as a paraplegic makes his recovery and social reintegration especially difficult. As a December 17, 1945, *Time* article reporting on World War II's more than 2,000 paraplegic cases explained, "The injury makes [the paraplegic] helpless as a baby" (88). Given the physical and psychological trauma of the injury and the obvious challenges that it presents to assuming a "normal" masculine role as husband and breadwinner, it is not surprising that Ken's first thought in the hospital is one of absolute despair: "I was afraid that I was gonna die. Now I'm afraid that I'm gonna live." Nor is the viewer surprised to learn that he has broken off his engagement to his fiancée, Ellen (Teresa Wright), on the grounds that he "is not a man anymore."

Set primarily in a Veterans Administration (VA) hospital—presumably Birmingham General in San Fernando Valley, California—the film might seem to promise an examination of the alternative abject masculinities produced by wounding. By focusing on the stories of wounded veterans not yet reintegrated into society and still physically vulnerable, the film indeed explores several relationships between male patients and examines masculinities not predicated on a whole, able body. Nevertheless, Zinnemann makes it clear through his title and dedication that the audience should not view veterans in terms of their vulnerabilities but should instead perceive them as warriors. While the title assures viewers that the veterans are still men (not helpless babies), the dedication positions them as active soldiers. After mentioning that in all wars "there have been men who have fought twice," the dedication explains that the subjects of the film are still fighting a war, though without their machine guns or usual weapons. The far greater battle of their recovery, the opening text suggests, "was fought with abiding faith and raw courage, and in the end Victory was achieved." Like advertisements and posters portraying wounded servicemen as still being "in the fight," the dedication invites viewers to see the veterans' wounds as marks of heroism and honor and assures us that their process of remasculinization will be successful. As if to reaffirm this perception of the men and their wounds, the opening scene depicts Lieutenant Wiloceck bravely leading his unit into battle, where he receives several gunshot wounds. The image of Ken behaving courageously enough to receive a Silver Star, then, provides a context for viewing the broken and despairing patient we see in the next scene.

After briefly showing the bitter and troubled Wiloceck receiving care from Nurse Robbins (Virginia Furmer), the film shifts its focus to Doctor Brock, the surgeon and physician charged with rehabilitating the paraplegic veterans. Following a lecture where Brock lays out the realities of the veterans' medical conditions for their family members and spouses, the audience soon sees the doctor in action, surveying the ward and monitoring the individual progress of his patients. While effectively depicting paraplegic veterans at every stage of recovery, the scene also serves to emphasize Brock's unquestioned authority and penchant for strict discipline. Not only does he reprimand one patient for the carousing that has ruined "perfectly good surgery," but he also scolds central characters Leo Doolin (Richard Erdman) and Norm Butler (Jack Webb) for not taking their rehabilitation seriously enough. "Blood and Bowels" Brock, as Norm jokingly names him, quickly decides that he and the hospital staff need "to get tough with Wiloceck" and places him in the general ward with Norm, Leo, and Angel Lopez (Arthur Jurado), where "those bench jockeys will ride him 'til he's saddle sore." Like Page's rehabilitation, Ken's recovery shifts from the feminine realm of Nurse Robbins's care to the firm, disciplined administration of Doctor Brock and the other veterans in the ward. Although he is initially received with a certain degree of compassion and understanding from Norm and Angel, Ken immediately realizes that he will receive neither pity nor coddling from his fellow patients. In response to Wiloceck's request to turn down his radio, for example, Leo replies, "What's a matter? You paralyzed or something? Turn it down yourself."

Although Ken's entry into the tough, masculine sphere of the ward is crucial to his recovery, it is Ellen's visit that ultimately sparks Wiloceck's desire for recovery. As in the case of his previous dealings with Ellen, Ken attempts to end their relationship on the grounds that he cannot fulfill his proper male role as husband and provider. Fearing that Ellen's true feelings stem from pity rather than love and worrying that she would have to wait on him hand and foot, Ken begs Ellen to move on with her life and to forget him. Ellen, however, convinces him that she needs him and that her every happiness depends on him. While moved by the idea of being needed, Wiloceck finally consents to resume his relationship with Ellen only after she reminds him that the government will provide him with a pension and transportation allowance and that the VA will pay half the costs of building a house. Assured that he can assume at least a semblance of his proper role as the family provider, Ken finally begins his rehabilitation in earnest.

Like *Broad Margin, The Men* suggests that the process of restoring veterans' masculinity is primarily dependent on the transformation of their bodies. By winning the "far greater" battle of physical rehabilitation, the dedication implies, the veteran necessarily regains his sense of masculinity along with the courage, determination, and self-reliance he displayed during the war. Not surprisingly, the film includes several lengthy sequences of Ken performing his physical therapy exercises and participating in group sports and other activities. To provide a benchmark for his dramatic recovery, Zinnemann shows the enormous effort that it takes for Ken to complete simple tasks such as pulling himself up or sitting up in bed. Although Marlon Brando's strained expression and the swelling background music reveal that Wiloceck's ability to sit on his own is quite an accomplishment, it is clear that he is still quite weak and physically dependent on others to complete the simplest tasks. The first series of physical reconditioning scenes likewise emphasizes Wiloceck's frailty and lack of stamina. The viewer watches Ken slowly and painfully doing sit-ups, push-ups, and upper body twists and lifting light free weights. Gradually, he takes on more physically challenging tasks and equipment, and he is pictured using pulley weights, tossing a medicine ball, climbing rope, and pulling his legs while walking on his hands. His increased fitness, though, still pales in comparison to Angel's; the latter scenes of this first reconditioning sequence juxtapose the two men exercising, showing the well-muscled Angel easily performing the same tasks that Ken struggles to complete. While serving as another yardstick by which to measure Wiloceck's final transformation, the scenes contrasting Angel's and Ken's fitness and ability also highlight the connections between physical rehabilitation and the restoration of masculinity. Following their varied success in climbing ropes, Wiloceck asks Angel why he has been working so hard—so strenuously, in fact, that even Doctor Brock keeps urging him to take it easy during his workouts. Angel explains that he needs to get home because he is "a papa now." With his father gone, he has to assume the role of patriarch and provide for his mother and six brothers and sisters. Outlining his plans to get a job and build a new house that will give his sixteen-year-old sister "a proper place to grow up," Angel demonstrates that his newly restored strength and physical abilities go hand in hand with regaining his proper male position as family provider.

The film's second rehabilitation sequence reinforces this association between strengthening the body and shoring up the veteran's masculinity. Just prior to the sequence, Ken explains to Norm that he is "gonna be married standing up," suggesting that he will not assume his role as husband until he is able-bodied enough to appear normal or nondisabled in social situations. With this newfound determination to "be a man" at his wedding, Wiloceck embarks on a much more vigorous reconditioning campaign. Instead of laboring to complete simple exercises, Ken now easily climbs the rope and moves forward across the parallel bars. His true strength, however, is conveyed by a series of weightlifting scenes where the bare-chested Brando easily bench presses increasingly heavier weights. Reminiscent of Barclay's ripped sailors and the well-muscled men of wartime recruitment posters, Wiloceck's carefully sculpted upper body reveals both his strength and heroism. Zinnemann also uses the sequence to demonstrate Ken's social integration and reinvigorated competitive spirit. Interspersed with the weightlifting and physical therapy episodes are brief sports scenes. The audience sees Ken bowling a strike, shooting a layup, and playing water basketball as he competes with other veterans. In keeping with the War Department's emphasis on sports in military reconditioning programs, the audience witnesses Wiloceck and the other veterans redeveloping "an aggressive fighting spirit, initiative, resourcefulness, team work, and group morale."[20] Ken appears more outgoing and confident among his fellow ward mates and seems more comfortable interacting with others outside of the hospital. In between successful athletic performances, viewers watch Wiloceck as he easily gets behind the wheel of a specially designed car and busily surveys the construction on his and Ellen's new house. In marked contrast to earlier scenes with Ellen driving, these images of Ken assure the audience that he is reclaiming his independence and forcefulness and that he should be capable of becoming the family provider. More importantly, though, the frequent portrayals of Ken driving help to rephallicize his body. Just as wartime advertisements and recruitment posters fused soldiers' bodies with weapons in an attempt to portray their strength and "steel-like" qualities, the hardness, speed, and technology of the specially designed car help counter some of the weakness associated with Ken's disability, rendering him both whole and mobile.

Although the wedding and his desire to stand at the altar motivates Ken's dramatic physical rehabilitation, it does not complete his process of remasculinization. Unlike *The Best Years of Our Lives,* which concludes with one wedding (Homer and Wilma's) and the promise of another (Fred and Peggy's), *The Men* does not present marriage and feminine curative powers as the solution to Wiloceck's problems. Hardly a happy honeymoon, Ken and Ellen's arrival at their new house after the wedding is one of the most tense and awkward scenes in the movie. The viewer almost immediately recognizes how out of place Ken seems in the thoroughly feminine domestic space; his wheelchair squeaks quite audibly, and he has difficulty moving around on the new carpet. As Ellen shows off the drapes, lamps, and ashtrays she has picked out, it becomes clear that she taken charge not only of decorating but also of running their home. To Ken's dismay, she has already started a family photo album filled with pictures from his college and football days. The minor disagreement over the contents of the album, however, quickly escalates into a confrontation after Ken roughly grabs the champagne bottle and spills some on the new carpet. Although the fight stems from Ken's perception of Ellen's misgivings about the marriage, the scene also highlights Wiloceck's uneasiness about moving into a situation where he seemingly lacks control. In contrast to the earlier scene where he confidently oversaw the design and construction of the house, here Ken feels displaced and anxious about the idea of settling into a space that has been solely Ellen's creation. As the film suggests, simply assuming the role of husband is not enough to restore the wounded veteran's manhood; he must prove his masculinity through rough, violent behavior, as he did in the war.[21]

After their heated argument, Ken returns to the hospital, still dressed in his wedding suit, and joins a group of veterans listening to a boxing match on the radio. In the first of a series of violent outbreaks, he disrupts the group's entertainment by smashing a window. Seeking male companionship and an escape from his apparently failed relationship with Ellen, Ken and Leo drive to a bar, where they can smoke, drink, and unwind. Their conversation, however, is interrupted by a World War I veteran who attempts to buy them drinks. Although they at first calmly rebuff the other veteran and dismiss his appreciation of the "great sacrifice you boys have made," the still-angry Wiloceck calls the man back to the table and promptly decks him with a mean right hook to the face. Ken finishes his spree of rough, dangerous male behavior by driving speedily and recklessly until he crashes the car on the way back to the hospital. Clearly intended to show Ken's lingering anger and continuing readjustment problems, the series of violent and dangerous encounters nevertheless help to restore his sense of masculinity. The muscles he has carefully rebuilt help him move easily whether in a car or wheelchair and allow him take out a fully able-bodied man in a contest of strength. Having successfully navigated the male terrain of drinking and brawling, Ken can finally return to his home and life with Ellen assured of his manhood. Wiloceck initially resists this return, opting instead to remain in the familiar and comfortable male sphere of the ward and Doctor Brock's discipline, but he ultimately realizes that his proper role is indeed husband and family provider.[22]

Although *The Men* never actually shows Ken gainfully employed, the film does suggest that his interactions with Ellen will be on different terms. Already physically transformed from a weak helpless patient into a strong, sometimes dangerous individual, Ken finally accepts his paralysis as well as his responsibilities toward Ellen. After receiving some stern but helpful advice from Doctor Brock, Ken leaves the hospital with a new sense of purpose and control. Driving slowly and carefully this time, he arrives at Ellen's parents' house to retrieve Ellen and reclaim his position as husband and family provider. Having already shown Ken's physical rehabilitation, rough masculine behavior, and his ability to perform regular daily activities with the help of modern technology and engineering, the film implies that Ken will play a more active and controlling role in marriage this time. More importantly, though, *The Men* suggests that Ken will be able to transcend any obstacle since he has already won a fight greater than any he faced during the war. Like *Broad Margin* and *The Flesh and Mary Duncan*, Zinnemann's film reassures viewers that the wartime damage done to American masculinity is both temporary and mendable. Even serious disabilities of paraplegic veterans can be overcome through discipline, physical reconditioning, and advances in U.S. technology.

MEDICAL NARRATIVES—PROSTHETICS, WHOLENESS, AND NORMALCY

While the rehabilitation of the wounded veteran's body and masculinity figured prominently in postwar literary and cinematic narratives, the impetus to restore wholeness to the injured serviceman's body was perhaps strongest within medical discourses. An examination of World War II and postwar prosthetic advances reveals that the war amputee initiated a revolution in the design, manufacture, and fitting of artificial limbs. This sudden research initiative on prosthetics—the greatest in the U.S. since the Civil War—was not motivated by a radical surge in the number of amputees. Although some 23,000 veterans were suddenly in need of artificial limbs, more than 100,000 American civilians lost limbs in industrial accidents during the war years.[23] In fact, since the First World War, more civilians lost limbs in any given year than did military personnel. In 1942 alone, a 1944 *Journal of the American Medical Association (JAMA)* article reported, U.S. artificial limb manufacturers "supplied limbs to 70,000 civilians, whereas the total number of amputations in our army during World War I was about 4,000."[24] Despite the relatively small percentage of total amputees that veterans comprised, however, the injured veteran provided the foremost motivation for advances in prosthetic research.

Because of the threat his wounded body posed to the national body politic and cultural narratives of masculinity, the serviceman's recovery took on special significance. Moreover, due to wartime constructions of combat wounds as badges of honor and marks of sacrifice, the injured veteran's body represented a debt that the public owed for its freedom. This certainly was the rhetoric employed by periodicals like *Time* and the *Washington Daily News* in their campaigns to condemn government treatment of veteran amputees. In its August 27, 1945, exposé on the state of prosthetic research, "For Neglected Heroes,"[25] *Time* criticized the "laggard government" and its poor efforts to help veterans (90). The *Washington Daily News* likewise took the side "of the men who have given their arms and legs for this country [who] feel deeply that they are not getting the proper appliances."[26] The consensus of the media and public was that the proper restoration of veterans' bodies and masculinity was worth any price. The *Washington Daily News* editorial reasoned that the poor state of prosthetic research and the inferior quality of veterans' artificial limbs reflected badly on the nation: "This country, which has made efficient airplanes and rocket bombs, apparently hasn't produced workable artificial arms and legs" (1115). Or, as F. S. Strong, executive director of the National Research Council's (NRC) Advisory Committee on Artificial Limbs, explained, the field of prosthetics needed to be advanced in order to bring it "in line with the scientific and engineering progress which has become synonymous with America in the modern world" (1). According to the press, the wounded serviceman—particularly the war amputee—had to be made whole, not just for his own sake but for the good of the nation.

This attitude toward the wounded veteran was apparently shared by the government. In March 1945, after the well-publicized return of several thousand veteran amputees, the National Academy of Sciences and the NRC jointly established a Committee on Prosthetic Devices under the guidance of the surgeon general. Charged with the task of applying and developing new technologies to aid in the construction, design, and fitting of artificial limbs, the committee united engineers, surgeons, professors of applied science, limb manufacturers, and corporate research teams. The committee sought to provide veterans with "the best possible prosthetic appliance that can be devised" and aimed to standardize parts, mechanisms, and repair procedures.[27] To ensure that the Committee on Prosthetic Devices (later called the Advisory Committee on Artificial Limbs) would have the financial resources needed, Congress implemented Public Law 729, which authorized "the expenditure of $1,000,000 annually to aid in the development of improved prosthetic appliances" (Strong 1) under the guidance of the VA. In designating the VA as the administrator of the funds, the law confirmed the privileged status of the wounded veteran in postwar prosthetic research. Although designed to advance prosthetic research and improve artificial limbs for *all* Americans, the Committee on Prosthetic Devices recognized that its primary goal was "to aid those who suffered loss of limb in battle where they were serving their fellows" (Klopsteg and Wilson v). When one considers that an existing amputee population of more than half a million had not been enough to motivate new prosthetic research, it becomes clear that the restoration of the wounded veteran's body was indeed a national priority.

Media coverage of wounded veterans' homecomings revealed to the public that prosthetic devices—especially those for the upper body—were woefully inadequate. Citing the fact that little research on prosthetics had been done in the U.S. since the Civil War, articles described the types of limbs servicemen would have received in 1944 or early 1945.[28] Amputees complained that limbs made out of steel and leather were heavy (artificial arms weighed as much as ten pounds). Veterans recited tales of artificial arms that fit "like a ten-gallon hat on a cherubic head"[29] and leather devices that were hard to wash and quickly stank. As *Time*'s "For Neglected Heroes" explained, "The overall fact is that modern prostheses are uncomfortable, ungainly, ugly. After months of operations and fitting, most amputees are disappointed" (90). Servicemen's complaints about the poor quality of their artificial limbs stemmed partly from the fact that they had to purchase permanent limbs themselves. Like their Civil War predecessors, veterans were fitted with temporary limbs at military hospitals and then were given money by the VA to purchase permanent limbs on their own. Men needing full-length legs were given $290, those with amputations below the knee, $165, and those with thigh amputations, $215.[30] Those in need of an artificial arm, *Time* reported, were given "about $150" ("Neglected" 93). Often these sums were not enough to purchase a decent limb from private firms that could charge as much as $450 for prosthetic devices. After veterans complained, however, the Department of Justice penalized the American Limb Manufac-turers Association (ALMA) and 79 other firms and individuals for violating the Sherman Anti-Trust Act. Following the trial, members of the ALMA were forced to lower prices and to avoid price fixing.[31]

Although civilian amputees might have resented their political invisibil-ity and the lack of prosthetic research prior to post–World War II initiatives, the advances of the Artificial Limb Program helped millions of amputees at home and abroad.[32] In addition to coordinating the Committee on Pros-thetic Devices, the VA also oversaw artificial limb research by the various military branches and hospitals. The mass coordinated program of research teams, later known as the Artificial Limb Program, allowed for specialized research on individual prosthetic devices. Instead of independent private limb manufacturers all producing the same products, research laboratories and hospitals across the country focused on specific problems while work-ing to standardize parts and treatment programs. Within the first two years, the program produced important technological advances. Program research led to the utilization of lighter materials such as new plastics and metal al-loys in limb construction and helped develop better technologies for con-trolling limbs. By August 1946 the program had, in consultation with the Northrop Aviation Corporation, developed lighter, more usable arms, using "airplane control cords, extensors, wrist rotation and wrist flexion" ("Pat-terson" 1364). Meanwhile, through the joint efforts of navy technicians and researchers at Walter Reed Hospital, the program also facilitated tremendous improvements in "natural looking," lightweight artificial hands, which could be tinted to match the patient's skin and incorporated a "1 pound cam mechanism hidden inside the hand . . . to permit natural finger movement" ("Navy Technicians" 1178). Prosthetic legs were likewise improved by studying foreign "hydraulic" and "suction socket" technolo-gies and by incorporating lighter materials and improved joints.

The program's advances were not restricted solely to the development of better devices. The philosophy behind limb production changed as pros-thetics were increasingly tailored for individual users and better rehabilita-tion programs were adopted. Through the development of a "team ap-proach," the program united physicians, prosthetists, occupational therapists, physical therapists, and psychologists in the limb-fitting and re-habilitation process. As the artificial hand developments attest, one goal of the Artificial Limb Program was to restore wholeness to the body by mak-ing the wearer of prosthetics as "normal looking" as possible. Doctors and therapists recognized, though, that it was equally important for the wounded veteran to feel "normal" while completing everyday tasks and interacting in social situations. To this end, the program utilized special training films, group therapy exercises, and individualized consultations with doctors to teach veterans to perform a wide variety of tasks with their prostheses. Although the army eventually developed its own training films, many veterans with amputations were shown *Back to Normal,* an upbeat film produced by the British Ministry of Information that featured war-wounded Britons working, dancing, playing tennis, billiards, and ping pong, and riding bicycles with their new prostheses.[33] Military hospitals also invited World War I veterans such as Charles McGonegal to give inspirational talks and to demonstrate how they performed daily tasks with their prostheses. In his extensive tour of army and navy hospitals in 1944 and 1945, McGonegal showed veterans how he used his two double-hook prostheses to write with a pencil, light a cigarette, play cards, use a telephone, and dance with a woman.[34] According to army spokespeople, these week-long demonstrations coupled with individualized physical therapy programs proved to be one of the most effective methods of restoring veterans' confidence ("New Limbs" 52).

While the appearance of a whole body and the ability to perform everyday tasks were crucial for restoring a sense of a patient's masculinity, prosthetic research programs were also interested in the "economic and social point of view" (Klopsteg and Wilson 2). Ultimately, the Committee on Prosthetic Devices's goal was to restore the veteran amputee "to his normal and rightful place in his environment" (Klopsteg and Wilson 2). Or, in the words of prosthetic specialist Atha Thomas, the purpose of an artificial limb was "to transform a helpless dependent into a useful member of society."[35] As *Broad Margin* and *The Flesh and Mary Duncan* highlighted, returning the injured serviceman to work was necessary both for his own rehabilitation and for the nation's return to normalcy.

The concern over wounded veterans' productiveness was not limited to the field of prosthetics, nor did it focus solely on veteran amputees. Although many rehabilitation films and programs were specially designed to help veterans with prosthetics relearn old trades and develop new expertise in drafting, carpentry, engineering, and other highly skilled occupations, military training courses were aimed at helping *all* injured veterans find suitable postwar work. The task of restoring injured servicemen to their "proper place" in society through work, however, was not restricted to military and government projects. Advertisements for Packard Engines and Revere Copper and Brass revealed that American corporations were also committed to putting wounded veterans back to work. While making an appeal to Americans to buy war bonds, the June 19, 1944, *Time* advertisement "The Japs Aren't as Cross-Eyed as You Think" (fig. 18) highlights the toughness of the Japanese enemy and the vast number of American lives and limbs lost at the hands of "the Japs." Using Chief Signalman Murphy's wounded body as a reminder of servicemen's sacrifices, the ad encourages war bonds purchases by outlining the ways in which the company is striving to repay and acknowledge these incredible sacrifices. The text explains that "Revere Copper and Brass Incorporated is working to analyze every job which men with physical disabilities could perform, so these jobs can be made available first to returning servicemen" (64). Although offering a sobering depiction of a veteran amputee and a staggering statistic about America's battle losses, the advertisement nevertheless promises a brighter future. Thanks to American "imagination and initiative," even the severely wounded veteran can become a productive worker and citizen again.

While companies like Revere Copper and Packard modified their workspaces to accommodate wounded veterans' needs, other companies went even further, offering specially designed training courses or even establishing machine shops at VA hospitals. The Bulova Watch Company, for example, offered on-site classes "tailored to each patient's individual work tolerance" in an effort to provide paraplegic veterans with skilled and semiskilled jobs at their and other watchmaking factories.[36] The Northrop Aircraft Company, meanwhile, set up a machine shop with carefully engineered equipment at Birmingham General Hospital. In his January 13, 1945, *Collier's* article "Department 99," Jim Marshall described the medical and social benefits of turning hospital wards into machine shops. After explaining that at "Department 99 of Northrop Aircraft" men worked more than three hours a day assembling parts for P-61s, Marshall reported that these veterans felt like valuable contributors to the war effort. As Marshall noted, helping to build a Black Widow night fighter wasn't "just play work, like weaving rugs or stringing beads. It's the real thing" (62). The veterans were doing "useful work" that kept them in the fight against the Axis, as well as working to restore their roles as breadwinners. For their labor the men received the same hourly wage that full-time workers received, and, Marshall explained, "some of the cured wounded have been given jobs at the main plant, following discharge from the Army" (62).

Creating these jobs for wounded veterans, however, involved extensive planning between Northrop executive LaMotte Turck Cohu, hospital commander Colonel Alvin Miller, and head of physical reconditioning Major Daniel Mishell. Employing even bed cases, Department 99 utilized an extensive amount of "rejiggered" machinery in order to enable injured veterans to work:

> They have drill presses that a man with one arm and one leg can operate by a foot pedal. They have hydraulic vises to replace the old type where you hold the material in place with one hand and screw the jaws together with the other. There are pulleys, conveyors, straps to help crippled boys work. Tables are built to special heights to make jobs easier. (62)

Although the men clocked in and out and got paid the same as people working at the plant, the wounded veterans were quite different from the plant's other workers. According to Marshall, they represented a "reversal of

"The Japs aren't as cross-eyed as you think"

"I count myself lucky. I just lost a leg.

"There were eighty of us. I'm one of four who survived. That's paying at the rate of 95%.

"When the Japs can do that with one shell, you've got to agree they're not as cross-eyed as some folks make out. Take it from me, they're tough!

"Thank the Lord they lack our imagination and initiative.

"We can't have too many ships, ships with a great big wallop behind them if we want to win soon. The Navy can deliver that wallop — but *you* have to provide it."

They gave 95%. Is 10% for War Bonds too much for you to give?

REVERE COPPER AND BRASS INCORPORATED is working now to analyze every job which men with physical disabilities could perform, so that these jobs can be made available first to returning wounded service men.

This is Chief Signalman Willard A. Murphy, of Oakland, Calif., whom we Americans sent to do our fighting with the U.S.S. Atlanta.

18—Offering one of the more sobering depictions of the wounded, this Revere Copper and Brass advertisement emphasizes the debt owed to veterans while highlighting the company's commitment to providing jobs for wounded servicemen. (June 19, 1944, *Time*. By permission of Revere Copper Products, Inc.)

the practice of fitting men into jobs. The jobs had to be rearranged to fit the capacities of the men" (63). What Department 99 and other programs like it signified is the vast cultural importance attached to restoring the injured serviceman's usefulness and sense of self-worth and masculinity. In reversing the usual pattern of man serving machine, the work program sacrificed efficiency in production to rebuild another product—America's damaged male bodies. Thus in both postwar prosthetic research and work rehabilitation programs, there developed an interesting pattern of technology servicing man to service technology. In order to restore normalcy to postwar America, both the wounded veteran and his able-bodied peers had to be socially rendered whole and useful.

While the wounded body represented a potential threat to America's wartime body politic, it also provided an important site for rethinking and reconfiguring cultural notions of masculinity and the "whole" male body. For some servicemen, wounds allowed them to experience an alternative abject masculinity, which enabled new relationships and exchanges with other men. Generally, though, the wounded body was remasculinized in cultural representations. In posters, advertisements, novels, and films, the bodies of wounded servicemen were literally and symbolically restored to wholeness through recodings of their injuries, prostheses, and labor. Often this restoration of wholeness and masculinity was presented as a self-generating process, wherein the veteran drew on personal qualities and behaviors such as determination, self-discipline, and hard work. In cases where a veteran could not be completely cured, technologies helped to rephallicize his body and render him socially useful again. As postwar prosthetics discourses and cultural narratives repeatedly demonstrated, the rehabilitation of the wounded veteran was necessary both for the serviceman's own recovery and for the nation's return to normalcy. Although popular and medical narratives placed special emphasis on rehabilitating the wounded bodies and abject masculinities produced by combat and military service, these were not the only alternate models of manhood that the war exposed. Indeed, wartime discourses about race and ethnicity created an even broader range of marginalized masculinities that both reinforced and challenged America's self-representations.

FOUR— "WHITE MAN'S WAR?"

RACE AND MASCULINITY IN WORLD WAR II

In many respects, discussion of ethnicity is always also by implication a discussion of gender and sexuality.

—Williams and Chrisman, *Colonial Discourse*

Like the first novel in James Jones's World War II trilogy, *From Here to Eternity*, *The Thin Red Line* contains a rich sexual subtext. In a book full of homosexual encounters and desires, sexual arousal during combat, and discussions of heterosexual sex and masturbation, Sergeant John Bell's worries about the possible infidelities of his wife, Marty, might seem commonplace. Bell's anxieties and resulting nightmare about his wife's sexual transgressions, however, uncover another subtext—wartime racial discourses.[1] While feverish during a malarial attack, Bell dreams that "he was in a maternity hospital delivery room" (408) awaiting the birth of his child. In the dream, Bell witnesses Marty's difficulties in labor and her anesthetization, which leaves him alone during the delivery of his child. Bell describes the birth:

> When it was out to the waist it began to wail in a feeble voice and the doctor swabbed it some more, and it was then that Bell realized it was black. Coal black. . . . Bell sat aghast in horror, embarrassed, disbelieving, and strangely acquiescent, and watched the coal black baby come lasciviously the rest of the way out of the beautiful, beautifully white, shaved crotch of his wife. (409)

As the delivery progresses, Bell is gripped with questions about his wife ("Had she suspected?"), the doctor, nurse, and anesthetist

("Had none of them noticed it was black? Or didn't they care?"), and himself ("Should he pretend?") (410). His anxieties, however, turn to embarrassment "when he looked back down, . . . [and] saw that it wasn't black it was Japanese. He could tell because it wore a tiny, bent Imperial Army forage cap, with a tiny, baby iron star" (410). The sight of the Japanese baby jolts Bell awake "with a ringing cry" (410) and forces him to examine the nightmare. While analyzing the significance of the baby's ethnic and racial identity—"why a *black* baby?" (410)—Bell contemplates both his unexpected sexual arousal and the horror that motivates him "to do anything in order not to go back to sleep and risk having that dream again" (411). Arriving at the reason for both responses, Bell realizes that it is "the lascivious sensuality of knowing, of being sure, of having proof" (411). He further reflects, "Perhaps that was why so many men thinking of their wives, hated other races. Because nobody wanted to know he was cuckold. Everybody preferred the painful doubt to the sensual luxury of knowing for sure. But if the baby was another color, there was no— . . ." (411–12).

While primarily intended to develop Bell's character and his concerns about Marty's fidelity, the dream and Bell's analysis of it uncovers the complex intersections between discourses of race, sexuality, and masculinity that occurred during World War II. By focusing on the delivery of a black/Japanese baby, the dream not only highlights America's renewed fears of miscegenation brought on by the threat of the "yellow peril" but also exposes the ways in which all persons of color were often collapsed into a generalized "other" against which whiteness was normalized. Moreover, Bell's reflections on his possible status as cuckold firmly link definitions of masculinity to race, suggesting that wartime racist behavior might be tied to fears about challenges to white masculinity. As bell hooks, Londa Schiebinger, Homi Bhabha, and Anne Cranny-Francis have shown, these intersections between race and sexuality are hardly new; they are connected to colonial stereotypes and racist behavior long practiced and institutionalized in the United States.[2] With its exotic jungle setting, focus on combat, and references to cannibalism and native villages, however, *The Thin Red Line* highlights the ways in which World War II presented a unique amalgam of racial, gender, and colonial discourses.

On all fronts, wartime discourses of race and masculinity intertwined and were played out in specific ways on the body, but in the Pacific theater, they often took on more overtly racist dimensions. Four particular sites reveal these interconnections and dynamics: the creation of an appropriate Japanese enemy, representations of "good" Asians and select "white" ethnic groups on the home front, popular accounts and depictions of Pacific "natives," and the Jim Crow military. In addition to highlighting the ways in which white American masculinity was expanded during the war, these topics reveal how whiteness was also solidified as servicemen defined their manhood in relation to foreign, racialized "others." Moreover, they expose the shortcomings of America's pluralistic, ethnically diverse self-representations. Before turning to these particular subjects, though, it is important to briefly explore World War II's complex racial dimensions.

Although scholars have long recognized that World War II was a race war for the millions who died in the Holocaust and for the thousands of Japanese Americans confined in internment camps, the full complexity of the war's racial dimensions have only recently received attention. Until the late 1970s and early 1980s, almost all discussions of race in World War II focused on Nazi Germany and the Holocaust. During the 1980s, however, revisionist historians uncovered the "hidden Holocaust" and the international eugenics movements that helped engender Nazi policies, and they began to expose the complex racial discourses of America's home front and the war in the Pacific.[3] Although most World War II scholarship continues "to be directed principally to the war against Germany" (James and Wells 10), authors such as Ronald Takaki, John Dower, George Roeder, Reed Ueda, and Susan Hirsch have begun to examine wartime racial conflicts at home and abroad, demonstrating that the war fundamentally changed cultural perceptions of race and ethnicity in the United States.

As historian John Dower asserts in *War Without Mercy*, race shaped the Pacific war in numerous and complex ways. Not only did the "the Allied struggle against Japan expose the racist underpinnings of the European and colonial structure," but it "fueled both Asian racial dreams and Western racial fears" (Dower, *War* 5, 6). Unlike the war with Germany, which was conceived as a "family fight," the war with Japan was placed "in an East-versus-West, Oriental-versus-Occidental, and ultimately blood-versus-blood context" (Dower, *War* 6, 161).[4] Although the Allies adopted a Germany-first policy and deployed only 15 percent of their men and materials to the Pacific war, the war with Japan provoked greater, more emotional responses from the American people (James and Wells 10). In many respects Japan *was* the enemy—not just to little boys who only shot Japanese soldiers when playing war, but to the majority of Americans. As one wartime survey revealed, 50 percent of American soldiers reported that they would "really like to kill a Japanese soldier," while less than 10 percent possessed the desire to kill a German soldier (Roeder, *Censored War* 87). The intense and particular hatred that most Americans had for the Japanese enemy was not merely a wartime response to Pearl Harbor; it was rooted more deeply in decades-old anti-Asian attitudes and legislation.

According to historian Reginald Horsman, these anti-Asian laws were part of a broader pattern of racial discrimination in the United States that began in the nineteenth century. By the late 1840s, Horsman asserts, most Americans "thought of themselves as the descendants of English immigrants, speaking English . . . or they thought of themselves as a superior, distant, 'American' race, drawn from the very best of the stocks of western and northern Europe" (301). This sense of a white, "American" race coupled with the convergence of scientific racism, the closing of the American frontier, and growing U.S. colonial interests led to a series of restrictive immigration laws in the late nineteenth and early twentieth centuries. Alarmed by the waves of "new immigrants" from Eastern and Southern Europe and Asia in the 1880s and 1890s, American lawmakers sought ways to "Keep America American"[5]—to prevent new ethnic stocks from "polluting" the "American Anglo-Saxon race" (Horsman 302). First targeting Chinese immigrants, Congress passed the Chinese Exclusion Act in 1882, which barred the immigration of Chinese laborers and set an important precedent for legislation targeting particular ethnic groups. Made permanent in 1902,[6] the Chinese Exclusion Act was followed by other anti-Asian legislation such as the 1907–8 Gentlemen's Agreement, which limited the immigration of male Japanese laborers, and the 1922 *Ozawa v. the U.S.* Supreme Court decision, which upheld a previous ruling that Japanese and other Asian persons were "ineligible for naturalization by reason of race" (Daniels et al. xv). The most sweeping and xenophobic piece of legislation, however, was the Johnson-Reed Immigration Act of 1924, which made permanent existing European quotas and banned East Asian immigration altogether. With quotas based on the 1890 U.S. Census, the 1924 act ensured that most immigrants would come from Anglo or Aryan nations like Great Britain and Germany, curtailing almost all immigration by Russians, Jews, Poles, Greeks, Italians, and Hungarians.

During this same period, the Jim Crow system of segregation was established to prevent miscegenation and to assert white supremacy. Between 1873 and 1898, a series of Supreme Court decisions gradually eroded the rights of African Americans and created the legal apparatus for "separate but equal" public and private facilities. Firmly in place by 1920, the Jim Crow system became more elaborate and further entrenched as the new Ku Klux Klan reached a peak of 5 million members during the mid-1920s (Coben 282). Strengthened by racial violence, the segregation code covered everything from seating arrangements, bathrooms, accommodations, and recreation facilities to laws curtailing black barbers' clientele. As the 1926 Atlanta ordinance prohibiting black barbers from bobbing women's hair attests, Southern lawmakers were concerned not only with preventing the mixing of the races but also with preserving white gender norms and fashions. Although racial tensions eased somewhat during the depression, the Jim Crow system was well entrenched on the eve of World War II.[7]

Despite the realities of segregation and a history of legislation targeting specific ethnic groups during the late nineteenth and early twentieth centuries, the government and media sought to present a diverse, pluralistic, and unified image of the United States during World War II. The OWI and other government agencies frequently utilized the idea of America as the great "melting pot" as they created an ethnically diverse body politic through posters and other propaganda materials. Hollywood meanwhile produced war films such as *Bataan, Lifeboat,* and *The Fighting 69th,* which featured multicultural platoons and units.[8] Faced with the pressing demands of total war and full-scale mobilization, the United States could no longer exclude certain ethnic groups from its self-representations; bond drives, conservation efforts, war industry work, military service, and other aspects of the war effort required the entire nation's cooperation. Further, this new pluralistic ideal was often presented in contrast to fascist ideologies and Nazi rhetoric about a "master" race, creating the image that America was a nation unified by the ideals of democracy and multiculturalism. According to historians Lewis Erenberg and Susan Hirsch, America's new pluralistic self-definition marked a turning point in the national consciousness. World War II, they contend, "made it official . . . that the national identity of the United States was no longer exclusively white or Protestant" (4).

While new pluralistic constructions of America contributed to record-breaking bond drive campaigns and an unprecedented 1.65 million natural-izations during the war, they did not eliminate racial tensions and conflicts (Ueda 202). In fact, the promises of democracy and unity within diversity actually engendered racial conflict, as African Americans protested the Jim Crow military and sought a "Double Victory" of freedom abroad and at home.[9] Inscribed upon decades of racist legislation and practices, America's new nationalism and its contradictions were destined to bring existing racial tensions to a head. During the war, race riots broke out in many major U.S. cities,[10] and the constitutional rights of Japanese Americans were blatantly disregarded through Executive Orders 9066 and 9102, which allowed the War Relocation Authority to remove 120,000 Japanese Americans (two-thirds of them citizens) from their homes and to place them in internment camps.

The amalgamation of new pluralistic ideals and propaganda, existing racial tensions, and the demands and scope of the war resulted in a complex set of wartime racial discourses. The contradictory discussions and representations of racial issues made it possible for magazines to run articles praising black servicemen's contributions one week and then overtly racist material the next. *Life's* October 28, 1940, issue, for example, printed a picture of a white sailor posing with three small Hawaiian children "for a joke." The caption reads, "Black babies posed with a sailor are always good for a big laugh back home" (127). Later in the war, the same periodical would publish glowing reviews of black troops' performances and pleas for increased combat opportunities for African American soldiers. Not having resolved the tensions between America's new ethnically diverse self-representations and past racist practices, wartime racial discourses remained constantly in flux. One element that remained relatively stable, however, was the popular equation of American masculinity with *white* manhood.

KNOW YOUR ENEMY—CREATING A JAPANESE FOE

Perceptions of wartime enemies played an important role in defining the United States' embodied self-representations. Images of a hypermasculin-ized Germany encouraged government agencies and the media to represent America both powerfully, through overly muscled, youthful bodies, and pluralistically, by including women and persons of color. Perceptions of the

Japanese enemy likewise contributed to national wartime self-definitions, as the U.S. constructed itself as a democratic nation fighting to avenge the "treacherous" attack at Pearl Harbor. Whereas depictions of the German enemy remained fairly stable, constructions of the Japanese changed over the course of the war, offering a shifting signifier against which to constitute American masculinity. Just as America had to revamp its body politic as it mobilized for war, it had to reinvent the Japanese enemy after Pearl Harbor and throughout the war to explain early U.S. losses in the Pacific and to provide an appropriate foe for America's fighting manhood.

Although the U.S. military had recognized the possibility of a Japanese attack and had been developing strategies for a war in the Pacific since the mid-1930s, the general perception of the Japanese in 1941 was that they were an ineffectual, weak people who posed no real threat to America. According to John Dower, before Pearl Harbor most Americans believed "that the Japanese could not shoot, sail, or fly very well" and that they certainly were not innovative or strong enough to qualify as a real world power ("Challenge" 180). Even their victories in China were minimized as conquests over another racially inferior people, won because of Japan's animalistic savagery.

Existing immigration laws likewise reinforced pre–Pearl Harbor perceptions that the Japanese did not offer a threat to U.S. security. Although tied to fears of a "yellow peril" (the idea that hordes of Asians might overrun the U.S.), the anti-Asian legislation of the nineteenth and early twentieth century was primarily based on the notion that Asians offered inferior racial stock. San Francisco's mayor, James Duval Phelan, speaking for the Chinese Exclusion Act, captured this sentiment with his comment that "the Chinese and Japanese are not bona fide citizens. They are not the stuff of which American citizens can be made" (qtd. in Daniels 9). With popular perceptions that the Japanese were a "feminized" nation of exotic but brutal "tiny men," Americans dreaded the Japanese and other Asians because of their sheer numbers, not because they believed that the Japanese possessed any real strength or military prowess. Recalling his wartime experiences, veteran Bill Stevens observed, "The white hang-up about the infinite superiority of the white man to any man of color did not prepare the American white for the Japanese" (qtd. in Motley 77).

Despite having considered the possibility of a Japanese attack, the U.S. military had bought into the myth of American superiority and, as a result, was completely unprepared the morning of December 7, 1941. In just two hours, the Imperial Japanese forces wreaked complete havoc on America's western-most stronghold. U.S. losses included 2,335 servicemen and nearly 100 civilians killed, 1,178 wounded, 18 ships sunk or damaged, the destruction of 188 aircraft, and damage to an additional 159 planes (O'Neill, *Democracy* 6). The Japanese, in contrast, had comparatively light losses: 29 planes and pilots and 6 submarines, 5 of which were midget subs (O'Neill, *Democracy* 6). During the attack at Pearl Harbor, the navy "lost more men than it had in the Spanish-American and First World Wars combined"

(O'Neill, *Democracy* 6). The successful Japanese attacks later that day on Guam, Wake Island, and the Philippines, coupled with numerous additional victories in the early months of 1942, quickly dispelled American myths about the Japanese as a weak, ineffectual people. The U.S. government, military, and popular press had to create new constructions of the Japanese enemy as it embarked on full-scale war.

Almost overnight a bevy of books and articles appeared after Pearl Harbor that attempted to characterize and explain the Japanese enemy. Early in 1942, various presses published books such as *Our Enemy Japan, The Japanese Enemy: His Power and His Vulnerability,* and the army's *The Jap Army,* while magazines like *Time* and *Life* ran articles offering a "Portrait of a Japanese" and information on "How Japan Wages War."[11] Implicit in these texts was not only the idea that Americans had misjudged the Japanese enemy but that they really did not understand him at all. Although many of the books promised to provide insights into the "Japanese character" and nation itself, a central theme of the works was that this particular enemy was somehow unknowable. As Lieutenant Colonel Paul Williams Thompson explains in *The Jap Army,* "It is safe . . . to say that no American understands the Japanese Army in the way that many Americans understand, say, the German Army" (8).[12] Whether authors attributed Japan's unknowability to racial, cultural, or language barriers, the perception of Japan as a decidedly foreign and exotic "other" allowed the Japanese enemy to become a shifting signifier in American wartime discourses of race, power, and masculinity. Recent military defeats could now be attributed to America's inability to interpret the Japanese enemy and its behavior instead of U.S. complacency and myths of white superiority. This is not to say, of course, that the United States did not look for internal scapegoats for the Pearl Harbor debacle; numerous historians have shown that there was an immediate move to assign blame for the disaster within the military and government. Nevertheless, military and popular constructions of the Japanese as a somewhat unknowable adversary enabled a rhetoric in which the Japanese could be reinvented as an appropriate foe for America's fighting manhood.

In the months following Pearl Harbor, the government, military, and media incited U.S. patriotism with pleas to "Remember Pearl Harbor" and endeavored to recharacterize its Asian opponent. The July 1, 1942, *Yank* article "Portrait of Pvt. Moto,"[13] for example, revealed that the military in particular was eager to discredit those "cock-and-bull stories about the Jap" and to masculinize an enemy that had been seen as a non-threatening "pip-squeak" (14). Devastating losses at the hands of such an enemy questioned U.S. military prowess and left little room for future American military defeats in the Pacific war. While striking a balance between confidence in U.S. martial force and respect for Japan's military threat, Secretary of War Henry Stimson promised Americans, "We'll defeat the Japanese in the end" but warned that they "shouldn't look at the war with [Japan] through rose-colored glasses" (qtd. in *Time,* "Portrait" 17).

Utilizing Stimson's comments and other OWI and military information about the Japanese, *Time*'s "Portrait of a Japanese" sought to reimagine the enemy. Explaining how the American public has underrated the "Japanese man as a fighting mechanism" (18), the *Time* article focuses on the bodies and skills of the average Japanese soldier. Although filled with racist generalizations, the respect accorded the Japanese soldier is immediately evident in the decision to describe him as a "man" and a "man-weapon" rather than in subhuman or bestial terms. Like symbolic representations of American soldiers, the Japanese soldier's strength is conveyed through bodily terms:

> Physically he is as tough as he is unhandsome. From the top of his shaved head to the bottom of his splayed-toed feet he is hard. His buttocks are big with marching. His arms are strong, and he can dig himself into a shallow trench quickly and neatly. His eyes are generally good, and there is no physical reason why his aim should not be clean. (18)

While still emphasizing the Japanese soldier's supposed ugliness and difference, the physical characterization places the enemy soldier within a broader category of fighting man machines. His physical hardness translates into other appropriate war-waging abilities and skills, and he is linguistically placed in the discourses of masculinity used to describe both U.S. servicemen and Germans. According to the article, he is a well-equipped, well-disciplined veteran who is "wiry and tough" (18). Military sources such as *The Jap Army* and "Portrait of Pvt. Moto" likewise offered similar descriptions of the Japanese soldier as a "brave, tough fighter" with "amazing physical hardness" ("Moto" 14).

The *Time* essay is also quick to note, however, that the Japanese soldier's racial and ethnic background puts him in a separate military category. The "badly wrapped brown paper package," the article claims, offers a particularly menacing military threat. Described as "ruthless, cruel, lascivious," the Japanese soldier is also purported to be the perpetrator of vicious actions: "When his officer is not looking he spits in the white prisoner's food. He has no compunction (since there has not been time to build prisoner's enclosures) in whamming his rifle down on the captive's insteps, to break bones and prevent escape" ("Portrait" 18). Playing upon Pearl Harbor rhetoric of Japan's "treachery," these lines also tap into racial and colonial discourses by noting the brown color of the Japanese soldier's skin and the whiteness of the prisoner's. Rather than merely describe the Japanese soldier's abilities and characteristics within discourses of masculinity and military prowess, the article calls attention to physical and cultural differences. The Japanese soldier is not only deemed ugly and sloppy in appearance but is also marked as "other" through his skin color and behavior. Although the article strives to undermine stereotypical pre–Pearl Harbor perceptions of the Japanese, it reinforces notions of Asian duplicity and Japanese fanaticism. Playing up these

19—One of many racist depictions of the Japanese enemy, this 1942 Office for Emergency Management poster plays on American fears of miscegenation by constructing the Japanese soldier as a potential rapist and colonizer. (Courtesy of the National Archives and Records Administration, Still Picture Branch)

stereotypes, however, serves to strengthen the virility and virulent nature of the Japanese foe while creating a space for future white American superiority.

The most important way in which the *Time* article masculinizes the Japanese enemy is by constructing the Japanese soldiers as rapists and potential rapists. After recounting the Japanese soldier's various cruelties, the piece warns that "he has raped Chinese girls and can't help wondering what white ones would be like" (18). This statement, reinforced by posters such as the Office for Emergency Management's 1942 "Keep this Horror from Your Home" (fig.19), invokes fears of miscegenation and the yellow peril and positions the Japanese soldier as a potential colonizer. As bell hooks and other feminist theorists have observed, rape has been perceived as "both a right and rite" of male dominating groups (57). Hooks argues that rape has been equated with "the terrorist act re-enacting the drama of conquest. . . . The intent of this act was to continually remind dominated men of their loss of power; rape was a gesture of symbolic castration" (57). Interpreted within this framework, the Japanese soldier's rape of Chinese women serves to mark both his power and status as male colonizer. Moreover, the threat of Japanese violations of white women's bodies also operates as a special solicitation to American servicemen—not only to avenge American defeats in the Pacific but also to protect their women, the purity of the "American" race, and their status as men. According to veteran Bill Stevens, many men fighting in the Pacific were conscious of this Japanese challenge to white manhood: "[The Japanese] were a colored people so the big bad American marines were going to kick their asses properly and put them back in their place" (qtd. in Motley 77).

While the American media was casting the Japanese enemy in more virile terms, there was a simultaneous movement to dehumanize them. By the spring of 1942, Hollywood had already implemented its "'Slap the Jap' policy," and newspapers, magazines, cartoons, and radio broadcasts were filled with racial epithets (Dick 230). Throughout the war, the Japanese were frequently portrayed in a variety of subhuman or animalistic forms; they appeared as monkeys, gorillas, rats, mice, bees, lice, snakes, dogs, mosquitoes, cockroaches, and other vermin. As in previous wartime propaganda campaigns, dehumanizing the enemy made it easier for servicemen to kill them and for the U.S. to justify military actions such as the firebombing of Dresden and the nuclear bombing of Hiroshima and Nagasaki. The dehumanization of U.S. enemies during World War II, however, was disproportionately directed toward the Japanese. The Germans generally received more nuanced treatment in wartime films, advertisements, and posters, allowing for good German characters and individualization, while the Japanese were almost always depicted as evil. Moreover, although Hitler was caricatured in animal form and German soldiers were still called "Krauts" and "Jerries," the German soldier was generally portrayed as human. Racist discourses led Americans—especially servicemen—to create unique categories for the Japanese enemy. As one marine fighting at Guadalcanal told writer John

Hersey, "[The Germans] are human beings, like us. But the Japanese are animals. Against them you have to learn a whole new set of physical reactions" (qtd. in Linderman 168).

While characterizations of the Japanese as insects or vermin were often linked to an exterminationist rhetoric, the more popular depictions of the Japanese as apes and other jungle creatures fostered metaphors of "the hunt." The hunt metaphor pervaded American propaganda about the Pacific war and was sometimes employed to make even a bestial Japanese enemy a worthy opponent for American servicemen. These metaphors frequently evoked ideas of the Old West and America's various Indian wars. Despite OWI disapproval, marine recruiting offices in Chicago issued "Jap hunting licenses" to enlistees, and numerous businesses posted signs "declaring 'Open Season on Japs'" (Dower, "Challenge" 174). From advertisements for beer and ammunition to novelty hunting licenses from the "Viper Exterminating Society," the metaphor of the hunt verbally and visually linked shooting Japanese soldiers to killing game, psychologically minimizing the human loss involved in combat. By evoking images of the Old West and more ancient manly rituals, the hunt metaphor also served to imbue the Pacific war with special masculine challenges. In fact, as historian Gerald Linderman has noted, the animalistic representations of the Japanese "sometimes seemed to enhance the danger he posed" (172).

Depictions of the Japanese as backstabbing monkeys or fierce gorillas helped combine the traditional masculine proving grounds of combat and the hunt in many servicemen's minds. According to Linderman's discussion of the Pacific theater in *The World Within War,* these representations and metaphors shaped many servicemen's perceptions of war in that theater. In contrast to the more conventional fighting of the European theater, combat in the Pacific seemed to offer U.S. servicemen a more unpredictable, animalistic enemy as well as more exotic terrain. In Linderman's text, many servicemen describe the challenges of facing a bestial enemy that could camouflage itself in the jungle and sneak up on its target. In the words of one marine, "You [had] to get used to their animal stubbornness and tenacity" (qtd. in Linderman 168). The jungle itself also contributed to the danger of the hunt. Linderman explains that to American servicemen "the jungle conjured darkness and danger, stealth and perdition; it was forbidding, even impenetrable" (170). Americans, used to open spaces and "American-style" warfare, had to adjust to what veteran Kenneth Davis described as "Jap kind of fighting in Jap kind of country—gloomy, tricky, full of sickness and a sudden stab-in-the-dark kind of death" (qtd. in Linderman 171). The jungle terrain and animalistic depictions of the Japanese transformed the Pacific war for many servicemen into a particularly menacing theater, which allowed servicemen "to reach the warrior ideal" (Linderman 180). Forced to rely on fighting prowess instead of technology, servicemen could more readily prove their worth as warriors through hand-to-hand combat.

Given the pervasiveness of the hunt metaphor and the general racist perceptions of the Japanese enemy, it is hardly surprising that men fighting in the Pacific collected body parts as trophies and committed more heinous atrocities than those fighting in the European theater. Although American servicemen all over the globe collected war souvenirs, the practice of taking body parts as trophies was far more prevalent in the Pacific war. Comparing the war in Europe to the one in the Pacific, George Roeder attests, "In reviewing thousands of censored photographs and uncensored ones, . . . I have never encountered one documenting that American soldiers took as trophies body parts of European soldiers" ("Censoring Disorder" 52). While historian James Weingartner has noted that only a small percentage of servicemen actually engaged in the practice of collecting corporeal trophies, the practice was widespread enough to be a stable feature in novels about the Pacific war such as *The Thin Red Line, The Naked and the Dead,* and *Battle Cry.* Gold teeth were by far the most popular body parts collected, but U.S. servicemen also gathered and sometimes sent home Japanese skulls, bones (often carved into items), pickled ears and noses, and scalps. Despite military and customs efforts to confiscate grisly souvenirs sent to the states, a number of newsmaking items did arrive; an Arizona war worker accepted a signed Japanese skull from her navy boyfriend that made *Life*'s May 22, 1944, "picture of the week," while F.D.R. received (and returned) a letter opener carved from a Japanese thighbone. These war trophies highlight a particular combination of racism and masculinity not generally found in the European theater.[14] As veteran Eugene Sledge explains, "It wasn't simply souvenir hunting or looting the enemy dead; it was more like Indian warriors taking scalps" (qtd. in Linderman 180). Like scalping, the degradation of Japanese corpses was caught up in an unconscious discourse of masculine bravado. The trophies both provided concrete markers of American dominance as well as props for combat stories and bragging. According to Sledge, servicemen "gloated over, compared and often swapped their prizes" (180).

James Jones's *The Thin Red Line* reveals that atrocities committed in the Pacific war were also sometimes used to make particular statements about the other side's masculinity. Detailing one of the novel's earlier combat scenes, the narrator describes the aftermath of 2nd Battalion's capture of Hill 209, in which the tortured and mutilated bodies of two men from George company are discovered. According to the unofficial reports spread throughout Charlie company and the rest of the battalion, one of the captured men had been "beheaded alive with a sword" (156). To send an additional message, the unofficial report states, "As a gesture of defiance, or hatred, of something, the Japanese after beheading him had severed his genitals and stuffed them into the mouth of the severed head" (156). That "something," the men's responses demonstrate, is a statement about their masculinity. While their reactions to the news range from rage to shame to physical sickness (158), the men are united in their outrage; clearly, the castration is an affront to their manhood. As the novel's narrator explains, however, the atrocity is not simply an insult to their masculinity; it is an attack on *white* manhood and its superiority:

> That they had perpetrated this sort of outrage in China and the Philippines on their own dark-skinned races was known too. But that they would dare to do the same sort of thing to civilized white American infantry, and specifically the—Regiment of the—Division, was almost too much to believe and certainly too much to be borne. (156)

Like the lines of the *Time* article describing the potential rape of white American women by the Japanese, this passage reveals the complex ways in which wartime discourses of race and masculinity overlapped. The utter disbelief that American manhood could be questioned is, as historian Gail Bederman has shown, linked to early-twentieth-century America's "widespread beliefs that male power stemmed from white supremacy" (5). Thus the castration of a white American soldier by Japanese soldiers raised questions both about U.S. superiority and its supposed masculine right to dominate "lesser" nations and peoples. Although the average serviceman in the Pacific war—U.S. or Japanese—did not articulate the motives for atrocities in these terms, complex statements about race and masculinity were inscribed on dead male bodies in that theater.

KNOW YOUR FRIEND—REIMAGINING ETHNIC IDENTITIES

Just as it was crucial to reinvent an appropriate Japanese foe after Pearl Harbor, the American government, military, and media had to offer new representations of Asian peoples such as the Chinese, who had to be recognized as a fourth member of the Allies, and the Filipinos, who fought beside U.S. troops against the Japanese at Bataan. Whereas prior to World War II American immigration restrictions such as the Asiatic Barred Zone clause of the 1924 Johnson-Reed Act effectively lumped all East Asians together— viewing them primarily in terms of race rather than nationality—after Pearl Harbor it suddenly became important to offer distinctions between "good" Asians and Asian Americans like the Chinese and the "evil" Japanese.[15] Given the long history of immigration restrictions and alien land acts targeting Asians and the general stereotypical and homogenizing depictions of Asians in popular culture, the tasks of reinventing Chinese and Filipinos as "good" Asians and of viewing Chinese and Filipino Americans as full-fledged citizens were challenging ones. Complicating these tasks was the racist logic behind the internment of Japanese Americans, which implied that it was too difficult to make distinctions between loyal and potentially traitorous persons of Japanese descent because they were all suspiciously foreign in relation to mainstream "American" culture. In the words of Asian American Studies scholar Lisa Lowe, "The Asian is always seen as an immigrant, as the 'foreigner-within,' even when born in the United States and the descendant of generations born here before" (5–6).

Attempts to distinguish persons of Chinese origin from the Japanese occurred almost immediately after Pearl Harbor. The December 22, 1941, issues of *Life* and *Time* printed the articles "How to Tell Japs from the Chinese" and "How to Tell Your Friends from the Japs" respectively. Written in response to recent hate crimes against Chinese Americans, the *Life* piece reports that the seriousness of the situation had forced the Chinese consulates to prepare identification buttons for their nationals and had compelled many individuals such as journalist Joe Chiang to wear a badge proclaiming "Chinese Reporter *NOT* Japanese" (81). In an effort to help the American public overcome their "distressing ignorance" and to "dispel some of this confusion," the article provides guidelines for distinguishing "friendly Chinese from enemy alien Japs" (81). Primarily consisting of a brief history of and physical anthropological distinctions between the two "races," the article is accompanied by a series of photographs of "typical" Chinese and Japanese individuals. To illustrate specific racial differences, the facial and body characteristics featured in the photographs have been carefully labeled with white ink. The first pair of photographs contrasts the faces of Chinese public servant Ong Wen-hao and General Hideki Tojo, noting that Wen-hao's face is "long and delicate boned, his nose more finely bridged," while Tojo's features reveal a "more massively boned head and face, flat often pug nose, yellow-ocher skin and heavier beard" (81). While generally associating Wen-hao with features more commonly considered European or Caucasian, the article and images also serve to link Tojo's physical characteristics with their "aboriginal antecedents," suggesting that he, a "representative of the Japanese people as a whole," is more primitive (81). The second set of images compares three "tall Chinese brothers" who possess the "lanky, lithe build" of many northern Chinese with two "short Japanese admirals" who exhibit "the squat, solid, long torso and short stocky legs of the most numerous Japanese anthropological group" (82). Once again attributing to the Chinese physical characteristics more in line with contemporary American norms of physical attractiveness, the diagrams and captions make the Chinese seem slightly less foreign.

More telling than the facial and bodily features of the Chinese and Japanese, the *Life* piece suggests, are the cultural differences that mark the bodies of these friendly and unfriendly Asians. Offering claims that clearly position the Japanese as aggressor and the Chinese as the victims of this aggression, the photo caption for Tojo's image notes that the "Chinese wear rational calm of tolerant realists. Japs, like General Tojo, show humorless intensity of ruthless mystics" (81). Even more so than the *Life* article, the *Time* guidelines indirectly ascribe cultural differences to innate racial differences. Many of *Time*'s claims, in fact, sound as if they could have been lifted from Nazi racial hygiene teachings. *Time* reports, for example, that "the Chinese expression is likely to be more placid, kindly, open; the Japanese more positive, dogmatic, arrogant" (33). The guidelines also note that Japanese are more apt to be "nervous in conversation" and that they "walk stiffly erect, hard-heeled" (33). The Chinese, meanwhile, are "more relaxed, have an easy gait, sometimes shuffle" (33). While purporting to provide the American public with new, helpful information on distinguishing friend from foe, the *Time* and *Life* pieces largely map existing stereotypes and perceptions onto the bodies of these "typical" Chinese and Japanese figures. The images and accompanying text simply reaffirm popular conceptions of the ruthless, warlike nature of the Japanese and the kind, peaceful character of the Chinese, firmly fixing their respective positions as enemy and ally. Although casting the Chinese in a more favorable light and removing the aggressive yellow peril associations inherent in the Fu Manchu stereotype, the articles nevertheless continue to recirculate certain characteristics linked to the Charlie Chan stereotype. Like Chan, "the controlled minority man" (Chan 67),[16] the Chinese men in the articles are still somewhat feminized. Described as "slenderly built," "lightly boned," "placid," and lacking facial hair, the Chinese are depicted in terms of feminine values and characteristics, albeit American ones.

Given the history of Chinese Americans' cultural position in the United States prior to World War II, these representations of the Chinese in the *Time* and *Life* articles are not surprising. As Lisa Lowe observes, "In conjunction with the relative absence of Chinese wives and family among immigrant 'bachelor' communities and because of the concentration of Chinese men in 'feminized' forms of work . . . Chinese male immigrants could be said to occupy, before 1940, a 'feminized' position in relation to white male citizens" in the United States (11–12). Over the course of the war, however, Chinese American men began to occupy a more culturally recognizable masculine position, though they never entered the exclusive hegemonic domain of white Protestant masculinity. Military service by Chinese Americans, the 1943 Magnuson Act, and popular wartime visual representations of the Chinese served to redefine Chinese American men within more masculine cultural terms. In contrast to the Japanese foe, who was masculinized as a potential rapist, colonizer, and jungle fighter, the Chinese and Chinese Americans became defenders of family, land, and freedom.

Like African Americans and other minorities in the U.S., Chinese Americans recognized that fighting for one's country often was accompanied by the rights of citizenship. Serving in the armed forces, therefore, could solidify a person's manhood as well as his national identity. As veteran Charlie Leong explains, "To men of my generation, World War II was the most important historic event of our times. For the first time we felt we could make it in American society" (qtd. in Takaki 116). Eager to be accepted as Americans and as men, Chinese Americans on the East and West coasts enlisted enthusiastically, and "excited crowds cheered wildly when the first draft numbers were for Chinese Americans" (Takaki 115). Chinese boys, meanwhile, tried to enlist in the military by giving their "Chinese age," which often made them appear to be a year older than what was listed on their birth certificates. According to historian Ronald Takaki, 13,499 Chinese Americans served in the military during the war, representing "22 percent of all Chinese adult males" (115–16). Although they would have been racially classified as "others" according to a Selective Service system that had categories for "White," "Negro," Japanese," "Puerto Rican," and "Others," Chinese Americans enjoyed a certain degree of racial privilege by serving in "white" units. Coupled with expanded wartime employment opportunities in the defense industry, which opened up numerous jobs outside of the restaurant and laundry businesses, military service helped Chinese American men shed their feminized status.

The active wartime participation of Chinese Americans also helped to revise the long series of immigration restrictions that had been placed on the Chinese. Although political pressure from Chiang Kai-shek and the recognition of China's strategic long-term importance in U.S. diplomacy ultimately forced Congress to pass the Magnuson Act in 1943, Chinese American groups such as the Chinese Women's Association and the Chinese Consolidated Benevolent Association of New York lobbied the Roosevelts and key congressmen, citing the wartime contributions of Chinese Americans. With its passage, the Magnuson Act repealed existing exclusion laws, making Chinese eligible for citizenship, and allowed for a quota of 105 Chinese immigrants annually.[17] The act also cemented early wartime constructions of the Chinese as "friend" and Chinese Americans as a model minority. The act, F.D.R. pronounced, "would give the Chinese a preferred status over certain other oriental people, their great contribution to the cause of decency and freedom entitles them to such preference" (qtd. in Dower, *War* 170).

Visual representations of Chinese soldiers and their families in posters and films also helped to masculinize and ennoble Chinese Americans, who were still perceived in terms of their ancestral homeland. Primarily designed to raise contributions for the National War Fund, United China Relief posters created sympathy for the Chinese people while offering fairly heroic depictions of them. Martha Sawyer's poster "China First to Fight!" for example, features a war-weary but determined Chinese family. Standing in the back behind his wife and small daughter, a Chinese infantry soldier in full uniform carefully holds a rifle on his right shoulder while he supports his wounded wife. With her left arm in a slightly bloodied cast and sling, the woman grips the hand of the couple's young daughter, who raises her free hand in a small "thumbs-up" salute. Clearly positioned as patriarch, the soldier is masculinized both by his role as family protector and by his stern expression. With his wife bearing the role as the victim of Japanese aggression, the soldier is left to be the source of national and familial strength. Like Frank Capra's 1942 award-winning documentary *Prelude to War*, the poster reminds viewers that China was the first Allied nation to battle against Japan. In keeping with Capra's narrative, which placed the start of World War II with Japan's September 1931 invasion of Manchuria, the poster constructs China as a long-standing U.S. ally worthy of support. Other United China Relief posters, such as Belridge's "China Carries On," reinforced messages about Chinese strength and perseverance. Against the gray, muted backdrop of a war-torn countryside, a Chinese soldier, armed with a rifle and bayonet, marches toward the viewer, almost stepping out of the poster's frame. Behind him stands a very young boy, looking stoically ahead toward the soldier. Once again protecting family and homeland, the soldier in Belridge's poster shows off his strength and physical vigor. With his shirtsleeves rolled up and his top buttons open, the soldier exposes his muscles and fighting fitness as he strides off to revenge his country's losses.

Although the soldier in Belridge's image shares many of the heroic physical characteristics featured in posters depicting American servicemen, it is important to note that his strong proportions do not approach the comic book–inspired aesthetics of his U.S. counterparts. Willing to accord a certain degree of masculine respect to the Chinese soldier, the American military and media were not ready to give him equal status or to let him enter the realm of white hegemonic masculinity. Frank Capra's 1944 film *Battle for China,* which was viewed by more than 4 million servicemen (Dower, *War* 18), praised China's "indestructible spirit" and commented that the country's soldiers were "toughened and trained" but primarily located China's strength in its vast population, raw materials, and size. Frequently shown in mass groups rather than as individuals, representations of the Chinese in Capra's film revealed that the legacy of yellow peril sentiment was still alive, though it had lost some of its negative associations. Other profiles of the Chinese solider, such as the ones printed in *Yank,* likewise reinforced China's ennobled status while clearly conveying U.S. superiority. Sergeant Lou Stoumen's October 20, 1944, *Yank* article "Report From China," for instance, praised the "fighting Chinese spirit" but reminded readers that the country lacked the benefits of superior Western technology (3). Stoumen noted that the Chinese "are good soldiers, as Americans who have fought beside them in Burma and China can testify. Without any of the heavy weapons of modern war, without even shoes and adequate food, they have fought bloody delaying actions against the modern Jap armies with dignity and heroism" (3). By carefully reminding Americans of China's lack of technology, Capra's film and the *Yank* article allowed U.S. servicemen to respect their ally without having to give up any of their own masculine status.

The war also had important repercussions for the ways in which Filipinos living in the U.S. and its commonwealth were perceived. Although they were not as consistently desexualized and feminized as Chinese American men were, Filipinos in the United States prior to World War II were stereotypically depicted as effeminate "house boys" or dangerous, lascivious criminals. Primarily, though, Filipinos were cast as primitive "little brown brothers," who had succumbed to the superiority of the U.S. military during the conquest of the Philippines. In the words of Theodore Roo-

sevelt, the American victory in the Philippines was a "triumph of civilization over the black chaos of savagery and barbarism" (qtd. in Dower, *War*
151). Such racist perceptions of Filipinos as a heathenish and backward
people no doubt contributed to the incredible brutality with which the U.S.
military put down the three-year insurrection in the Philippines at the turn
of the century. Killing more than 20,000 Filipino soldiers and approximately 200,000 civilians, the American conquest of the Philippines was driven by a ruthlessness steeped in racial hatred (Dower, *War* 151). Not surprisingly, Japanese propaganda campaigns in the Philippines exploited
American racism and past atrocities. A series of "Remember Caloocan!"
leaflets were distributed in the Philippines, reminding Filipinos of the May
1900 "slaughter" of soldiers and civilians.[18]

The past "savagery" and military inferiority of the Philippine people,
however, was quickly replaced with new images in the early months of
1942, as American news stories about Bataan recast Filipino soldiers as
heroic defenders of freedom and liberty. Fighting alongside 12,500 U.S.
troops, some 67,500 Filipino soldiers inflicted heavy casualties on the
Japanese as they valiantly held out for several months in the Bataan penin-
sula (Dear 114). Almost overnight, the Filipino soldier became a respected
brother in arms, and Eleanor Roosevelt praised the fighting as "an excellent
example of what happens when two different races respect each other."
"Men of different races and backgrounds," she pronounced, "have fought
side by side and praised each other's heroism and courage" (qtd. in Takaki
121). Magazines, musical scores, posters, and films likewise highlighted a
newfound American respect for Filipino fighting prowess. The June 1942
cover of *The American Rifleman,* for example, featured a photograph of a Filipino soldier raising his rifle in a combat pose, while composers Frank Grey
and G. R. Montemayor paid tribute to Filipino heroism in their respective
works "Brave Heroes of Bataan" and "See You in Manila." The Office of Special Services, meanwhile, commemorated Filipino bravery with its 1943
poster "The Fighting Filipinos," which offered a dramatic visual representation of a Filipino soldier holding a tattered Philippines flag in one hand
and a grenade in the other. Very much in keeping with physical characteristics generally ascribed to U.S. servicemen, chiseled pectoral muscles bulge
beneath the soldier's open and torn bloodstained shirt. Like his Chinese
counterpart, though, the soldier's body is conspicuously hairless, offering a
mark of racial difference that sets him slightly apart from models of American virility. Filipino soldiers also won glory on the big screen in MGM's
1943 film *Bataan.* Recast as a World War II version of the Alamo, however,
the true heroes of the movie were Americans who upstaged the two Filipino
soldiers fighting with them.

As Ronald Takaki has observed, the stories of Filipino exploits at Bataan
had a tremendous impact on perceptions of Filipino Americans and their
involvement in the war. Initially denied entry into the armed services because they were still classified as "nationals," Filipinos in the U.S. enlisted

enthusiastically once the Selective Service changed the draft laws. According to Takaki, "In California alone sixteen thousand—40 percent of the state's Filipino population—registered for the first draft" (122). Serving in the military allowed many Filipino American men to break free from effeminizing stereotypes and led directly to rights of citizenship and changes in immigration exclusion laws. Previously barred from naturalization, Filipinos serving in the U.S. armed forces were made eligible for citizenship during the war, and a year after the war Congress revised the 1934 act barring Filipino immigration and naturalization and established a new immigration quota of 100 for the Philippines. As in the case of the Chinese, the war opened new spaces for Filipino masculinity in mainstream American culture. Although neither Chinese American nor Filipino American men entered the elite realm of white hegemonic masculinity, they began to occupy less of a marginalized cultural position as they became distanced from much-maligned Asians like the Japanese.

Just as World War II forced the American military, government, and public to redefine popular perceptions of Asians, it also forced Americans to complicate their definitions of whiteness. The Johnson-Reed Immigration Act, which banned East Asian immigration, also curtailed almost all immigration by Russians, Jews, Poles, Greeks, Italians, and Hungarians. Thus within the category of "white" America existed groups of "good" immigrants such as the English, Swedes, and Germans, who helped keep the population Anglo-Saxon and Protestant, and "bad" immigrants such as the Italians, Jews, and Poles, who complicated this profile of white America. These immigrants from Eastern and Southern Europe failed to speak English and practiced "alien" religions and often lived in separate ethnic neighborhoods and communities. Although these immigrants were recognized as Caucasians, leaders of the Americanization project of the 1920s and 1930s viewed these persons from Eastern and Southern Europe as separate from the white "American" race. As educator and Americanization proponent E. P. Cubberly explained in his goals for the program, "Our task is to break up their groups or settlements, to assimilate and amalgamate these people as a part of our American race, to implant in their children the Anglo-Saxon conception of righteousness, law and order, and popular government" (qtd. in Coben 287).

While Americanization classes and programs worked to assimilate Southern and Eastern European immigrants and their American-born children, in the 1920s the Ku Klux Klan's 5 million members sought to disenfranchise recent immigrants along with African Americans and other minorities. In addition to acts and threats of violence, the Klan helped defeat Catholic and Jewish political candidates, imposed bans on "indecent" films, books, and school curriculums, and generally protected the narrow domain of white hegemonic masculinity. Thanks to Klan actions and the broader anti-Semitic sentiments in the general population, on the eve of the Second World War Jews were frequently barred from resorts, social clubs, and certain types of employment. Though not nearly as pervasive as the Jim Crow system of segregation against African Americans, anti-Semitic policies positioned Jews as outsiders to American mainstream white culture.

The exigencies of total war and full-scale mobilization, however, meant that the United States could no longer exclude certain ethnic groups from its self-representations; every segment of the population was needed to keep America's war machine running. Drawing on World War I propaganda campaigns, members of the OWI along with filmmakers, artists, and reporters sought to celebrate America's ethnic and religious diversity. The famous "This is America . . . Keep it Free!" poster series, for example, paired images of ethnically diverse schoolboys with claims that "every boy can dream of being President" and promised Americans that they could "pray to God in your own way, according to your own beliefs." In keeping with OWI guidelines, individual states and cities issued posters publicizing the contributions of Americans from diverse backgrounds. Massachusetts printed the poster "Americans All," which featured an image of smiling racially diverse Americans and the plea, "Don't ever forget this war was won by the contributions of Protestants, Catholics and Jews—Negro and White—AMERICANS ALL." The City of New York, meanwhile, created a sobering poster of a wartime cemetery with graves marked by crosses and Stars of David. With the names "Adams, Kelly, Müller, Cohen, Svoboda, Santelli" boldly printed over the sea of graves, the poster encouraged peaceful pluralism at home by reminding viewers, "They died together— So that we may live together." Giving equal space to names associated with persons from Southern and Eastern Europe and those from Western Europe, the poster also helped collapse earlier cultural distinctions between "good" and "bad" immigrants.

Like New York City's stirring reminder of its ethnic diversity, wartime films presented an increasingly diverse America—especially in combat movies, where the idea of the multicultural platoon became firmly entrenched in the American imagination. Popular films such as *Hollywood Canteen, Lifeboat, Purple Heart, The Fighting 69th,* and *Stagedoor Canteen* emphasized the ethnic diversity of men in uniform by mentioning and including Italian, Jewish, and Mexican American characters. MGM's film *Bataan,* in fact, went so far as to present an integrated unit by including a young black private in the already ethnically diverse white group of soldiers. Created in late 1942, the unit was pure Hollywood fabrication, since no combat units had been integrated at this point in the war.[19] Perhaps the greatest cinematic testament to America's ethnic diversity and the expansion of whiteness was Capra's 1944 *War Comes to America,* the seventh installment in the *Why We Fight* series. Designed to inspire and inform U.S. servicemen, the film spends a good deal of time defining the "we" of American identity for its audience. After citing key events, battles, and patriotic figures in American history, the film focuses on the idea that the United States is a nation that has been built by generations of immigrants seeking a better life in the "land of opportunity." Following a reminder that "all men are created equal," the film offers several sweeping shots of the Statue of Liberty while the narrator recites the inscription at the statue's base. Capra's film then proceeds to offer a panoply of images of ethnically diverse Americans, naming their countries of origin as they appear. Departing slightly from typical immigration narratives, *War Comes to America* describes the immigration of the English, Dutch, Scots, Italians, French, Swiss, Danes, Norwegians, Swedes, "Negroes," Welsh, Spaniards, Mexicans, Greeks, Portuguese, Germans, Hungarians, Russians, Irish, and "Slavs" respectively. Although the film generally privileges an Anglo-focused narrative of American history and notably excludes Asian and Native Americans from the collective American "we," it carefully collapses distinctions between older and more recent immigrant communities, creating more inclusive and egalitarian versions of America and whiteness.

Wartime and postwar novels also frequently presented ethnically and religiously diverse characters as they explored the trials of American servicemen at home and abroad. Although certainly not the first fictive work to feature such a cast, Leon Uris's best-selling 1953 novel *Battle Cry* offered the multicultural unit par excellence. Focusing on a squad of radiomen in the Second Marine Division of the Sixth Regiment, the novel's narrator, Mac, self-reflexively notes that the story is full of stock war story characters: "There was the company clown, the farmer, the wanderer, the bigot, the boy with the mission, the Texan. Huxley's Whores had its gambler, its tightfisted quartermaster, its horse-ass officers, its lovers, its drunks, its braggarts, its foul-ups" (2). Primarily, though, the narrator and other characters identify the principal players in terms of ethnicity and religious beliefs. Andrew Hookans is described as "a big dumb musclebound Swede with two left feet" (4); Joe Gomez, the "renegade trouble maker" (5) is known as Spanish Joe throughout the book; Connie Zvonski, nicknamed "Ski," is identified as "the little Polack" (20); Shining Lighttower, "that Injun" (4), is described as "a skinny, hunched over, deflated redskin with a nose off a buffalo nickel" (4); and later squad additions Red Cassidy, Jake Levin, and Pedro Rojas are respectively called "a stocky redheaded Irishman" (248), "that Jew boy" (287), and "the Mexican" (294). With the exception of Danny Forrester, "the All-American boy" (5), the remaining white characters are identified in terms of their interests, professions, or behaviors. Cyril "Seabags" Brown is "the farmer" (5); Marion Hodgkiss is "a music lover" (5); and Mortimer "Speedy" Gray is "a drawling Texan" (99) and "the bigot" (2). Presumably of Western European origin, these non–ethnically marked characters reinforce distinctions between old and new American ethnicities, subtly reminding readers that "whiteness" is still hierarchical despite its new wartime inclusiveness. By carefully designating the middle-class, golden-haired, star football player Danny Forrester as "the All-American boy," the novel highlights that Anglo-Saxon Protestants were the original members of the exclusive club of white American manhood.

Despite its obvious ethnic stereotypes, *Battle Cry,* like Capra's film, cele-brates the notion of unity within diversity forged through hard work, coop-eration, and the rigors of training and combat. Tracing the men's individ-ual developments and the group's collective exploits, the novel follows the radio squad members from their early bonding moments in basic training to their first combat experiences at Guadalcanal through their adventures and losses in New Zealand, Tarawa, and Saipan. Although Danny remains the novel's central figure and one of the squad's three survivors, *Battle Cry* devotes fairly equal treatment to the various characters and does not main-tain ethnic distinctions when meting out honors and moments of heroism.[20] Pedro and Ski, for example, are singled out for their gallantry in combat by winning Navy Cross medals. Further, former boxing champions "Spanish" Joe and Jake Levin both turn down invitations to join the division boxing team in order to stay with the outfit, proving both their loyalty to the group and their willingness to fight in combat. Already endowed with a certain mascu-line toughness because of the boxing titles, the decisions to remain with the squad help counter their potential marginal status as ethnic and racial "oth-ers," reminding the group that they want to "be Marines like the rest of us" (312). In an interesting departure from many cinematic and fictive combat narratives where the "All-American" boy emerges as the true hero, *Battle Cry* tries to endow each of the central characters with heroism and strength, ex-panding the parameters of American masculinity to include a broader spec-trum of "white" men as well as select men of color.

While collapsing certain boundaries within white American masculinity, the novel nevertheless maintains other hierarchies. In keeping with a climate of wartime prejudices and hate crimes against Latino men such as the famous 1943 Zoot Suit Riots, Pedro informs Mac that their outing in New Zealand "is the first time I have been able to walk into a restaurant or bar with a white man" (305). And Lighttower reminds his squad mates of their white privilege by frequently addressing them as "white man." Jake Levin and Connie Zvonski, however, are given the opportunity to join Danny Forrester's club of white American manhood, largely because they are fighting against a vilified Japanese enemy. In relation to such a foreign, racially marked "other," their status as white Americans seems much more assured. As the narrator's frequent descrip-tions of battle reveal, the real conflict took place when "fanatic yellow men and fanatic white men locked in hand to hand combat" (468). The intense, racially inscribed hatred of the Japanese enemy not only contributed to the divergent treatment of Italian, German, and Japanese resident aliens,[21] but also, in casting the war in the Pacific as a race war between "white" and "yellow" men, helped level hierarchies within the category of whiteness in America.

THROUGH "NATIVE" EYES

The newly expanded white American manhood solidified itself in rela-tion to "natives" encountered abroad as well as in contrast to African American soldiers in a Jim Crow army. Just as wartime constructions of the Japanese enemy served as important "others" against which white American masculinity could be defined, so too did representations of the "natives" that servicemen encountered in their overseas ventures. As Gail Bederman has argued in *Manliness and Civilization,* this standard colonial practice had been occurring in the United States since the late nineteenth century when America rose to the ranks of an imperial power. Indeed, by the end of World War I, the U.S. had territorial holdings in Alaska, the Aleutian Islands, Midway, Wake Island, the Hawaiian Islands, Cuba, the Dominican Republic, Puerto Rico, the Philippines, Guam, American Samoa, the Panama Canal Zone, and the Danish West Indies, and it had come to see its dominance of "inferior" nations as an index of its power and civilization. Nevertheless, in addition to persons fighting the Spanish-American War, only a handful of anthropologists and manly adventurers like Theodore Roosevelt had the opportunity to explore these "exotic" locales.

With World War II, however, more Americans came into direct contact with foreign cultures, persons, and customs than ever before. No longer restricted to the pages of *National Geographic* or specialized publications, images and accounts of "natives" began to fill the pages of popular and military periodicals like *Collier's, Life, Harper's, Time,* and *Yank* as Americans took an increased interest in the places their family members and friends were stationed. In fact, there was such a strong interest in foreign lands and cultures that a new hybrid genre, the "pop ethnography," emerged during the war.[22] While these pop ethnographies professed to provide information about "natives" and their customs, like most mid-twentieth-century anthropological and ethnographic studies, the essays ultimately revealed more about Americans than their supposed objects of study. A brief examination of pop ethnographies provides further insights into the complex intersections between wartime discourses of race and masculinity and highlights the particular ways in which U.S. masculinity was marked as white via comparisons with racialized others.

One of the most obvious ways in which these wartime articles about Pacific "native" others sought to reaffirm American manhood and superiority was through the constant rearticulation of colonial stereotypes. Even while attempting to dispel stereotypes about indigenous populations, these essays functioned to preserve the boundaries between civilized (white) American society and other primitive worlds. Like much of colonial discourse, the articles maintain the fixity of racial and ethnic stereotypes by telling readers what they already know. As postcolonial theorist Homi Bhabha explains, in colonial discourse, "we always already know that blacks are licentious, Asians duplicitous . . ." ("Other Question" 80). In *Yank's* May 12, 1944, article "GI's meet the ex-cannibals," for example, staff writer Sergeant Barrett McGurn attempts to disassociate Solomon Islanders from cannibalistic practices but ultimately remythologizes them as cannibals. In addition to the article's title, which immediately conjures up an array of stereotypes of the primitive cannibal, the human interest piece devotes its first seven paragraphs to descriptions of past cannibalistic practices. Thus, although the article focuses on how the Solomon Islanders have learned the secrets of capitalism and have come to admire their G.I. "companions," the opening section plays upon the primitive mystique, describing "the best parts of a man [to eat]," unsuspecting missionaries dining on "a native feast," and past head-hunting practices (McGurn 8). Given this information, the reader is forced to define the Solomon Islanders in the terms from which they are supposedly dissociated.

Although he represents the Solomon Islanders as primitive ex-cannibals, McGurn describes the "natives" positively because of "their admiration for things American" (8). This rhetorical move emphasizes America's cultural superiority both by contrasting civilized Americans with the mostly nude, ex-cannibal "natives" and by revealing the Solomon Islanders' desire for American goods and lifestyles. Complementing the article's detailed discussion of bartering between the Solomon Islanders and servicemen is an "interview" section, which reveals the extent of this "native" desire for civilization. Next to drawings of various "natives" are the following responses to questions about Americans and their lifestyles:

> **Duga** (aged 9): Like American women and American children. Like to see in American pictures they run all over the house. House is big, lots of people. Big place to run in. American women wearum clothes, children shoes. Very nice.
> **Gunnith:** All native like Americans. They're good to native people. They give us food, clothes. They give us all we need—knife, flashlight. No like Japs. Japs no good.

Once again, the article reinforces American superiority through the respondents' primitive speech patterns, their envy of American wealth and goods, and their approbation of Americans themselves. Like many other wartime pop ethnographies, the *Yank* piece reinvents and recirculates stereotypes of the civilized colonizer, the loyal native, and the exotic other in order to position America as the "good" imperial power in the Pacific war.

Adopting a double function of asserting American superiority and Japanese and "native" inferiority, many pop ethnographies also described loyal "natives" who risked their lives saving Allied pilots, tracking the Japanese, and caring for wounded Americans. Patrick Maitland's February 1943 *Harper's* article "Under Fire on Guadalcanal," for instance, tells the story of Sergeant Major Vouza, a "fuzzy-headed blackamoor" Solomon Islands police officer who refused to reveal American positions despite brutal Japanese torture (271). Vouza's tale, Maitland avers, "could be duplicated twenty times" (271). Although often intended as informative representations of indigenous peoples' character, these tales of loyalty serve as endorsements of Euro-American colonial rule and the Allied war effort. Moreover, they reinforce Japanese inferiority by highlighting the reasons Japan could not keep its "temporary empire." Using the "natives" as objective parties, the pop ethnographies repeatedly privilege American goods, technology, and values over the savage ways of the Japanese.[23]

In keeping with the stereotype of the loyal native, many pop ethnographies explicitly cast American servicemen in the role of the civilized colonizer. In the January 1944 *National Geographic* article "At Ease in the South Seas," for instance, Major Frederick Simpich glowingly describes "the American way of life our troops have brought to the coral and jungle of these far places" (79). Pointed out as a sign of great progress is "a native-owned 'beanery' in Fiji . . . [with] a blackboard menu offering hamburgers, cheeseburgers, and vanilla ice cream" (Simpich 79). Bragging that American servicemen were not "changed by their weird environment of head-hunters and gooney birds," Simpich notes the ways in which U.S. military personnel have transformed the local landscapes: "There are baseball diamonds set in jungle glades to the specifications of Abner Doubleday, daily news mimeographs filled with the latest communiqués—from Hollywood, and bomb shelters on advanced bases with electric lights and poker tables" (79). Like McGurn's piece, Simpich's essay highlights the ways "natives" have embraced American habits, dress, and, of course, the wonders of capitalism. Along with offering descriptions of local laundry and souvenir businesses, the article includes photographs of New Caledonians and Samoans donning military clothes and using American machinery. Always positioned as readily embracing American goods and civilization, the "natives" are also portrayed as willing workers who happily agree to serve U.S. military personnel and their war effort. The caption below the photograph of one New Caledonian laborer reads: "Taking orders from this private, the tractor driver is typical of the fine physical specimens who have helped build our installations. In contrast to his mechanical aptitude, his fuzzy hair is stained red in primitive style" (Simpich 91). The "willing, intelligent" helper, as Simpich describes him elsewhere, not only readily respects the command of the army's lowest ranking servicemen but also welcomes the opportunity to become modernized. His "primitive style" hair and body, however, will always betray the fact that he is only "semicivilized" (Simpich 91). Throughout much of his essay, Simpich continues to position "natives" as natural laborers of the white man and, in fact, offers advice taken from military pamphlets such as "The Native and You" on how American soldiers and sailors should handle their workers. Quoting from "these widely studied booklets," Simpich informs the servicemen and other readers, "Joke with him by all means (but) don't deliberately descend to his level. He will consider it unfitting. . . . Give him something for services rendered, even if it is only a half stick of tobacco, a fishhook, or a razor blade" (81). More pointedly, though, Simpich offers his own blunt advice: "Don't abuse him and don't nag. If you find yourself especially irritated by the way your laborers are behaving, take some more quinine and a dose of salts" (82). Underlying much of this advice is the notion that the American serviceman must always remember his superior position as he deals with childlike "natives" who will exasperate him because of their inability to grasp American technologies and cultures. Like the civilized colonizers, the serviceman must be a benign and patient boss during the U.S. occupation of various islands.

In addition to providing a generally positive lens through which to view the United States and its culture, wartime pop ethnographies offered a subtle vehicle for constructing white American masculinity. Unlike representations of American cultural superiority, which were developed through direct comparisons of cultures, constructions of white masculinity were often constituted indirectly in terms of female bodies. As Gail Bederman and Michael Kimmel have noted, since the turn of the century American masculinity was predicated not only on the physical strength and fighting prowess of a man but also on his capabilities to control his emotions and physical passions. While combat offered American men the opportunity to prove the former, encounters with Pacific "natives" often provided the latter.

Drawing on several centuries of scientific racism, wartime materials reinforced the myth that the "primitive" people GIs encountered abroad were more sexual than their civilized European and American counterparts. While some accounts described "native" women as "ugly" or unsuitable for white men, many narratives objectified their bodies, marking them as sites of sexual desire. E. J. Kahn's *New Yorker* article "The Army Life: Somewhere in New Guinea,"[24] for instance, focused on "native" women's natural sexuality and availability:

> Though for some reason or other we saw no little girls, we passed plenty of older ones, many of them as becomingly undressed as if they had just finished posing for the *National Geographic*. They were, inevitably, subjected to admiring whistles. Some of them seemed unmoved by these tributes, but others, on the shy side, retreated modestly behind the trees. (128)

Like the women on the pages of *National Geographic*, these women are always already commodified as sexual objects available to the white male gaze. According to definitions of civilized (white) masculinity, however, American manhood was more effectively demonstrated by *not* having sex with these "native" women. As journalist Margaret Halsey's wartime volume *Color Blind* explained, in civilized societies "much of the energy which the primitive puts into simple, direct gratification of sex is diverted into other channels—invention, exploration, art, wit, education, friendship, family ties" (110). In order to preserve American manhood, Halsey implies, the "civilized man" had to "postpone gratification in order to achieve a sense of power and mastery" (111).

While the actual sexual practices of American servicemen in the Pacific theater are almost impossible to document, military and media representations endeavored to preserve notions of masculine self-control—especially in discourses concerning "native" women. In an October 28, 1940, *Life* photo essay on servicemen's experiences in Hawaii, for example, the magazine staff carefully foreclosed any suggestions of miscegenation. Describing a photograph of three sailors posing with "a Hawaiian girl," the caption mentions that "sailors find little to do in Hawaii." The text continues: "There are almost no white girls whom the sailors can meet, and since the average of the enlisted men are high-school trained, ambitious and self-respecting, they do not want to have dates with native girls or underworld whites" (40). In reality servicemen in Hawaii were not as chaste as the caption alleges, and their sexual encounters were not confined exclusively to women of the same racial background. However, the military and the American media sought to maintain the perception that rigid racial and ethnic boundaries existed across sexual lines. Recalling his wartime experiences, Lieutenant Colonel Alden Jacobs noted that "we had policies issued by the commander in chief in the Pacific against fraternizing with native women anywhere" (WWII Survey). While not always enforced, these nonfraternization policies could be used to forbid racially mixed marriages and to regulate brothels overseas so that white men only had access to light-skinned women.[25] The American media likewise persisted in its declarations that American men controlled their sexual urges and/or saved them for women of the appropriate (same) race. Despite white servicemen's own cartoons and jokes about miscegenation, popular articles reassured the American public that their men were only posing with those "native girls"[26] for fun, that they were really dreaming of a "white mistress."

Although largely absent from the Pacific theater, white women's bodies also played important roles in the constructions of white American masculinity. *Yank* articles, photographs, and cartoons revealed that a salient feature of white American manhood was its privileged access to white women. Just as they validated notions of U.S. cultural superiority by reporting "native" admiration for all things American, pop ethnographies also demonstrated "native" desire for white American women. *Yank*'s March 12, 1943, cover photograph, for example, featured a group of Fiji Islanders with nose rings and body paint, collectively examining a copy of *Yank* with a white Women's Army Corps (WAC) sergeant on the cover. The photo offers a striking contrast between the white woman on the cover and the six dark-skinned "natives" who gaze at the magazine with great interest. While the photograph itself suggests a simple cross-cultural encounter, the caption below highlights the idea of "native" desire for white women. The caption reads, "On one of the Fiji Islands, natives (not the Hollywood variety) are evidently finding plenty of interesting things in a copy of *The Army Weekly.* By the way, howdaya like the pin-up, bud?" (1). The informal "howdaya like the pin-up, bud?" removes the innocence of the encounter, positioning the cover subject and inside pin-up women as shared objects of desire.

McGurn's "GI's meet the ex-cannibals" likewise performs this rhetorical move. Quoting from Suru in the interview section, the text informs *Yank* readers that Solomon Islanders "likkum white hair (blond)" (12). The rest of Suru's quotation reveals his implied preference for American women over "native" women: "American women very nice, wearum good clothes. Native boy likkum women wear clothes. Native women want wear clothes all time, not get any" (9). After representing "native" desire for American women, the *Yank* pieces carefully note the impossibility of "native" men gaining access to white women. As if to assure readers of this impossibility, McGurn ends his article by noting that although "plenty of natives want to go to the States after the war ends . . . few are likely to realize these ambitions because of British restrictions of native travel and U.S. immigration laws" (9).

By reinventing the myth of black men's desire to have sex with white women, the *Yank* pieces and other pop ethnographies reaffirmed white American men's status as protectors as well as their cultural and masculine superiority. While, because of their cultural privilege, they had access to women of any color, they also had the luxury of constructing a one-way color line in sexual relations. As Beth Bailey and David Farber have noted, the importance of limiting men of color's access to white American women was so great that during the war most madams on Hotel Street in Hawaii "removed all chance of racial conflict by simply refusing to serve men of color" (103). Like representations of the Japanese enemy, wartime pop ethnographies problematized America's pluralistic, ethnically diverse self-representations. Despite presenting friendly relations and goodwill between U.S. servicemen and local "natives," as well as moments of homosocial bonding across racial and ethnic lines (as in the case of the *Yank* pin-up), these articles generally reinforced boundaries between black and white, nature and culture, civilized and primitive. Time and time again, the pop ethnographies constructed American manhood in terms of whiteness as they defined American masculinity in relation to foreign, racialized "others."

THE JIM CROW MILITARY

Despite the military's early efforts to preserve its fighting ranks as a domain of white manhood, none of the service branches was exclusively white. According to the *Fourth Selective Service Report,* by the war's end, "1,056,841 Negro registrants were inducted into the armed forces," and, with the exception of the Marine Corps, African Americans constituted approximately 11 percent of all inductees (Hershey 187). Moreover, thousands of other racially and ethnically marked men served as well; by the end of 1945, the armed forces had inducted approximately 33,000 Japanese Americans, 45,000 Native Americans, 13,499 Chinese Americans, 1,320 Hawaiians, 11,506 Filipinos, and 51,438 Puerto Ricans.[27] In addition to these inductions, "by June 30, 1945, a total of 125,880 aliens of various nationalities had enlisted or been inducted into the Army or Navy" (Hershey, Vol. 4: 189). While these inductions were in keeping with the pluralistic wartime self-representations the U.S. government and media created, they posed key problems for the existing structures, prejudices, and definitions of the military.

Despite the fact that blacks and other men of color had served in the U.S. military in every major war, on the brink of World War II, the military was reluctant to accept full minority participation. According to historian Bernard Nalty, "Less than 2 percent of the combined strength of the Regular Army and the National Guard consisted of blacks as the 1930s drew to a close" (133). Moreover, as the War Department prepared for the draft and future enlistments, planners drew up quotas that created "a wartime Army that would be roughly 6 percent black, even though blacks made up almost 10 percent of the population" (Nalty 133). Not only would the full participation of blacks and other ethnic minorities force the military to address issues of segregation, but it would also raise broader questions about issues of citizenship. Since the Civil War, African Americans had recognized the connection between the right to fight for one's country and the attainment of other rights of citizenship, and they viewed World War II as another potential battlefield for gaining additional civil and legal rights. In addition to obtaining voting, employment, and other social rights, black Americans desired to confirm their status as men, to exercise their manly right to prove themselves in battle. The policies of America's World War II Jim Crow military, however, presented sizable obstacles in the path of achieving these goals.

For many servicemen, the Second World War, like others before it, offered an important proving ground to demonstrate their masculinity through combat. The issue of black participation in combat, then, became a particularly vexed one, as white military leaders sought to preserve this domain primarily for white American manhood. If blacks were allowed to prove their fighting prowess as the 367th and 369th infantry regiments had in France during World War I, then the military would be forced to change its policies restricting black participation, and America as a nation would be compelled to question its assumptions about white superiority. Even after authors of the 1940 Selective Service Act rejected the War Department's initial quotas and mandated that "any person, regardless of race or color, between the ages of eighteen and thirty-six, shall be afforded an opportunity to volunteer for induction into the land or naval forces" (qtd. in Lee 73), the military still found ways to limit black participation. In the summer of 1940, on the eve of "the greatest expansion which the Army of the United States had known," the War Department decided that blacks would be inducted and mobilized only in "proportions equal to their representation in the nation's manpower of military age" (Lee 49). The War Department further ruled that the military would keep its units segregated, that additional officers (50 percent more than in white units) would supervise black troops, and that no black officers would ever command white troops.

Despite a 1940 decision stating that blacks were to be given combat assignments in the same ratio as whites, the War Department was slow to place blacks in combat units and failed to let them enter the more prestigious areas of service like the Army Air Corps and the Marine Corps. By the end of 1941, only 5 percent of enlisted men in the infantry were black, and

African Americans were still barred from certain branches of the military. It was not until Roosevelt issued Executive Order 9279 in December 1942 that all branches of the service were forced to end restrictions on black military participation.[28] Nevertheless, ending restrictions and placing blacks in combat units did not necessarily ensure that they would have a chance to demonstrate their fighting abilities; military leaders were slow to organize, train, and send black combat units overseas. Black servicemen readily recognized that their lack of combat opportunities was tied to the boundaries and definitions of white masculinity. As veteran Bill Stevens, member of the 25th Infantry Regiment of the 93rd Division realized, "Blacks were not going to be given a chance to prove themselves in combat in the Pacific. From where I sat they weren't going to get a chance even if it caused the death of every cracker in the Pacific to keep it that way. The glory boys had to be white!" (qtd. in Motley 76). This injustice, Stevens notes, further perpetuated myths about blacks' "faulty" manhood; denying blacks the right to fight fostered the myth, "perpetuated by whites, that the black man is a big zero as a fighting man; he is a coward" (qtd. in Motley 77). These myths reached to the top echelons of military command. Lieutenant General George Patton "was convinced that blacks lacked the reflexes for armored combat" (Nalty 177), while Secretary of War Stimson made numerous remarks in private about blacks' inferior combat abilities.[29]

Ultimately, black combat units such as the 99th Fighter Squadron, the 761st Tank Battalion, and the 614th Tank Destroyer Battalion were organized and put into action despite a general reluctance on the part of the military to utilize African Americans in combat. The 99th Squadron, the first black unit to see combat, was not activated until the spring of 1943, and, even when infantry divisions like the 93rd finally saw action in the Pacific, it was often to do "mopping up" work (Buchanan 95). Despite white commanders' unwillingness to take on black troops and their limited combat opportunities, black servicemen performed well enough to be considered for integrated units by 1945. When a shortage of white infantry troops arose in Northwest Europe, more than 5,000 black troops volunteered for the 2,500 positions fighting alongside white soldiers. Wartime and postwar reports in which 84 percent of white officers and 81 percent of white sergeants said that blacks fighting in integrated units had performed "very well" (Nalty 178) no doubt contributed to Truman's Executive Order 9981, which desegregated the armed forces in 1948.

Under the guidance of the OWI, the American media helped the military maintain the perception that America's fighting manhood was still racially coded as white. Although war bond campaigns and various posters emphasized the heroism and bravery of black servicemen like Dorie Miller, Joe Louis, and Obie Bartlett, the wartime achievements of most African Americans were minimized by the press. As George Roeder has noted, "Photographs of wounded soldiers from African-American units . . . ended up in the files of censored materials because of army resentment of an alleged 'tendency on part of the Negro press to unduly emphasize' the achievement of those units" (*Censored War* 79). In addition to slighting African American participation through censorship, the mainstream white press also frequently criticized the *Pittsburgh Courier* and other members of the black press for their coverage of African American units, further undercutting African American contributions.[30] Moreover, when describing black combat assignments, articles such as the September 20, 1943, *Time* report on the 99th Fighter Squadron, "Experiment Proved?" denigrated the basic idea of black combat troops. The article described the combat assignments of black troops as "one of the Army's biggest headaches" and noted that "high command has trouble finding combat jobs for them" (68). Further, the piece questioned whether the black soldier would ever "develop his potential as an airman or soldier," ending the article with "a question as old as U.S. independence . . . : Is the Negro as good a soldier as the white man?" (68). Although the white press was slow to recognize the military accomplishments of blacks, it readily noted America's democratic values and pluralism when it did report blacks' wartime accomplishments. The achievements of the 103rd Division, for example, became the stuff that would give Hitler a "hemorrhage": "white boys . . . going out on mixed patrols, sleeping in the same bombed out building, sweating out the same chow line with Negro GIs."[31] Thus black accomplishments were not about masculinity and fighting prowess but rather about America's success as a democracy.[32]

Denying blacks combat opportunities was not the only way in which the military sought to privilege white manhood over black masculinity. The complex Jim Crow system of segregated units, blood supplies, facilities, and buses worked to lower black morale and to create racial hierarchies of white over black at every turn. The various injustices of Jim Crow segregation worked in subtle, Foucauldian ways to remind blacks of their disenfranchisement and lack of masculine status. In his July 24, 1943, letter to African American General Benjamin Davis, Private W. C. Ross provided an extensive list of ways that blacks were treated as second-class citizens at Fort Clark, Texas.[33] In addition to describing poor theater seats, inferior food, and the absence of a pool, chapel, and cafeteria for black soldiers, Ross noted that "our colored officers swim once per week in the lily-white pool and they empty the water that night so [whites] will not swim in the contaminated water the next day." More importantly, Ross complained, "we are called boys, birds and guys instead of soldiers and troopers by rank." Discussing conditions at Camp Lee, Vancouver Barracks, and Fort Riley, meanwhile, First Lieutenant William Knox recalls that black officers were not permitted to attend their class graduation dance, buy black newspapers on the post, or use recreational facilities that were available to German POWs. Moreover, they were subject to demeaning lectures like the one at Fort Riley where "a white officer speaking to black troops at a Troop Information Hour stated that blacks could not be fully accepted in our nation because 'they had not proven themselves'" (World War II Survey). These daily indignities were reinforced by the rulings of the military courts, which often endorsed white privilege and violence against blacks.[34] In one noteworthy case, Air Force Colonel William Colman was charged with "careless use of firearms" after shooting a black private in the head. Outraged that the motor pool had ignored his standing order of "no Negro drivers," Colman shot the private when he reported to the officers club to retrieve Colman. The court sentenced Colman to a reduction in rank (from colonel to captain) and barred future promotions for three years.[35] It is no wonder that a 1943 Special Service Division study reported that only one in five black soldiers felt they had received fair treatment by local police, while approximately three-fourths of white soldiers recounted fair dealings with law enforcement.[36] Faced with these sorts of rulings and other injustices, black servicemen often proved Foucault's point that where there is power, there is also resistance. Though often minimized or ignored by the press, racial conflict erupted on bases throughout the U.S., often leading to violence, sometimes resulting in death. In June 1943 alone, Truman Gibson, civilian aide to the secretary of war, reported "riots of a racial character" at more than seven army posts and noted that there was "a smoldering unrest which is quite likely to erupt at any time."[37]

Just as assumptions about race and masculinity influenced military decisions to keep blacks out of combat, they also shaped the types of assignments blacks were given. During World War II, black servicemen, like their First World War predecessors, were generally assigned to work and supply units. In the navy, for example, blacks could only work as mess attendants until Roosevelt's Executive Order 9279 opened up additional positions. Even then, the navy was slow to assign blacks to non-service roles; in fact, Navy Cross recipient and national hero Dorie Miller was still waiting tables when his ship, the *Liscome Bay,* sank in November 1943 (Nalty 186). While they fared a bit better in the army, blacks were still disproportionately placed in the Engineering, Quartermaster, and Chemical Warfare Service Corps. According to Ulysses Lee's *The Employment of Negro Troops,* during the first half of 1942, in which the army inducted more than 200,000 black troops, "the proportions of Negroes in the Quartermaster and Engineer Corps increased to the point where it appeared that every nontechnical unit in those branches would soon be Negro" (111). Further elaborating on this placement, Lee notes, "It was generally agreed that Negro troops could be employed to advantage in such units. By April 1942, 42 percent of all engineer and 34 percent of all quartermaster units were Negro" (128). Although blacks were primarily given menial positions as chauffeurs, cooks' helpers, and orderlies and were readily placed in baking, fumigation, and salvage collection units, abroad they played an invaluable role building roads and airfields and maintaining supply lines. Recounting these important capacities, veteran William Knox writes:

The 'Red Ball Express' manned mostly by 1,500 black truck drivers, provided the supply backbone for the Normandy drive in 1944. Black troops made up 60 percent of the 15,000 soldiers who carved the Ledo Road out of dense jungle, and then drove convoys over it to China. Approximately 3,700 black soldiers, one third the labor force, helped build Alaska's Alcan Highway. (World War II survey)[38]

While crucial to the Allied war effort, these services did little to contribute to blacks' perceptions of their masculinity. As veteran Ray Carter points out, "We black servicemen of World War II can set down and talk and laugh about the war, but we know deep down inside the war struck at our manhood by trying to make menials out of us at every opportunity" (qtd. in Motley 110). Using the same logic that placed WACs in clerical positions, the military's assignment of blacks to service jobs essentially freed white men to fight. Service jobs, therefore, were "feminized" in relation to the more dangerous and manly combat positions.

While the disproportionate military assignments of blacks to service and supply positions reproduced civilian work practices and racist social norms, it also reinscribed the gendered and racialized nature of the mind/body dualism. Philosopher Susan Bordo has noted that throughout history European and American scholars have constructed blacks and other non-European "races" as "'primitive,' 'savage,' 'sexually animalistic,' and indeed more *bodily* than the white 'races'" (*Unbearable* 9). By placing blacks primarily and disproportionately in service and labor positions, the military continually associated blacks with the body instead of the mind. Henry Stimson confirmed the implications of black service assignments in a letter to Representative Hamilton Fish. Explaining the disproportionate number of black service and supply units, Stimson remarked, "It so happens that a relatively large percentage of the Negroes inducted in the Army have fallen within the lower educational classifications, and many of the Negro units accordingly have been unable to master efficiently the techniques of modern weapons" (qtd. in Buchanan 94). While specific to World War II, Stimson's comments can be interpreted as part of a larger racist discourse associating technology, intellect, and combat abilities with whiteness and servitude with non-white races. Like treatments of "natives" in pop ethnographies, these representations of black Americans reduced them to physical laborers and supporting roles. Other remarks to General Marshall reveal Stimson's belief that blacks simply did not possess necessary military mental skills. According to Stimson, "Leadership is not imbedded in the Negro race yet and to try to make commissioned officers to lead men into battle . . . is only to work a disaster to both" (qtd. in Blum 185). Under the direction of the War Department, African Americans were routinely passed over for officer commissions; less than 1 percent of blacks in the army received commissions compared to 11 percent of whites. Through work assignments and limited opportunities for commissions, the military subtly reinforced racist notions that blacks were somehow more embodied than their white peers. While strong bodies were indeed prized by the military and associated symbolically with strength and manhood, without being accorded intellectual capabilities, black masculinity could only be perceived as inferior to white masculinity.

Black servicemen were further constructed in more corporeal terms through rumors and statements about their sexuality. Margaret Halsey's 1946 book *Color Blind: A White Woman Looks at the Negro* captures prevailing wartime myths about black sexuality. Describing the fictions she heard while managing New York's integrated military canteen, Halsey writes:

> white people take it for granted that Negroes are more musical, more rhythmical, better co-ordinated muscularly, more impulsive, more spontaneous, closer to the child and the pagan than white people are; and from this they infer the sex life of the Negro is more uninhibited and more gratifying than the sex life of white people . . . the belief is widely held, both in the North and the South, that Negro women respond instantly and enthusiastically to all sexual advances and that Negro males have sex organs which dwarf those of white men. (107)

Paired with the myth of their supposed ardent desire to rape white women, these perceptions of black sexuality served to construct black men as more embodied beings, controlled by base passions. Although these myths were rooted in decades of racist characterizations of blacks in America and their origin could hardly be attributed to the military, the U.S. military skillfully exploited them to reinforce notions of white superiority and to maintain its Jim Crow system abroad.

As veteran and former venereal disease control officer William Knox recalls, "During World War II our nation's medical profession taught that blacks had a greater propensity for getting venereal diseases than whites. This was so stated in army manuals" (WWII Survey). Lee's *The Employment of Negro Troops,* for example, attributes blacks' higher venereal disease rates to their supposedly superstitious and backward nature. According to Lee, although both blacks and whites were subject to superstition, "Negro troops were the more likely to have learned that it is impossible to contract venereal diseases during the full moon or that drinking lemon juice was the cure for gonorrhea" (279). Further, Lee contends, black servicemen had trouble understanding the "charts and technical terms" and would misuse the prophylaxis kits (279). Constructing black servicemen as backward, sexualized beings led not only to "officers' letters requesting transfers" from their command of black troops but also to additional myths that "the Negro troops were personally careless and dirty" (Lee 277). In a system already entrenched in discrimination and notions of white superiority, these myths further discredited blacks and their status as soldiers.

More sinister, however, was the circulation of myths about black service-men's sexuality abroad in order to influence people who had, according to military leaders, "little or no racial consciousness" or "knowledge of the ne-gro."[39] Although World War II did not offer many black servicemen the op-portunity to demonstrate their fighting abilities, it did provide many with the possibility of experiencing more racially tolerant societies. In places such as England, Belgium, and Italy, black servicemen could eat, dance, and socialize with white Europeans and were sometimes preferred over white servicemen for their manners and company. For example, after white ser-vicemen started fights with black soldiers for walking with and dating white British women, some British restaurant and pub owners turned the Jim Crow system on its head by displaying signs that read, "For British Civilians and U.S.A. Negro Forces Only" (James et al. 312).[40] Fears of misce-genation and postwar unrest at home, though, led the military to curtail interactions between black American servicemen and foreign civilians—es-pecially women. Privileging racial boundaries over national boundaries, the U.S. military attempted to export its Jim Crow system of segregation wher-ever it went. Recognizing that it would be impossible to ensure the "ab-solute segregation of the races," which they saw as "the only real solution," military leaders turned to rumor campaigns and other strategies to prevent fraternization across racial lines (Carter 2).

Although military rumors about black sexuality were not limited to any one area or theater, they were particularly prevalent in places with more racially tolerant mores. In Hawaii, for example, white servicemen circulated rumors that "if a black man and a local woman had a child, 'the baby would be a monkey'" and scared locals with tales of blacks' animalistic sex-uality (Bailey and Farber 150). In England, British officials and the U.S. mil-itary worked together to prevent black servicemen from dating white women. An army report titled "The Racial Problem in Britain" outlined plans for "the importation of negro female personnel as hostesses in Service Clubs, waitresses, clerks, stenographers, etc.," so black servicemen could date "members of their own race" (Carter 2). The army plan likewise tried to encourage increased allotments by black troops, separate on-base recre-ation facilities, and passes for "a designated area at a specific time" as ways of curtailing fraternization (Carter 2). It was the British Foreign Office, though, that unofficially started "a programme of rumour-spreading about the black GIs" (Smith 195). The BBC learned of the whispering campaign and ran a story in August 1942 suggesting that various women's groups "had been told not to entertain black GIs in private houses 'owing to the prevalence among them of venereal disease'" (Smith 195). Ultimately, inter-racial dating did occur in England, but the OWI largely prevented Ameri-cans at home from learning of blacks' interactions with white women over-seas. After a 1943 *Life* photograph caused a stir by showing black soldiers dancing with white British women, the War Department censored all pho-tographs of black soldiers interacting socially with white women.[41]

Through a variety of methods, then, the U.S. government and military succeeded to a certain degree in exporting its myths about black male sexuality and its Jim Crow system of segregation.

The policies and practices of America's Jim Crow military add another interesting facet to wartime discourses of race and masculinity. While the segregated facilities, blood supplies, and training facilities demonstrated beliefs in white superiority and basic racial hierarchies, efforts to keep blacks out of combat and away from white women exposed a certain degree of anxiety about white manhood. To allow black servicemen to prove themselves in combat or to date white women would force white Americans to question the supposedly innate superiority of their manliness and to accord blacks full rights as men and citizens. The recent expansion of white American masculinity to include new ethnicities and religious affiliations no doubt contributed to the tenacity with which military and government officials fought to maintain Jim Crow segregation. Having already given up some of its privilege, white hegemonic masculinity would still need a range of marginalized masculinities in order to retain its elite position.

Ultimately, however, World War II opened up important new avenues for dismantling the Jim Crow system. Not only did black troops and war workers begin to fight for social change through demonstrations, writing, and the Double V campaign, but also many white servicemen who fought alongside blacks in integrated units began to protest U.S. racism in letters to *Yank* and *The Stars and Stripes*. Moreover, the global dimensions of the war led to breakdowns in the military's ability to enforce Jim Crow segregation. In addition to the more egalitarian treatment black troops received abroad, the challenges of mobilizing forces in U.S. commonwealths such as Hawaii, Puerto Rico, and the Virgin Islands made it difficult to maintain clear racial boundaries. As an August 1943 War Department memo explained, army authorities had to reclassify hundreds of men in Puerto Rico because "Units, officially called white, include a large percentage of men who have to ride the jim crow car in this country."[42] Even after assigning new racial designations on their Selective Service cards, the military still had to create racially mixed units in Puerto Rico and the Virgin Islands because of local failures to respect America's "one drop rule" for determining race. Although the military was partially successful in exporting its Jim Crow system of segregation, other cultures' social acceptance of black troops and refusals to recognize U.S. racial classifications made it impossible to maintain consistent, strict racial boundaries overseas.

The intersections between wartime discourses of race and masculinity were often complex, layered, and contradictory. In many respects, government and media representations of the American people were more racially, ethnically, and religiously diverse than ever before in U.S. history. Not only was the category of white American masculinity expanded to include persons of Eastern and Southern European descent, but also previously feminized Asian Americans such as the Chinese and Filipinos were granted new respect as men and U.S. citizens. Despite wartime celebrations of American diversity and pluralism, numerous race riots, the internment of 120,000 Japanese Americans, the Jim Crow military, and racist laws and practices revealed that American masculinity was still primarily constructed as *white* manhood. Like John Bell's anxious dream about miscegenation and cuckoldry, white American masculinity revealed its insecurities. Time and again, white American manhood had to be solidified and defined in relation to foreign racialized "others" such as the Japanese enemy and Pacific "natives" encountered abroad as well as in contrast to African Americans in the Jim Crow military.

FIVE—(RE)MEMBERING THE DEAD

FROM THE BATTLEFIELD TO THE HOME FRONT

If our soldiers remain anonymous in our useful buildings, that is because they are already anonymous, being inseparable from the nation out of which they sprang. How then can one give them added life except in the life of that nation?

—Joseph Hudnut, *The Atlantic Monthly*, 1945

In its July 5, 1943, issue, *Life* magazine marked the nation's Independence Day by listing the names of 12,987 servicemen killed in action during the first 18 months of the war.[1] Despite falling short of the 15,132 confirmed battle deaths recorded by the army and navy, the list, which also noted the men's home towns, managed to fill 23 pages. The length and simplicity of the list conveyed great loss, but it was the roster's accompanying materials that heightened the names' emotional impact. A photograph depicting a funeral service in a Tunisian wheatfield preceded the list, while an editorial followed the names, attempting to shed light on the roll's "larger purpose."

Together the photograph, list, and editorial provide insights into America's experience with war dead during the Second World War. Resulting in 407,318 military deaths (292,131 from combat and 115,187 from accidents, disease, etc.), World War II produced the greatest number of U.S. war-related casualties since the Civil War (Wallechinsky 206). Although these losses comprised but a tiny fraction of the estimated 55 million persons killed during the war, they were, like the list, overwhelming to a nation not accustomed to foreign-war deaths.[2] Despite the abundance of corpses created by the war, pictures of America's war casualties remained largely absent from public view—especially during the first 21 months of the conflict when the OWI banned such photographs. Even after images of U.S. corpses did appear in September 1943, the media continued to portray America's war dead as sanitized entities whose status was communicated by symbols and circumstances rather than by the reality of the flesh. As the July 1943 *Life* editorial reveals, however, even sanitized representations of corpses could have enormous symbolic potential. Attempting to discover what has "called them over the Big Hill" and to understand the purpose of the servicemen's deaths, the editorial conjures up pictures of "Mom bending over the stove," baseball diamonds, cars, and "a good life" called "freedom" (39). The dead servicemen on "the roll call of the Adjutant General" (39), in short, become agents of freedom, the American dream, and democracy.

In addition to illustrating the euphemisms, the general sequestering of death, and the patriotic rhetoric that accompanied most discussions and representations of casualties, the editorial highlights the ways in which America's war dead became "texts" on which the meanings of war and nation could be inscribed. After pragmatically noting that the dead can no longer define American life or the meaning of their deaths, the editorial asserts that it is up to the living to define these things: "It is for us to decide whether [they] died for the fulfillment of a purpose, like the boys of the American Revolution, or whether [they] died for the fulfillment of practically nothing like the boys of World War I. The dead boys will become what we make them" (39). Although their lives had fixed limits, the bodies of America's Second World War dead have no fixed meaning. Indeed, with the construction of a national World War II monument, World War II monument, the "dead boys" are still becoming "what we make them."

Just as living servicemen's bodies became important sites around which debates about the health and future of the nation unfolded, America's World War II dead shaped national self-representations and policies of war and peace. Like their living counterparts, dead bodies were also subject to complex military processing and classifications, and their presence affected servicemen on the battlefield in profound ways. As evidenced by their symbolic evocations in the media, civic ceremonies, and monuments, representations of dead American male bodies also had significant effects on those on the home front. Five particular subjects reveal the ways in which U.S. war dead continued to create meaning and concerns for other Americans: the military's handling and burial of the dead, servicemen's confrontations with corpses, home front representations of dead servicemen's bodies, postwar "living memorials," and the burial of World War II's Unknown Soldier. When analyzed together, the latter three subjects highlight the ways in which representations of America's World War II casualties both produce and are shaped by our cultural memory of the war. The former two topics meanwhile provide insights into the less examined material dimensions of America's human losses. Ultimately, these material elements were often effaced in America's evocations of its World War II dead, allowing the dead to become equated with abstract ideals of heroism, justice, and democracy.

Like the achievements of their living counterparts, the memory of U.S. World War II dead was called upon to demonstrate national strength and righteousness during the cold war.

DEATH—THE MILITARY WAY

Although World War I ushered in an era of modern man-made mass death and changed Western perceptions of and attitudes toward dying, it was the Second World War that radically altered the theater of death on a global scale.[3] World War II's 55 million dead not only exceeded "the number killed in all the other wars of the modern age together" (Overy 120) but also forever changed notions of total war. Blurring the lines between home front and battlefront, World War II pitted entire populations against each other and claimed civilian lives in record numbers. Whereas civilian casualties comprised only 5 percent of total deaths in World War I, during World War II they accounted for 44 percent of war deaths (Craig and Egan 1). Nazi concentration camps alone killed approximately 12 million people, including 6 million Jews, and were responsible for introducing the term "genocide" and new modes of organized, mass killing. The firebombings of Tokyo and Dresden and the war-ending atomic explosions at Hiroshima and Nagasaki further altered conceptions of death. With the advent of the atomic age, entire populations could be exterminated in an instant. According to literary critic Alan Friedman, the madness and mass destruction of World War II made "the Great War seem retrospectively Victorian . . . Trench warfare's lunacy seemed almost reasonable after the Holocaust" (124, 125).

For American servicemen and other combatants, advances in military technology meant new, more destructive ways of injuring the body. The advent of tank warfare coupled with more effective air power, mines, and artillery produced more battlefield corpses and made violent dismemberment more likely. World War II scholars Paul Fussell, Stephen Ambrose, and Gerald Linderman have noted that the Second World War battle death was a far cry from the neat bullet in the heart or bayonet wound popularly depicted in Hollywood. Bullet wounds, in fact, caused only 10 percent of casualties; most wounds (over 75 percent) resulted from artillery shells and mortars.[4] Fussell, one of the greatest critics of the sanitized, "Disneyfied" versions of battle death that the American public received, has noted "the lack of public knowledge of the Graves Registration form used by the U.S. Army Quartermaster Corps with its space for indicating 'Members Missing'" (*Wartime* 270). Moreover, Fussell adds, "You would expect front-line soldiers to be struck and hurt by bullets and shell fragments, but such is the popular insulation from the facts that you would not expect them to be hurt, sometimes killed, by being struck by parts of their friends' bodies violently detached" (*Wartime* 270). With the additional terror of corpses being booby-trapped by the enemy, dead bodies in wartime could hardly be counted on to be whole or safe.

In addition to the occasional personal hazards that dead bodies offered, more than 400,000 American corpses also presented the U.S. military with enormous logistical problems. For reasons of sanitation and troop morale, corpses had to be removed from the sight of the living as soon as combat conditions would allow. Further, American military and funerary traditions dictated that each corpse be properly identified, processed, and buried; dead bodies could not be disposed of in hasty graves as convenience might prescribe. By World War II, the United States had a fairly long-standing tradition of honoring its war dead, which mandated that the government properly acknowledge the "ultimate sacrifice" of its citizen-soldiers.

Kristin Ann Hass, George Mosse, and Kurt Piehler have shown that the First World War ushered in new modes of and expectations for burying and memorializing the common soldier in Europe.[5] Before World War I, most European nations left their common soldiers on the battlefield, burying them later in scattered mass graves with no markers for individual servicemen; grave markers and monuments were reserved for officers and more general celebrations of victory. However, with the rise of nationalism and the advent of the citizen-soldier—the volunteer or conscripted soldier—the common soldier's corpse could no longer be treated so callously. According to Hass, "Nations promised the soldier a hallowed place in public memory in exchange for his life" (39). This practice of publicly and ceremoniously memorializing battle deaths also contributed to what Mosse calls the "cult of the fallen soldier."

In the United States, this new, more individualized way of memorializing the common soldier had its roots in the Civil War, an armed conflict also fought by citizen-soldiers for ideological reasons. Although many Union and Confederate soldiers were buried in unmarked mass graves and no organized graves registration service was ever developed, the U.S. government and the army took steps toward the future memorialization of all its soldiers. In 1861 the army mandated that all soldiers be buried in registered graves, and the following year Congress established the National Cemetery System. While most Civil War regulations were "largely experimental" and "ineffective" (Steere and Boardman 15), they laid the basic groundwork for the more organized graves registration corps officially established in 1917. Nevertheless, important burial sites and memorials were constructed at Gettysburg in 1863 and Arlington in 1864, forever changing military burials and memorials. The status and symbolism of servicemen's corpses changed as well; the dead Union soldiers at Gettysburg became important emblems of sacrifice to preserve the Union, while dead Confederate soldiers buried years later at Arlington became symbols of a healed nation.

As Kristin Hass observes in *Carried to the Wall*, the memorialization of common Civil War soldiers was not entirely politically motivated; the burials were also part of a larger cultural movement that advocated professional funerary practices, individual memorialization, and burial in park-like rural cemeteries. The increasingly elaborate, professionalized American funeral, which required a well-preserved, "life-like" corpse, fueled the embalming business during the Civil War, as bodies began to be chemically preserved for their journey home, and led to Americans' demands for repatriation of their war dead during the Spanish-American War and World War I. The demand was so great that after the First World War approximately 60 percent of corpses interred in Europe were eventually returned to the United States. With the modern professional funeral firmly established in American culture by 1920, the dead bodies of World War II had to be handled with great care; it was likely that Americans would again demand repatriation and individual memorialization.[6]

As it had during World War I, the American Graves Registration Service (AGRS), under the authority of the quartermaster general, was in charge of collecting, identifying, processing, and burying most World War II dead. While the navy, Coast Guard, and Marine Corps kept their own records and often buried their dead in temporary graves, during World War II the AGRS had jurisdiction to act for all branches of the armed services as well as for all civilian and government agencies. With a war spanning six continents and numerous islands and seas, the military needed a central service to deal with the demands of death in global war. In the end, the AGRS would travel more than 25 million miles to recover American corpses from isolated graves and temporary cemeteries distributed "within the borders of 86 nations" (Steere and Boardman 35).

Although the AGRS was responsible for handling most details concerning the processing and burying of dead bodies, the initial tasks of collecting corpses on the battlefield often fell upon medics, stretcher bearers, local labor, prisoners of war, and other servicemen from the deceased men's units. (With the standard assignment of one AGRS platoon per combat division and one AGRS company per corps, graves registration personnel were usually occupied with identification and burial work.) Every effort was made to remove corpses as soon as possible from the front lines, and the more mobile fighting of World War II generally allowed for faster evacuation than during World War I, when bodies were sometimes left for several days or weeks. Depending on the location and scale of fighting, dead bodies were either buried in temporary, shallow isolated graves or left for immediate collection by an AGRS platoon.

From these hasty battlefield burials, the corpses were transported to central AGRS collection points in the rear echelons. According to historian Stephen Ambrose, graves registration crews charged with retrieving dead bodies often "became callous" and sometimes drank to make their job bearable (317). Despite the media's portrayal of careful burials and tender care of the dead, corpses were often handled roughly as they were tossed into trucks. The irreverent treatment of corpses led cartoonist Bill Mauldin to remark of one crew that they "'could have played the gravediggers in *Hamlet*'" (qtd. in Ambrose 317). Retrieval practices and graves registration assignments also reveal interesting racial dimensions. In keeping with the

military's policies of restricting African Americans to service jobs, many retrieval and burial crews were black. Like other service jobs, the task of collecting corpses helped to associate black troops with the body and provided AGRS
crews with daily reminders that African Americans were not being given the
opportunity to shed blood for their country. Only in death, it seems, was the
military willing to relax the color line of Jim Crow segregation.

Once bodies arrived at rear collection points, AGRS personnel began to
process and identify remains. Although Reports of Death would have been
initiated by the deceased men's units, additional paperwork was required
for military processing; AGRS technicians filed Reports of Interment, and,
when pertinent, medical corpsmen updated emergency medical tags. Additionally, the AGRS initiated a card record for the Adjutant General's Office,
which listed the name, rank, organization, and serial number, date of
death, and date of evacuation for each body that passed through the collecting point (Steere 122). Morticians and other specially trained AGRS personnel meanwhile searched the remains for personal effects and identifying
marks. Bodies with clear identifying items like ID tags or attached certificates were then transported with their paperwork to a nearby temporary
cemetery. At this point, the dead servicemen's personal effects "were removed, inventoried and shipped from collecting points to the Effects Quartermaster," a centralized office in Kansas City, Missouri (Steere 106). More
often than not, however, friends on the battlefield would have screened a
man's personal effects. Gerald Linderman has noted that "things that
would have been painful for his family to see . . . pornographic books or
pictures, indiscreet letters, things of that sort" would have been removed to
uphold "the character of the dead" (319).

In cases of uncertain or unknown identification, bodies were put aside
for additional examination. While identifying techniques varied at different collection points, bodies were generally fingerprinted (when possible)
and searched for identifying marks or items like laundry tags, paybooks,
bracelets, and rings. The Army Signal Corps often photographed bodies so
that pictures could be shown to surviving friends. In some AGRS companies like those attached to the Third Army, morticians "spen[t] many hours
reconstructing the face and removing battle scars to make remains recognizable before pictures were taken" (Steere 123). After bodies were identified or every means of identification was exhausted, these corpses were likewise transported to temporary cemeteries with their paperwork, and, in the
case of an unknown, its personal effects. During the postwar final disposition program, anthropologists, police detectives, and other technicians at a
centrally located identification laboratory examined unknowns more thoroughly. By the close of the program, almost 97 percent of all recovered
World War II remains were positively identified.

Once at a temporary cemetery, bodies were placed in already-dug graves,
were given last rites and military honors, and were buried with either a white
cross or a Star of David grave marker. Although some servicemen killed early in

the war were placed in wooden coffins, most received a "soldier's burial," in which the uniformed body was wrapped in a shroud or blanket and placed directly in the ground. Because the bodies would need to be exhumed for permanent burial after hostilities, AGRS platoons avoided expensive caskets, concrete vaults and headstones, and elaborate landscaping. Upon burial, AGRS personnel completed the paperwork accompanying bodies and carefully recorded the exact location of each man's grave. AGRS technicians then filed burial reports and record cards after compiling their daily reports.

Until V-J Day, all corpses remained in one of 454 temporary cemeteries or registered gravesites. After the cessation of hostilities, the lengthy process of final disposition began, and the dead servicemen's families became involved in burial decisions. Following a World War I precedent, the War Department and Congress approved a plan that covered all repatriation and burial expenses and allowed the dead servicemen's next of kin to decide where they would be interred. All expenses for interring bodies in national cemeteries at home or abroad were absorbed by the military; families wishing to bury servicemen in local plots, however, received a flat fee for burial expenses. The casket and flag were provided by the military. A serviceman's marital status determined the degree of kinship order that was used in these decisions. In the case of unmarried servicemen, burial decisions fell to his relatives in the following order: father, mother, brother, sister, other relatives. For married servicemen, the decision went to a widow, a child, then other relatives in the order designated for unmarried servicemen.

While decisions concerning the final burial of servicemen were exclusively private matters, public debates over whether to return the war dead appeared on the pages *Collier's, Life, Reader's Digest, The Saturday Evening Post,* and numerous other publications. Most debates focused on the idea that families had to choose between fulfilling personal memorialization needs and allowing their men to provide further service to the nation. Proponents of interring the bodies in one of fourteen military cemeteries abroad often argued, as F. W. Graham did in his November 1946 *Rotarian* article "Let Them Lie in the Ground They Hallowed," that servicemen would have preferred the more masculine "soldier's tradition" of lying near his comrades "in the ground made sacred by [their] sacrifice" (20). These proponents also suggested that the presence of buried servicemen abroad would carry diplomatic symbolism, providing both a promise of commitment to Europe and U.S. territories and a sign of America's young strength and democratic values.[7] Advocates for repatriation, meanwhile, stressed the importance of visiting the dead and the symbolic, patriotic value the graves would have for future Americans. While arguments for returning war dead often conceded that overseas World War I cemeteries were both dignified and well-kept, advocates for repatriation stressed that many Second World War dead were lying in soil that was foreign and potentially distasteful to some Americans. For example, while discussing overseas burial sites in his August 11, 1945, *Collier's* article "They're Coming Home," Quentin

Reynolds disparaged "the miserable, ugly coral, lava and jungle . . . where the feet of Japanese once trod" (19). By the end of the military's final disposition program in December 1951, approximately 172,000 bodies of servicemen killed in action were returned to the United States, while 93,240 were interred in the 14 permanent overseas military cemeteries (Nishiura 6–7).[8]

CONFRONTING CORPSES—DEATH IN *THE THIN RED LINE*

World War II certainly stands as a watershed event in the modern theater of death; it not only ushered in new forms of man-made mass killing but also produced new, more elaborate programs and techniques for locating, identifying, and repatriating U.S. war dead. Like other wars before it, World War II's mass destruction also had a tremendous impact on the living—especially servicemen and civilians who had to confront corpses on a regular basis. Although a fictional account, James Jones's *The Thin Red Line* offers some remarkable insights into servicemen's wartime encounters with corpses and the impact these experiences had on their embodied subjectivities. When examined in relation to servicemen's firsthand accounts and 1940s attitudes toward death in the United States, the novel provides an especially thoughtful text for exploring death's impact on combat soldiers as well as the corpse's unique symbolic status.

Theorists Maurice Blanchot and Julia Kristeva suggest that the corpse, with its haunting simultaneous presence and absence, occupies "the position par excellence" (Blanchot 256). By marking the threshold of subjectivity, the space between life and death, the corpse establishes "a relation between here and nowhere" (Blanchot 256). Neither its meaning nor place, Blanchot contends, can be fixed because the corpse "escapes common categories" (256). As Blanchot explains, "Something is there before us which is not really the living person, nor is it any reality at all. It is neither the same as the person who was alive, nor is it another person, nor is it anything else" (256). Thus the corpse becomes the ultimate signifier, "the anonymous and impersonal place par excellence" that haunts the living and calls into question any fixed notions of the self. For Kristeva, the corpse likewise represents an impossible, haunting space; it is "the utmost of abjection," marking the border of subjectivity, where death "infects" life and threatens "identity, system, order" (4). Like other forms of abjection (wounds, bodily fluids, waste, etc.), the corpse produces fear and loathing because it reminds the subject of its own otherness, its own death (Kristeva 3–4). Moreover, sociologist Philip Mellor asserts, an existential encounter with a corpse produces dread because it calls "into question the meaningfulness and reality of the social frameworks in which [the subject] participates, shattering their ontological security" (13).

Given the corpse's haunting and powerful presence, it is hardly surprising that modern deaths have become "characteristically private, institutionalised and professionally controlled" (Turner 232). As Phillipe Ariès, Jessica Mitford,

David Stannard, James Farrell, Philip Mellor, and Anthony Giddens have
shown, death in America has, since the early twentieth century, become increasingly hidden. Due to medical advances and changes in funerary practices, by the middle of the twentieth century it was possible for a person to
reach adulthood without having a close friend or family member die, and
death itself had become a taboo topic. By the 1940s the average life ex-
pectancy had reached 65, dying had come to be associated with old age,
and death, when it did occur, was sequestered from the rest of society. Explaining this "American way of death," David Stannard notes, "Death is . . .
avoided as much as possible, and when it is no longer possible—when a
body must be confronted and dealt with—it is turned over to professionals
who provide their own special skills in the effort of denial" (viii). Thus, although the open casket played (and continues to play) a central role in
most American funerals, the corpse was transformed back into a "living"
image of the deceased through embalming, makeup, and other mortuary
techniques. With few World War I veterans in the service and a general sequestration of death, most American G.I.s heading off to the Second World
War, then, had little firsthand experience with corpses. Combat offered servicemen the potential for their own deaths and presented them with profound existential encounters.

Lauded by Paul Fussell as the most realistic and perhaps best combat
novel of World War II, Jones's *The Thin Red Line* is, among other things, a
study of various servicemen's encounters with combat-related death. Although this topic is hardly new (death is, after all, a staple element of any
war novel), *The Thin Red Line* creates a unique space for exploring these existential encounters. As John Limon has observed in *Writing After War*,
Jones's second novel "is the war book that comes closest to having no context"; it is, in many respects, a "pure" combat novel (136). Unlike Mailer's
The Naked and the Dead with its Dos Passosesque "time machine" sections
or Uris's *Battle Cry* with its inclusion of long-distance romantic relationships, the characters in *The Thin Red Line* have no history outside of the
war. Limon notes that "the one character with continuous memories of a
home life—John Bell—literally receives a Dear John letter . . . and thereafter
has no home life either" (136). Focusing on one company's participation in
the Guadalcanal campaign, the novel creates a world within war and emp-
ties its characters of thoughts beyond the campaign. In short, *The Thin Red
Line* provides an ideal space for exploring a range of servicemen's reactions
to mortality and the general anesthetization to death that accompanied
many servicemen's combat experiences.

In the front matter of the novel, Jones foreshadows the omnipresence of
death by noting "Replacements" in the company roster and by including
the music and lyrics for "Don't Monkey Around with Death." Like Kristeva's description of corpses, the song links death to abjection by associating it with dirt and waste. The lyrics warn the listener not to "monkey
around with death," offering the following reasons:

It will only make you dirty;
Don't futz around with the reaper
He will only make you smell
Have you got B.O.?
Then do not go fiddling with that Scytheman
Because your best friend with not tell you
Don't monkey around with death
You will only wind up soiled (xiii–iv)

Although designed to lend a proto-postmodern absurdity to the theater of death and the world of combat, the lyrics set up the grim realities of death in jungle warfare: the sickening smell of corpses, the shallow graves, and the grime and decay of combat. By combining the abject dimensions of the corpse and the absurdity of modern warfare, the song sets an appropriate mood for the study of death in the rest of the novel.

Chronicling the activities of C-for-Charlie company from its prelanding preparations on November 10, 1942, until the end of its involvement in the Guadalcanal campaign, the novel traces the company's shifting attitudes toward death and the ways in which combat experiences alter the men. On the opening pages of the novel, the narrator records their precombat thoughts on death: "As they prepared themselves to go ashore no one doubted in theory that at least a certain percentage of them would remain on this island dead, once they set foot on it. But no one expected to be one of these" (1–2). Typical of many servicemen's prebattle thoughts, this conviction of one's invincibility and faith in survival not only captures the typical soldier's "psychic defense against war's destructiveness" (Linderman 7) but also registers the remoteness of actual death. Despite Welsh's fatalistic thought that "almost certainly, nearly all of them would be dead before this war was over" (Jones 23), there is a general denial of death among the members of C-for-Charlie company; many refuse to discuss or even name the possibility of death.

As their "baptism of fire" (1) begins, however, death becomes a reality, albeit a distant one, for Charlie company during their landing, when a Japanese plane bombs one of the transports and an adjacent LCI. Near the aid station, the men of Charlie company huddle into the safety of their five platoons and watch the freshly wounded men with "an almost sexual, morbid curiosity" (46). Describing their collective thoughts, the narrator remarks:

Here were men who were going to die, some of them before their very eyes. How would they react? . . . C-for-Charlie, as one man, was curious to see: to see a man die. Curious with a hushed, breathless awe. They could not help but be; fresh blood was so very red, and gaping holes in bared flesh were such curious, strange sights. It was all obscene somehow. Something which they all felt should not be looked at, somehow, but which they were compelled to look at, to cluster closer and study. (46)

Through this passage, Jones establishes the way in which death had become a taboo subject in 1940s America and begins to explore the profound effects of confronting corpses in war. His frequent references to the "curiously sexual" (69) nature of these encounters here and elsewhere heighten the taboo and highlight the "animal" drives that the confrontations uncover. The dying men fascinate and horrify Charlie company because they occupy the liminal space of the corpse "between here and nowhere" (Blanchot 256) and call into question the boundaries of their own embodied subjectivities. Watching the wounded men die forces C Company to realize that "the human body was really a very frail, defenseless organism" and that "these men might have been themselves" (Jones 46). The experience ultimately silences the entire company on their six-mile march, forcing them to contemplate their own vulnerability. Like real-life Guadalcanal veteran Grady Gallant, the men "had not been taught to die. They had been taught to kill" (qtd. in Linderman 12); nothing in their training had prepared them for the experience.

More than a stock first confrontation with death, the experience at the aid station sets up two other immediate encounters with dead bodies and remains. Shortly after erecting their first campsite, a group of 20 Charlie company men go off on their own to explore the surrounding jungle. Led by the heavily muscled and imposing "Big Queen," the party stumbles upon a bloodstained khaki shirt on top of a root cluster. The men, still reeling from their earlier encounter with the wounded men, gather excitedly around the shirt. Because none of them "had ever seen material remains of a man killed in infantry combat," the shirt offers a new encounter with death (Jones 66). The distinctive army chino brings the man's death closer to home; the shredded sleeves made to resemble buckskin fringe force the men to realize that the dead man had preferences and habits like their own. As the narrator explains, "The sight gave Big Queen, who had owned and worn a buckskin jacket . . . a particularly painful twinge" (67). Although the men can distinguish between the shirt and "the guy who was in it" (69), the dead man's presence is still bound up in the shirt, and the remains cause "a curious sense of unreality [to] come over all of them" (70). Nevertheless, the men, still untested by combat, cannot assimilate the "facts" of war and dying:

> Each man each time he tried to imagine his own death; tried to conjure up the experience of that bullet keyholing through his own lung; found himself being tricked by his own mind. The only thing he was able to picture was the heroic, brave gesture he would make when dying. But the rest was unimaginable. (70)

Despite having relinquished their invulnerability, the men nonetheless cling to Hollywood constructions of the noble battle death and associate dying with myths of war and heroism. Although the shirt further underscores their own mortality, their lack of actual combat experience allows them to deny the realities of combat death.

Shortly after the encounter with the shirt, the scouting party happens upon an abandoned Japanese position with a long mass grave. The narrator explains, "It was here that the delayed emotional reaction to the death shirt caught up with them in the form of a sort of wild horseplay or bravado" (72). In an attempt to dam up their recently confronted vulnerability, the men begin to desecrate the Japanese bodies, searching for souvenirs. Where they stood earlier in awe and reverence, the men now adopt a "strange arrogance" and begin "laughing loudly, each trying to outbravado the other" (73). Big Queen, once again leading the men, attempts to disinter a corpse by pulling on its leg. Reflecting on the motives for Big Queen's desecration, the narrator notes, "He only wanted to show them, and himself, that the dead bodies—even Japanese ones afflicted with God knew what horribly dirty Oriental diseases—held no terror for him" (74). While the men's actions are no doubt shaped in part by wartime hatred of the Japanese, they also mark a new, hardened phase in dealing with death—at least in the case of enemy dead. To survive combat, they need to numb themselves to the horror of corpses and add "layers of callus" (Linderman 77).

By including three separate encounters with dead bodies and remains on Charlie company's first day of the campaign, Jones clearly establishes that *The Thin Red Line* is not merely the tale of war's survivors. Instead, his novel is built around the shared community of the dead and the living and their complex interactions. Although he does not give a voice or consciousness to the dead, Jones does grant his corpses a certain agency, a presence that affects other subjectivities in significant ways. Whether through the Japanese corpses' resistance to being unearthed or their fetid, area-clearing smell, dead bodies have an unmistakable presence in the novel that, like Blanchot's conception of the corpse, extends beyond the physical place of the remains.

After setting up the corpse's signifying power and haunting presence, Jones spends the rest of the novel exploring the nature of combat death, individual soldiers' reactions to death and dying, and the gradual psychological hardening that communing with the dead requires. Like *The Naked and the Dead* and later American postmodern World War II fiction, *The Thin Red Line* portrays combat death as a random, fairly meaningless event, exploring the elements of chance, luck, and fate involved in deciding who crosses the line between life and death. While recording individual characters' contemplations on death's randomness, the novel also examines a broad range of reactions to death and dying, focusing on the ways in which characters define their masculinity through the experience.

Although, as the narrator points out, there are "as many various reactions as there were men" (93), encounters with corpses, killing, and dying often serve as ways to define or question constructions of masculinity. Indeed, the novel seems to offer the realm of combat as a privileged space for examining the construction and performance of masculinities. Resisting neat dichotomies that would align killing with active, forceful masculinity and dying with passive, weak masculinity, the novel reveals that both spaces of dying and killing can be used to demonstrate a character's masculinity. In dying, for example, Big Queen is able to shore up his sense of manhood, which had come into question through his earlier hesitancies in combat. His stoic, tough performance while dying wins the respect of his buddies, who promise to write Big Queen's wife and tell her that he "died like a man" (447). Acts of killing, meanwhile, offer possibilities for eroding one's sense of manhood. Following his deadly hand-to-hand confrontation with a Japanese soldier, Private Bead, the company's young assistant clerk, becomes ashamed of his performance. He vomits after killing the soldier and resolves not to tell the other men in Charlie company about the murder because of his botched performance, which does not live up to what he "had been taught by movies to expect" (170). Despite most of the men's desires to encounter corpses and killing in culturally accepted masculine ways, the novel reveals a range of reactions from Mc-Cron's breakdown to Tella's fear and pain while dying to Storm's ultimate admission of cowardice.

The novel's primary exploration of the impact of death on combat soldiers, however, is its study of the psychological hardening the men achieve as they become combat veterans. While simultaneously examining individual reactions to death, *The Thin Red Line* also explores the collective change that confrontations with death produce in Charlie company. Shortly after their initial encounters with the death shirt and the mass grave, Charlie company's lives literally become threatened first by air raids and then by infantry combat. At the start of their combat phase, the narrator notes that from their "dirtcaked faces . . . human eyes still peered" (88), indicating that the men of Charlie company still had not lapsed into combat numbness. Although they have already adopted strategies for dealing with the dead, "during the next two weeks they changed more" (88), eventually entering that liminal space between human and automaton. To survive combat and deal with dead bodies, they would have to deaden themselves, striving for an emotionless, semiconscious state.

Charlie company's subsequent encounters with dead bodies provide a barometer for measuring the men's layers of callus, their lapse into numbness. Although still outraged by news of Japanese atrocities visited upon two George company men and shaken by the first deaths in their own company, the men register increasingly less horror in reaction to corpses as the novel progresses. While preparing for their assault on Hill 210, for example, Charlie company discovers a dead body left from the previous day's attack on Hill 209. Though they are initially disturbed by the medics' rough handling of the corpse as they take it away, the men of C Company note their own callousness: "At the same time, they were aware that their own reaction smacked of irreverence too. *Nobody* wanted the poor bastard now" (165). As the unit participates in more battles, Charlie company realizes that "when a man is hit and killed outright, there was nothing anyone could do" (232); the men come to treat corpses more coldly and focus on the living. Ultimately, as John Bell observes, they cease "to feel human" (275) and begin to care for little more than their survival. Their ultimate numbness, however, is registered in their encounter with a cannibalized body and five other ragged corpses in an abandoned Japanese camp. Noting this change, the narrator remarks that "curiously enough nobody was shocked or horrified by the cannibalism. In this mad world of mud, perpetual wet, gloom, green air stink [from corpses], and slithering animal life, it seemed far more normal than not normal" (446). By the time they bury Big Queen hours later, they have almost completely deadened all emotions and consciousness; they learn that "once they had covered his face and bare hands first, it wasn't so hard to fill in the hole over the rest of him" (448).

The novel illustrates, though, that this numbness is a temporary state reserved primarily for combat itself. During their first break from combat, for example, it takes about two or three days for the numbness to diminish and humanity to return to their "haunted faces and pooldeep, seadark eyes" (351). Nevertheless, as Bell and Welsh observe, there is the possibility that the men of Charlie company are forever changed, that "if pursued long enough and often enough, [combat numbness] might really become a permanent and mercifully blissful state" (510). Following Welsh's remark about the blissfulness of combat numbness, Jones ends the novel with two brief sentences that highlight future landings and the eventual composition of a "book about all of this" (510). The abrupt ending and promised repetition of events suggests that Jones is offering Charlie company's experiences as a microcosm of sorts for the war's broader theater of death. Although a specific exploration of the Guadalcanal campaign, the novel examines the blurred lines between sanity and madness, civilian and soldier, and living and dead associated with combat and death all over the globe.

SANITIZED DEATH AND THE HOME FRONT

In comparison to servicemen's encounters, Americans living on the distant, unbombed home front experienced war deaths in a drastically different and sanitized way. Although World War II proved to be more candid in its media coverage of wartime casualties than the First World War, which banned photographs of dead U.S. servicemen for the entire 19 months of American involvement, its reporting was nevertheless carefully controlled by the military and the OWI. For practical reasons, the grim realities of war had to be minimized to prevent problems with morale and resistance toward participation. If citizens spent too much time mourning and focusing on the deaths, they would not only derail the war effort but might be prompted to call for a peace settlement with Germany.[9] As it had during the First World War, the government asked families "not to wear black when mourning the loss of a son killed in the nation's service" but instead "to display a distinctive Gold Star to express their sacrifice" (Piehler 171). Various factors such as the absence of servicemen's corpses (their return was delayed until after the war due to shipping restrictions), the management of information, and the cultural sequestration of death created a general wartime displacement of death. Nevertheless, when images and symbols of dead servicemen's bodies were shown, they proved to be powerful tools of motivation in the war effort.

Although the military and government managed to maintain a complete ban on the publication of photographs of U.S. war dead during the first 21 months of its involvement, by September 1943 it became increasingly apparent that they could no longer hide this grim facet of war from the American people. The public had grown skeptical of war coverage in which no Americans "get badly shot or spill any blood" (Roeder, *Censored War* 10) and had, according to OWI officials, grown too complacent in their war effort duties. Further, with recent victories in North Africa and Italy, the road to Allied victory seemed shorter and less costly than it really was. In an attempt to provide more candid coverage, to combat public complacency, and to renew home front enthusiasm for the war effort, the OWI and the War Department's Bureau of Public Relations loosened restrictions on the publication of photographs of dead and wounded servicemen. In September 1943, several dozen photos previously confined to the "Chamber of Horrors" were cleared for release (Roeder, *Censored War* 12). Because of the long-standing prohibitions on showing images of U.S. war deaths, the carefully selected images held enormous rhetorical power—especially when accompanied by patriotic text. Although the September 1943 clearance of photographs ushered in a more candid approach to reporting war news, it did not unleash a flood of gory battle casualty pictures. Dead and wounded bodies remained largely intact in pictures that did appear, and many "newspapers and magazines declined to run them" at all (Roeder, *Censored War* 13). When photographs of dead servicemen were printed, their bodies became privileged symbols of sacrifice from which the goals of nation and the war could be discerned.

Life's September 20, 1943, publication of George Strock's photograph of three dead servicemen on a Buna beach, for example, reveals the ways in which wartime rhetoric often displaced the realities of death. Because it was one of the first photographs of U.S. servicemen's corpses to appear, the editors of *Life* felt compelled to accompany the picture with a full-page editorial on page 34, explaining their reasons for publishing the photograph. Beginning with the decision to print the image, the editorial briefly meditates on the failure of language to convey the realities of war. According to the editors, the photo provides a way for the American people to enter "into the presence of their own dead," to understand the "reality that lies behind the names" on casualty lists and monuments. While it does present a bit of the reality surrounding the circumstances of the three deaths, the editorial quickly shifts the picture from a site of mourning to one of sacrifice and strength. Despite the obvious loss of life recorded by the picture, the editorial provides an interpretation of the bodies that focuses on "why it is that

American boys win." Thus the running assault on the beach is transformed into a "sense of high optimism," the position of the first man's body reveals his "relaxed self-confidence, and the bodies still collectively reveal "the fury of their attack, the hard muscles driving forward, the hot blood surging." After discussing the bodies in terms of their noble, living characteristics, the editorial further displaces their deaths by shifting to patriotic images that apparently lie beyond the frame of the photograph. Missing from the picture, the editorial asserts, is an America complete with Mom, apple pie, baseball scores, a harvest moon, a young girl's promise, and majestic hills, rivers, and cities. With the broader "picture" complete, the editorial then positions the dead bodies as part of America's body politic; they become "three parts of a hundred and thirty million parts, three fragments of that life we call American life: three units of freedom." Having completed the shift from the grim realities of their individual deaths to their status as "units of freedom," the editorial ends with a message to its readers. They must understand that in order for freedom "to live, [soldiers] must be willing to die," and readers must focus on efforts to "give meaning to their death."

Like the Strock photograph and *Life* editorial, images of U.S. war deaths appearing in other forums were rarely shown for the sake of candor. Carefully managed by the War Department and the OWI, the images performed certain war functions: to prepare civilians for heavier casualty rates with the European invasion as well as to sell bonds, motivate workers, and request additional civilian sacrifices. While military and government agencies could not control the reception of all these images, they could direct particular responses through posters. In its 1943 poster "This Isn't War . . . It's MURDER" (fig. 20), for example, the army utilized an image of five Japanese soldiers bayoneting an already-wounded U.S. serviceman to spur production at home. Combining wartime racial hatred and general feelings of revenge, the poster creates an emotionally charged plea. While the yellow background offers suggestions of a yellow peril, the slumped, heavily pierced body of the serviceman is reminiscent of the martyr St. Sebastian. By including both the Japanese perpetrators and the serviceman's martyred body, the poster ennobles the production cause and provides the emotional incentive for stepping up industrial output.

Other posters used images of U.S. war deaths to send different messages, though the goal of increasing civilian involvement in the war effort generally remained the same. Stanley Frederic's 1944 poster for the Citizens Service Corps, for instance, relies on the viewer's feelings of guilt. Featuring an image of a dead serviceman lying facedown on the ground, the poster uses a series of questions to offer the viewer a specific way of interpreting the body. In Frederic's poster, the sacrifice of life and body is contrasted with the viewer's war contribution, and the civilian onlooker is forced to consider the question "What have *I* done today for freedom?" By suggesting that the viewer's contributions cannot compare to the serviceman's "ultimate sacrifice," the poster effectively places the onlooker in a position to increase his or her wartime contributions by joining groups such as the Citizens Service Corps. Relying on a more powerful and realistic image, the army's famous 1945 poster "This happens every 3 minutes" likewise equates civilian actions with battlefield outcomes. By showing a photograph of a bullet-riddled corpse, the poster utilizes a serviceman's dead body as a motivational tool. Instead of playing on feelings of revenge and racial hatred, the poster promises an end to war's horrors if workers will "stay on the job."

Despite a trend toward increasingly grimmer depictions of dead bodies and the incorporation of actual photographs of U.S. war deaths, the American public nonetheless had a relatively sanitized experience with death during the war. Often posters like Adolph Treidler's "What You Make Can Prevent This" (fig. 21) relied on symbols of death rather than on representations of corpses to convey their messages. Issued in 1944, Treidler's war bonds poster evokes the same emotional responses as those incorporating corpses, but it employs the specter of the dead to convey its message. Like the bloodstained khaki shirt that the men of Charlie company encounter in *The Thin Red Line,* the helmet atop a cross suggests death generally while still representing the individual subjectivity of its deceased former owner. The unmarked cross forces the viewer to imagine the identity of the dead serviceman and to contemplate the possible loss of a family member, friend, or neighbor. Other posters such as the OWI's 1943 "They Did Their Part" and "Americans Suffer" utilized even more abstracted symbols of death, offering images of the Sullivan brothers and grieving parents in front of a service star respectively. Working in tandem with other images of dead servicemen's bodies and the cultural sequestration of death, these images are powerful, nevertheless, because of the corpse's haunting power. These posters and other representations of death on the American home front reveal that the public's experiences with war death were both sanitized and carefully regulated. It also becomes apparent that the bodies of servicemen were pressed into additional wartime service even after death. Whether urging civilians to increase production, to minimize "careless talk," or to join the Citizens Service Corps, posters featuring images of battle deaths demonstrated that U.S. war dead had tremendous symbolic potential and could move people to action.

LEAVING DEATH BEHIND—LIVING MEMORIALS

Even before the bodies of dead servicemen were returned home or reinterred abroad, various military, government, and private organizations were making plans to commemorate U.S. war deaths. As in the case of previous wars, the monuments they erected would be shaped by a combination of popular attitudes toward the war and government agendas. World War I set certain precedents for commemorating U.S. war deaths, such as the burial of an Unknown Soldier and the creation of overseas military cemeteries;

20—Part of a larger late war trend of showing more graphic images of America's war dead, this 1943 army poster uses an emotionally charged combat scene to increase civilian participation in the home front war effort. (Courtesy of the Hoover Institution Archives)

however, the Second World War and its unprecedented destruction demanded certain departures from earlier traditions of memorialization.

Although next-of-kin preferences determined that some 93,000 dead
U.S. servicemen would remain buried overseas, the symbolism attached to
their graves was largely determined by the military and government. As
historian Kurt Piehler has noted, the military and the American Battle
Monuments Commission (ABMC) used the selection of the 14 permanent
overseas cemetery sites to symbolize U.S. commitments to certain countries
and territories. While practical reasons like accessibility and the percentage
of servicemen killed in Europe dictated that several of the cemeteries would
be located there, Europe nonetheless became home to a disproportionate
number (ten out of the fourteen) of the cemeteries. According to proponents
of overseas interments such as Quentin Reynolds, parents would feel "satis-
fied to know that their sons were buried in the lovely countryside of France or
Belgium" (19), and the U.S. could maintain and strengthen its ties with European allies.[10] The remaining four cemeteries likewise were politically distributed; one was built in Tunisia, a French colony at the time, and three were
constructed in the Pacific to solidify relations with current and former territories in Alaska, Hawaii, and the Philippines. Despite the great number of bodies interred on islands like Iwo Jima, the military and ABMC ultimately selected the Philippines because they wanted to emphasize the "importance of
political ties with the former U.S. colony" (Piehler 130).

In the eyes of the U.S. military and government, the bodies interred in
overseas cemeteries not only symbolized American commitments and past
sacrifices but also transformed the land itself. Like their predecessors who
had "hallowed the ground" at Gettysburg, World War II's American dead both
sanctified the ground and renationalized it. Granted "in perpetuity by the
host government to the United States," the cemetery lands became, in the
eyes of most Americans, U.S. soil (Nishiura 7).[11] Thus the selection of cemetery locations offered a clear statement about America's postwar diplomatic
goals while simultaneously renewing the covenant between citizen-soldier
and state; by refusing to place cemeteries on former enemy soil or other remote, politically uncertain lands, the military and the ABMC could honor foreign and domestic promises through the proper care of its war dead.

While World War II overseas cemeteries performed many of the same
functions that First World War military cemeteries had, their layout and designs offered new messages. With fears that the memorialization of World
War I and the "cult of the fallen soldier" had promoted the militaristic
ideas and regimes that led to the Second World War, the U.S. took steps to
promote new forms of commemoration within both its own cemeteries and
those in other nations. Architect James Mayo has noted that the U.S. overseas cemeteries of World War I and their "rectilinear plotting provide an almost military feeling" (101). Seeking to convey a more tranquil message,
the designers of World War II cemeteries relied on curvilinear patterns and
tried to break up seas of "marching" crosses despite the larger numbers of

WHAT YOU MAKE CAN PREVENT THIS

21—Adolph Treidler's 1944 War Bonds poster employs a popular strategy of sanitizing American war deaths by using symbols to suggest loss of life. (Courtesy of the Hoover Institution Archives)

war dead. According to Mayo, the smaller grave sections and curvilinear patterns convey the message, "Our cause was just, but more importantly we are now at peace" (101).

In addition to adopting new modes of commemoration in its overseas cemeteries, the U.S. helped shape more peaceful memorialization practices in former Axis nations. Under the terms of Allied occupation, both Germany and Japan were prevented from building military cemeteries, and many earlier militaristic monuments were razed. Both nations were also encouraged, for the time being, to forget the war and to focus on the war's victims instead of its heroes. Although the seeds of the cold war had already been sown in the liberation and postwar occupation of Europe, the horrors and widespread destruction of World War II left former combatants longing for peace and normalcy.

A desire for peace likewise influenced trends in memorialization on the home front, where efforts to commemorate the war emphasized the future and the living rather than the past and the dead. Although the return of some 172,000 dead servicemen's bodies in the postwar years brought private grief to millions of Americans, there was little public memorialization of these "ultimate sacrifices." The initial, larger shipments of returned war dead to New York and San Francisco brought a certain amount of military pageantry, but, for the most part, the final interments of servicemen's bodies were often simple yet dignified affairs. Exhausted by a lengthy war and years of their own sacrifices, veterans and civilians alike were eager to put the war behind them and share in America's growing prosperity. It is not surprising, then, that Americans primarily chose "living memorials" to commemorate the war. Initially introduced but not widely erected in the years following World War I, living memorials often took the form of utilitarian structures such as community centers, playgrounds, and stadiums that aimed to preserve the memory of the war dead while primarily serving the living. In addition to these fairly standard construction projects, living memorials could also assume the forms of scholarships, gardens, tree-lined roads, parks, forests, and other projects.

Just as World War II's mass destruction led to new cemetery designs and memorialization practices in Europe, it also brought about a shift away from erecting traditional war monuments such as statutes, columns, and arches in the United States. For veterans and civilians wishing to forget the horrors of war and the new threats of the atomic age, living memorials offered a welcome change from militaristic forms of commemoration. As cultural critic Lewis Mumford explained in his January 1945 *Good Housekeeping* article "Monuments and Memorials," many of America's earlier war monuments heightened the effects of war. The "cast-iron monuments that celebrated the heroes" of the Civil War, he claimed, "almost added to the horrors of war," while the sculptures of the First World War "put into the very center of the monument the tanks and machine guns our men used," providing additional focus on destruction (17). While Mumford called for new sculptural designs rather than new forms of memorialization altogether, many proponents of living memorials felt a complete break with tradition was necessary. Living monuments in the form of parks, community centers, and churches, they argued, promised to further beauty, democracy, and peace rather than war and destruction.

The ways in which the war was fought and packaged to the American people also contributed to the trend toward living memorials. Defined as a good and necessary war and recorded in careful detail by the media, World War II seemingly did not require monuments to justify its cause or remind U.S. citizens of victory. The war's memory would be preserved in the minds of Americans through film reels and pictures, and the unconditional surrender of the Axis would assure the world of the Allies' victory—there would be no ambiguity or lack of consensus as there had been with World War I. Yet despite the unmistakable victory and the binary terms of good and evil in which the war was framed, Americans were already examining the war with a prescient postmodern sensibility, realizing that the "good war" could not be reduced to a singular narrative or coherent national story. As one proponent of living memorials pointed out, "No one monument could be adequate to commemorate the sacrifices of this war."[12]

In his September 1945 *Atlantic Monthly* article "The Monument Does Not Remember," Joseph Hudnut, dean and professor of architecture at Harvard University, provides a more philosophical reflection on war monuments and the needs of a postwar "fragmentary world" (55). After offering a brief history of war monuments and a meditation on architecture's symbolic qualities, Hudnut reflects on the failure of both language and images to convey the horrors of modern war. He writes, "There is no realism which can encompass war, this horror and madness, this confusion, pain, filth, and waste; neither is there any symbol which will invoke the smallest part of it" (57). Specifically commenting on one of the early sculptures in Times Square of marines raising the American flag on Mt. Suribachi, Hudnut remarks, "You have not seen the flag raised over Iwo Jima until you have seen the black smoke and red flames of our guns, . . . the enemy tortured by tank and flame thrower, . . . the noise and stench, the loneliness and desolation which covered that narrow island" (57). Like other proponents of living memorials, Hudnut offers the incomprehensibility and horrors of war as reasons to shun traditional war monuments. Further, he addresses the importance of having memorials that can shift their meaning in a late modernist age. Lamenting that a "people in continuous and accelerated change covers its land with fixed and static symbols" (59), Hudnut argues for World War II memorials that "live" because they will constantly be "unfolding, conscious of change and of the necessity of change" and will resist "old systems and thoughts and usages" (59). According to Hudnut, World War II, with its new theater of death, renders the very idea of a monument obsolete. Thus the only way to remember the servicemen who died is "to give them added life in the life of the nation" (58).

Many other supporters of living memorials were more pragmatic in their motives for adopting new forms of commemoration. A generation raised during the depression, veterans and their families brought their practicality to bear on postwar memorial decisions. The depression and war had stalled the building of much-needed facilities and recreation centers, and many communities found themselves scrambling to keep up with necessary construction projects after the war. Housing shortages and community needs were seemingly more pressing than monuments to the war dead. As landscape architect Janet Darling asked in a January 1945 *House Beautiful* article, "Do you believe your town can afford to build an imposing monument to World War II, while just around the corner children are playing in the streets?" (42). Moreover, Americans also recognized that the war effort had been successful because an entire nation had contributed; the war's casualties were not the only sacrifices that could be commemorated. Reflecting on the new demands of modern war, living memorial proponent James Dahir wrote, "Modern war, which mobilizes the entire population and re-creates for emergency periods the functioning of the community, should end in the erection of community buildings dedicated to lasting community and personal rehabilitation—this is indeed an eminently appropriate concept" (16). Thus for a nation looking to the future and prosperity, the best ways of remembering the war and its people's sacrifices would be the GI Bill of Rights and local, community-based living memorials that served all its citizens.

The trend toward living memorials coincided with other efforts to strengthen the postwar body politic. Just as remasculinizing and restoring the wounded veteran's body had become a postwar priority, so did the continued rebuilding of the national body politic. Living memorials, which frequently took the form of community recreation centers, gymnasiums, parks, and sports fields, were seen as important tools in creating a stronger, fitter nation. The Committee on Physical Fitness, created in response to high Selective Service rejections, sponsored the Commission for Community War Memorials for Physical Fitness. With FSA backing, the Commission lobbied America's towns and cities through pamphlets, books, articles, and brochures, encouraging them "to make America stronger by making Americans stronger."[13] As James Dahir noted in his review of various living memorial ideas, "When it is remembered . . . that 4,500,000 men were rejected for military service because of physical and psychoneurotic conditions, and that of those accepted only 5 percent were in top condition [recommendations for fitness-based memorials] take on a different meaning" (19).

Not all Americans, of course, favored living memorials. Critics such as Margaret Cresson and Lewis Mumford blasted their impermanence in articles and editorials and accused Americans of selfishly serving themselves instead of the war's heroes.[14] Enough military, government, and public backing also existed to erect sculptures based on Joe Rosenthal's famous photograph of marines raising the flag over Iwo Jima in New York, Washington, D.C., Arlington, and elsewhere.[15] These sculptures—especially the

78-foot Marine Corps Memorial in Arlington—conveyed the heroism, honor, glory, and ideals of traditional monuments and demonstrated that despite its horrific dimensions World War II was still the "good war" and a symbol of American victory for many Americans. As the postwar period quickly turned into the cold war and then another hot war in Korea, the community-based nature and practicality of living memorials soon gave way to other forms of national commemoration.

COLD WAR CONCERNS—HONORING TWO MORE UNKNOWNS

Like many postwar memorializations that focused on peace, prosperity, and the goals of the living, the initial plans for interring an Unknown Soldier killed in World War II were relatively simple. Originally approved by Congress on June 24, 1946, and updated on July 23, 1948, the plans specified that the Second World War's Unknown Soldier would be selected by the president in a Washington, D.C., ceremony by May 28, 1951. Five candidates—one from each of the five zones of operation—would be involved in the selection process, and the chosen Unknown would lie in state at the Capitol before a May 30th burial at Arlington National Cemetery. These plans, however, were put on hold with the outbreak of hostilities in Korea in June 1950.[16] By the time the World War II Unknown was interred at Arlington Cemetery on May 30, 1958, not only had the ceremony and selection plans changed but so had the symbolism of the Unknown's body. Selected from 19 candidates and buried with his Korean counterpart in an elaborate military ceremony, the Unknown Soldier of World War II became literally and symbolically linked to the cold war.

At first glance, the ceremonies for America's World War I Unknown and those for the World War II and Korean Unknowns are remarkably similar in form and significance. Like earlier British and French services, the U.S. ceremonies focused on preserving the anonymity and symbolic potential of the selected Unknowns. With utter anonymity assured through an elaborate selection process, the Unknowns became privileged signifiers of their wars' dead. Because nothing was known about the Unknowns' class, race, religion, age, or branch of service, they embodied the democratic spirit of America while simultaneously representing all the specific sons, brothers, husbands, and friends killed in the various conflicts. By honoring these Unknowns with medals, speeches, and elaborate rites, then, the government was able to fulfill its contract with its citizen-soldiers and their families by demonstrating proper gratitude for their sacrifices. While both ceremonies were designed to satisfy the needs for public mourning and the official commemoration of war sacrifice, they also held larger political significance. Like their counterparts pressed into additional national service via their placement in overseas cemeteries, the Unknown Soldiers of both World Wars continued to serve national interests through their selection and interment ceremonies.

While the burial of World War I's Unknown helped communicate America's rising international status and aims for peace, the ceremonies involving the Second World War and Korean Unknowns helped reassure Americans about their nation's military strength and position in the nuclear arms race.[17] Authorized via Public Law 975 in August 1956, concrete plans for the burial of a Korean and a World War II Unknown did not take shape until 1957 and 1958. The general tensions of the cold war and the specific anxieties caused by the events of late 1957 influenced the interment of the Unknowns, turning the original simple plans of the late 1940s into an elaborate military display.

In the year prior to the interment of the World War II and Korean Unknowns, several developments in the arms race left Americans feeling uneasy about their nation's future. News of the Soviets' successful testing of an intercontinental ballistic missile in August 1957 introduced a new vulnerability in American defense systems, while the October 4, 1957, Sputnik launch brought on genuine panic. The Soviets not only had displayed long-range missile capability, which meant they could soon target U.S. cities directly in a nuclear attack, but also had leaped ahead of the United States in the space race. Fears that America was lagging behind the Soviets in the military and space races were further exacerbated by the November launch of Sputnik II and the fall publication of the Gaither and Rockefeller reports. Sputnik II revealed that the Soviets could launch even bigger satellites than the first Sputnik and that they could send a living being—a dog named Laika—into space; the Gaither and Rockefeller reports, meanwhile, alleged that America had serious defense weaknesses and claimed that the Soviet Union was far outspending the U.S. in weapons technology. These initial reports, coupled with the dozens of other defense analysis reports and the Vanguard fiasco,[18] led politicians and private citizens alike to call for increased military spending and new efforts to keep pace with the Russians. Under enormous political pressure, Eisenhower secured an additional $1.37 billion for weapons technology and production "and submitted a 1958 budget with defense increases that bloated the budget to a record peacetime figure of $73.9 billion" (Oakley 346).

Although the initial plans for America's second interment of Unknown Soldiers were in place before the Sputnik scare, the scope, media coverage, and specific details of the events were shaped by America's need for reassurances of military strength. Even before the World War II and Korean Unknowns arrived in Washington, their selection ceremonies, transportation, and honors displayed impressive military organization and fanfare. Since World War II had been fought on a global scale, the selection process of its Unknown necessitated a complex, international affair. Preselection ceremonies and careful mortuary examinations at overseas military cemeteries assembled American candidates that had been killed in action and that were absolutely unidentifiable. To ensure the complete anonymity of the various candidates, military officials destroyed all records pertaining to the

Unknowns to prevent any future speculation about the chosen individuals. In the weeks prior to the Memorial Day burial, selection ceremonies involving members of all five military services, the press, government officials, and the public took place at Hickam Air Force Base in Honolulu and the Epinal American Cemetery in France.[19] Chosen from six and thirteen candidates respectively, the transpacific and transatlantic Unknowns represented unidentified servicemen in every U.S. overseas cemetery.

Although all branches of the military participated in the various selection ceremonies and transportation of possible candidates, the navy was responsible for the final selection ceremony and for conveying the Unknowns to Washington. Carrying the Korean and transpacific Unknowns, the USS *Boston* rendezvoused with the USS *Canberra* and the USS *Blandy*, which transported the transatlantic Unknown, off the Virginia Capes for the final selection ceremony. Through this convergence of ships, the navy showed the press America's newest destroyer (the *Blandy*), the "world's first combatant guided-missile ship" (the *Boston*), and the world's "second vessel to be converted to a guided-missile cruiser" (the *Canberra*) (Defense Department, *The Unknowns* 12, 13).[20] The elaborately staged transfer of caskets to the *Canberra* and the impressive full dress ceremony that followed further displayed military precision and prestige. Numerous reporters and other invited guests witnessed the final selection of the World War II Unknown, the transfer of Unknowns to the *Blandy*, and the dignified sea burial of the unchosen World War II Unknown. For an America still trying to catch the Soviets in the military and space races, the ceremonies provided reminders of U.S. military achievements and highlighted the unity of its armed forces.

The final services and events surrounding the burial of Unknowns likewise provided the American public with elaborate displays of military organization and technology. With minute guns sounding from the Washington Monument grounds continuously except during the two minutes of silence, the ceremonies offered a spectacular military ensemble. More than 6,000 service men and women participated in the Memorial Day ceremonies, with 216 Medal of Honor winners joining the Unknowns' procession. Having rehearsed their duties multiple times in the previous weeks, the military assured that "final ceremonies all went off with clocklike precision," including the perfectly timed passing of 20 jet fighters and delta winged fighter bombers as the caissons crossed the Memorial Bridge (*Unknowns* 41). While the ceremonies were primarily intended to honor the Unknowns, top military leaders "were eager to obtain the widest possible coverage of the events" (*Unknowns* 42). Utilizing press stands, briefings, press kits, prepared stories, and a National Press Club conference, the government and military achieved extensive coverage of the event, employing the ceremonies as a way to both reaffirm American military strength and to honor publicly the nation's contract with its citizen-soldiers.

While only the latter goal was stated during the 34-minute funeral service, President Eisenhower reinforced the former in his earlier address to the 216 Medal of Honor winners, who had been invited to Washington for the funeral and lying-in-state services at the government's expense. In the process of trying to pass the Defense Department Reorganization Bill, Eisenhower used the informal preceremony gathering to link past valor and military success to the future of the nation. After thanking the Medal of Honor recipients for defending "those ideals and those principles on which America stands," the president noted America's cold war aims as well as the other "rocks" on which America stood.[21] In order to preserve ideals like "freedom and liberty" and to prevent America "from getting overrun by atheistic communism," Eisenhower contended that it would be necessary to maintain both economic and military strength. Underscoring the significance of the Memorial Day military display, Eisenhower remarked, "Our military strength, costly though it may be, is one of the rocks today on which we must rest our hope for peace. No weakness must be allowed to appear in the American shield." As the military and government hoped, the afternoon ceremonies and events leading up to them reassured the nation that "the American shield" was still intact and that it operated with perfect precision and inter-service cooperation.

The circumstances and events surrounding the burial of the Second World War Unknown reveal that World War II's dead servicemen were still serving the nation symbolically during the late 1950s. By burying the World War II Unknown alongside his World War I and Korean counterparts, America gave continuity and meaning to all three wars. The "good war," with its lofty ideals and just cause, not only resolved the conflict that sprang from World War I's settlement but also lent its noble "good versus evil" framing to Korea and the cold war. Moreover, the services for the World War II and Korean Unknowns provided the nation with a reassuring military spectacle and source of pride. The American people could not only renew their faith in the American military but could feel justified spending millions of dollars on weapons and technology because of the righteousness of World War II. For this continued service, the World War II Unknown and the war dead he represented received the Medal of Honor but no national memorial of their own.

It is clear that the dead bodies of U.S. servicemen continued to create meaning long after their living subjectivities had expired. On the battlefield, U.S. corpses had a profound impact on living servicemen as they confronted their own mortality and the horrors of abjection. For many veterans, these confrontations with corpses and the loss of friends during the war continue to be things they "cannot forget."[22] On the home front, sanitized images of U.S. war dead offered incentives for higher production, war bond sales, and greater participation in the war effort. The massive scale and badly maimed condition of U.S. war dead likewise forced the military to invent new procedures for identifying and processing bodies. The postwar program for returning and reinterring U.S. war dead proved to be the most elaborate and expensive program of its kind, demonstrating the government's strong commitment to honoring its dead citizen-soldiers. This commitment was renewed with the elaborate 1958 burial of the World War II Unknown, which honored the war dead's sacrifices in a simultaneous display of cold war military strength.

Although their bodies held special meaning for Americans, the U.S. dead were also inextricably bound to the Second World War more generally and to the other 54.5 million people who died in it more specifically. Immediate postwar memorialization practices such as the trend toward living memorials reflected these associations, as they tried to focus on the living and to recognize the conflict's incomprehensibility. Given the enormous scope and multiple facets of the war, it is not surprising that in the nearly six decades that have elapsed since V-J Day numerous World War II monuments have been erected, each highlighting a different dimension of the war. In addition to local memorials throughout the country, there are national and regional Holocaust museums; monuments to separate service branches in Washington, D.C.; coastal memorials recording the missing in New York and San Francisco; monuments commemorating specific battles in overseas cemeteries; and changing museum exhibits that highlight all other facets of the war—from Japanese-American internment camps to women's participation to minority involvement in the war effort. Collectively, these World War II "monuments" reveal that both the meaning of the war's dead and the war itself are irreducible to any single memorial.

In 1993, however, Congress decided that it was time to create a National World War II Memorial to honor not just those who served in the armed forces but the entire World War II generation. In many respects, the memorial, completed in 2004, offers a synthesis of the goals of postwar living monuments and the form of traditional, state-sanctioned monuments. Like earlier living memorials, the new World War II monument has been funded entirely through private and corporate donations and seeks to commemorate an entire nation's sacrifice rather than just the sacrifices of the war dead and injured. Moreover, through various inscriptions on the parapet walls, iconography, and sculpture, the memorial also promises to commemorate the high-minded idealism of the World War II generation and the vision of America they sought to preserve in their postwar living memorials. At the same time, though, the monument is a vehicle of the state. Charged with designing and constructing the memorial, the ABMC has chosen to reinforce notions of World War II as the "good war" as it attempts to define the war for national memory.

While monuments always exceed their intended, sanctioned meanings through personal interactions and the passage of time, the new World War II memorial offers insights into the ways in which America has attempted to fix and define the meaning of the Second World War. By placing the memorial on the Mall between the Washington and Lincoln Monuments— considered by many to be the most hallowed land in the nation—the ABMC has constructed World War II as one of the most important events in

U.S. history. According to Hayden Williams, chairman of the ABMC's site and design committee, Friedrich St. Florian's revamped monument design conveys a "[great] sense of monumentality, one that respects and complements its historic surroundings, and one that is appropriate and commensurate with the momentous events being remembered."[23] With two 43-foot granite arches, four bronze eagles holding victory laurels, two flagpoles flying the American flag, and a memorial plaza embraced by 56 stone pillars—symbolizing U.S. states and territories at the time of the war—the design focuses on "victory and valor" as it attempts to communicate the "unity and strength of the nation." Although it commemorates those killed during the war with a cenotaph and acknowledges the many sacrifices of the World War II generation, the memorial is mainly celebratory. As the National World War II Memorial homepage explains, the memorial "celebrate[s] the American spirit that brought [the] victory of democracy over tyranny, light over darkness."[24]

While the commemorative area acknowledges the "contribution of our allies" and the "suffering of all human kind" along with U.S. war deaths,[25] the memorial largely ignores the multiple, complex lenses of social and revisionist history. The memorial's design reinforces notions of World War II as "the good war," a conflict with a just cause, a clear-cut victory, and an aftermath that positioned the United States as a political and economic superpower. In many ways, the memorial offers a return to the binary good-versus-evil framework in which the war effort was constructed between 1941 and 1945, eschewing the postmodern sensibility that the war engendered. This return to the past, no doubt, is an attempt to provide a moral reference point for a nation that has since experienced conflicts and events such as Vietnam and Watergate, which have caused Americans to mistrust their government and to question the ethics of U.S. foreign policy and global interventions.

What the new memorial does not and cannot capture is the monumentality of death that also surrounds World War II's memory. There is not enough room to record the names of all 407,318 U.S. servicepersonnel killed during the war or to convey the magnitude of the war's 55 million total deaths. This mass scale of death is, however, beyond the scope of the intentions of the memorial. The memorial attempts to secure the memory of the "good war," not to explore modern war's impact on the body. In time, perhaps, films like *Saving Private Ryan* and new memorialization traditions such as those practiced at Holocaust museums will collectively commemorate America's World War II dead in their full embodied and gendered complexity.[26] Or perhaps, as Paul Fussell contends, "the real war will never get into the books" (*Wartime* 267).

CONCLUSION

Susan Jeffords writes in *The Remasculinization of America* that we can not fully comprehend "war and its place in American culture without an understanding of its gendered relations" (182). Although commenting specifically on the conflict in Vietnam, Jeffords's statement reminds us that wars are important subjects for gender analysis not only because they often radically reconfigure "male" and "female" social roles but also because they highlight existing cultural gender relations. Throughout U.S. history, wars have expanded social and economic opportunities for women and men of color who took over jobs and responsibilities traditionally held by white men. Despite the freedoms and social advancements won by women and minorities, wars and their cultural representations have also served as important catalysts for consolidating hegemonic masculinity. After armed conflicts such as the Civil War and the Vietnam War, which divided the nation and left significant political scars, popular representations and reinterpretations of the wars led to a remasculinization of America.[1] In other instances, wars themselves have served as processes for reimagining the nation in explicitly masculine terms. Like the Spanish-American and Philippine-American wars, which allowed men to reassert their fighting prowess and chivalric ideals at a time when the New Woman threatened to feminize the public sphere, the Second World War provided a crucial opportunity for men to demonstrate characteristics such as strength, bravery, and usefulness that had been called into question during the 1930s.

Although many of Roosevelt's New Deal programs had taken steps to counteract challenges to masculinity precipitated by the Great Depression, it was not until World War II that American men, the media, and the government began to imagine the United States in explicitly masculine terms again. Integral to this shift in perception were the widespread wartime representations of powerful, youthful male bodies in posters, advertisements, and other public images. With their comic book physiques and implied steel-like force, these images communicated messages of national strength as America mobilized for war and prepared to battle the hypermasculinized Nazi fatherland. Although more powerful representations of women in posters like Miller's "We Can Do It" also appeared during the war, their visible muscles and toughened facades reinforced rather than undermined the perception that wartime America was primarily a *masculine* nation. Uncle Sam's ubiquity and near complete eclipsing of female national symbols Lady Liberty and Lady Columbia in public imaging campaigns further bolstered the idea that the war had remodeled the American body politic.

The physical transformations of American bodies that accompanied the symbolic changes in public representations of masculinity also contributed to the sense that World War II had reinvigorated and masculinized the nation. Millions of servicemen improved their bodies and overall health through military training programs and regular nutritious meals. Wartime programs inspired by early army rejection figures led to better civilian health and fitness as well. In addition to inspiring new national physical fitness and x-ray screening programs, the physical examination of more than 18 million men served to position the draft-age American male body as the literal and symbolic index of the nation's health. Indeed, wartime public health discourses served to reinforce perceptions of the United States as a preeminently masculine nation. Capturing this sentiment, Cabel Phillips wrote in a 1941 *New York Times* article, "An American Army is something more than a cross section of our manhood, it is a living mirror for what we, as a nation, are."[2] While civilian fitness programs revealed that the health of all American bodies was crucial to wartime and postwar success, the repeated privileging of servicemen's bodies and military physical ideals in national health debates highlighted the fact that the "generic" American body was implicitly young, strong, and male.

Although combat and military training accidents produced hundreds of thousands of mutilated male bodies and abject masculinities, representations of wounded bodies generally did not undermine America's recently retooled images of national strength. Thanks to censorship policies and the carefully controlled visual experiences of most Americans during the war, wounds were often presented as badges of honor or as tangible marks of masculinity proved on the battlefield. The media likewise sanitized images of dead bodies and used representations of death to promote patriotism, encourage wartime sacrifices, and symbolize "American" ideas such as freedom, bravery, and democracy. Rather than providing threats to the recently rebuilt body politic, images of dead and wounded bodies often provided additional spaces for wartime and immediate postwar re-masculinization. Some popular magazine articles and films revealed cul-tural anxieties about the wounded veteran's ability to reclaim his proper masculine position in postwar life; however, many more narratives about re-turning veterans presented the wounded body as a site of self-regenerating masculinity. Like the bodies of actual veterans that were rehabilitated and rendered useful again through prosthetics, these fictional figures demon-strated that any threats to American masculinity were both temporary and mendable.

Just as they became important indexes for evaluating and improving the nation's wartime health, American servicemen's bodies continued to serve as privileged instruments for measuring national strength and returns to normalcy in the postwar period. Although the government and military ceased to exercise control over servicemen's bodies after separation, they es-tablished guidelines to protect the fitness and health improvements men made during the war. Exit examinations similar to initial inspections en-sured that servicemen left the military without diseases and other physical defects. The level of scrutiny varied greatly at these examinations, but, as ex-sergeant Merle Miller reported in a 1945 *Yank* article, even minor physi-cal problems such as high blood pressure or cavities could delay a man's separation from the service.[3] Although proposed nationwide health and fit-ness programs to keep former servicemen in their prime physical shape were not adopted,[4] Congress did pass other legislation to protect the well-being of returning veterans. The Servicemen's Readjustment Act of 1944, more popularly known as the GI Bill of Rights, provided continued medical care, counseling, VA loans, insurance, educational opportunities, and other benefits to ensure successful physical and mental readjustments. Whereas the triumphs of American technology were literally inscribed on the bodies of veterans who received state-of-the-art prosthetics,[5] other markers of U.S. postwar strength were measured by the "new, young, eager middle class" spawned by the GI Bill (Blum 337). Moreover, the GI Bill reflected the privi-leged position that servicemen continued to occupy in postwar American culture. As historian Michael Sherry notes, outlays on veterans' benefits and services through the GI Bill averaged $7 billion per year from 1947 through 1950, "more than triple all other spending on social welfare, health, housing, and education" (110).

Comprising one quarter of the population in 1947 (Blum 339), World War II veterans and their immediate family members also shaped U.S. poli-tics and culture in crucial ways. In addition to helping elect seven World War II veterans to the presidency after Truman, they helped create and pre-serve a victory culture that left little room for national self-reflection and introspection after the war.[6] In building practical living memorials that only vaguely commemorated the war, Americans seemed to accept the clear-cut victory and framing of the war presented by the government and media. An emphasis on a rapid readjustment and return to normalcy likewise left heroic, hypermasculinized national self-representations unquestioned. Susan Faludi and Suzanne Clark have examined the stakes of preserving World War II masculine ideals during the postwar and cold war periods. For Faludi, the greatest problem stemming from the preservation of wartime ideals and the lack of introspection in postwar victory culture was the lack of communication between World War II veterans and their sons. Explaining this phenomenon in *Stiffed*, she writes, "Postwar culture denied its returning soldiers the opportunity to grapple publicly with their horrific secret burden . . . thereby denying them a moral knowledge to pass down to their sons. All they could instruct their sons to do was to rerun the moment of victory" (378). This failure to educate their sons about war and the complexities of manhood, Faludi contends, was a key underlying cause of the crisis in American masculinity in the 1980s and 1990s. For Suzanne Clark, the victory culture's inability to relinquish its warrior ideal led to "the hypermasculinity of national policy" during the cold war and to "a politics resistant to postmodern complexities of gender, sexuality, or race— or of representation" (3). According to Clark, a cold war culture built on wartime ideals offered additional rugged masculine figures such as the cowboy and the frontiersman to the national mythology and created a cultural canon that largely excluded women and people of color.

Perhaps the greatest legacy of America's postwar victory culture and preservation of wartime masculine ideals, however, is that it fostered the idea of "the good war" and firmly positioned World War II as the nation's most commonly agreed upon moral reference point. By unproblematically adopting the clear-cut, binary framing of the war offered by the OWI, postwar narratives naturalized these stories, turning propaganda into truth and fiction into fact. The popular resurgence of the war film during the late 1940s was especially vital in perpetuating World War II's almost mythical status in the American imagination. Describing this process and the appeal of the late 1940s Hollywood combat film, Karal Ann Marling and John Wetenhall write, "World War II seemed clean, straightforward, refreshingly unambiguous in a Cold War world of espionage and ideology. In less than a decade, World War II and its symbols came to stand for the postwar ideal, for things as they should have turned out: American valor and know-how supreme; America always victorious" (127). At the forefront of this wave of new World War II films was Republic Pictures' 1949 film *Sands of Iwo Jima*. With John Wayne playing Sergeant Stryker, the film introduced a somewhat troubled and unconventional protagonist but still managed to celebrate the hardboiled, "blood-and-guts" heroism of American men. Cashing in on the patriotic fervor the movie created, marine recruiters set up booths in the lobbies of theaters following the film's March 1, 1950, general release. And in at least one theater, the R.K.O. Keith's in Richmond Hill, New York (where my father saw the film), young men were enlisting enthusiastically. Many of them would no doubt go on to serve in the Korean War.

As the second half of the twentieth century unfolded, the memory and representations of World War II were invoked time and again to legitimize America's other wars or to justify continued involvement in armed conflicts. The burial of the World War II Unknown Soldier helped reframe the Korean War in terms of the Second World War's good-versus-evil constructions, and the memorial services assisted Eisenhower in his efforts to pass the Defense Department Reorganization Bill and to reassure the American people amid cold war anxieties. During the Kennedy and Johnson administrations, military leaders, diplomats, and the presidents themselves used their experiences in and memories of the Second World War to shape American policy in Vietnam. Johnson, for example, recounted his largely exaggerated and greatly embellished war story "to help persuade congressional leaders to support his foreign aid spending and his policy toward Vietnam" (Dean 52). Commanding General William Westmoreland, meanwhile, employed "World War II as the standard of measurement" for waging aerial warfare in Vietnam and frequently offered analogies to the Second World War in his memoirs, as he compared events like the Tet Offensive alternatively to Pearl Harbor and the Battle of the Bulge (Sherry 271, 268–69).

Although he could not invoke the memory of combat experience as Kennedy and Johnson had, Nixon also frequently positioned World War II as the touchstone for Vietnam. In televised speeches on April 20 and 30, 1970, Nixon addressed the implications of his Vietnamization program and his decision to invade Cambodia, justifying his policies in terms of America's power and past military victories. During the April 20th speech on Vietnamization, Nixon avowed, "We are not a weak people. We are a strong people. America has never been defeated in the proud one-hundred-ninety-year history of this country, and we shall not be defeated in Vietnam" (qtd. in Carroll 11). Ten days later, employing more cold war rhetoric, Nixon asserted that "the world's most powerful nation" could not afford to act "like a pitiful helpless giant"; freedom throughout the world was in jeopardy (qtd. in Herring 236).[7] As historian Peter Carroll has noted, during the ten-day period between speeches, Nixon "ordered several screenings of the movie *Patton,* a film which celebrated military toughness, high risk attacks, and the disregard of formal channels" (11). While screenings of *Patton* offered inspiration for his unauthorized attacks in Cambodia, they also remind us that Nixon, like his predecessors, was haunted by the specter of World War II. In contrast to the "bad war" (Vietnam), the "good war" had more definitively become "the culminating myth of the American experience and national character" (Isaacs 7).

During the Gulf War, George H. Bush, himself a decorated hero of the Second World War, capitalized on the different places Vietnam and World

War II occupied in America's cultural imagination. Repeatedly asserting that "this will not be another Vietnam," Bush differentiated Operation Desert Shield from the "bad war" while he simultaneously invoked the memory of the "good war" through his frequent comparisons between Saddam Hussein and Adolph Hitler. More recently, George W. Bush and the media invoked the Second World War through allusions to Pearl Harbor and other World War II events after the September 11, 2001, terrorist attacks. Despite frequent assertions that the United States would be engaging in a totally new kind of war for the twenty-first century, World War II's specter once again haunted the government and media's framing of America's attacks on the Taliban and Al Qaeda network in Afghanistan. From initial claims that September 11 was another "day that will live in infamy" to Bush's binary framing of the conflict, the Second World War was evoked to lend its aura of righteousness to yet another American war—the United States' "war on terror." While primarily capitalizing on the memory of September 11, the George W. Bush administration used references to World War II to marshal support for Operation Iraqi Freedom, citing both the appeasement policy of the 1938 Munich Conference and the postwar occupation of Germany and Japan as reasons to invade Iraq.

Although most mainstream cultural representations of World War II have reinforced the "good war's" status in the national imagination, since the 1960s important revisionist narratives have questioned the framing and ideals put forth by the postwar victory culture. While Nixon was touting his new vision and plans for the war, another process of Vietnamization was taking place: the "Vietnamization" of World War II in American literature.[8] Kurt Vonnegut's 1969 novel, *Slaughterhouse-Five,* and Thomas Pynchon's 1973 masterpiece, *Gravity's Rainbow,* revealed that the war in Vietnam was shaping representations of World War II just as the legacies and cultural narratives of the Second World War were influencing policy in Vietnam. Following the lead of Joseph Heller's *Catch-22* (1961), *Slaughterhouse-Five* and *Gravity's Rainbow* deconstructed the binary framing of America's "good war," offering a "Vietnamized" version, full of discontinuities, fragmented bodies, and multiple shades of gray. World War II scholarship during the late 1960s and early 1970s also presented more complicated, revisionist visions of the "good war," as scholars began to examine topics such as the "hidden Holocaust," the internment of Japanese Americans, wartime racial conflict, and the wartime experiences of women and persons of color.

Following in this tradition of critical reexamination, this study has sought to provide a fuller account of the American male body and representations of masculinity during World War II. Although World War II films such as *Saving Private Ryan* and *The Thin Red Line* have provided the American public with more graphic representations of the grisly realities of combat, the Second World War's broader impact on the American body politic has remained largely unexamined. By investigating the ways in which wartime gender ideals and particular embodied national self-representations were produced, we can begin to see these World War II ideals as the historically located constructs that they are. Until we recognize both war's true impact on the body and the countless abject masculinities that existed alongside the hypermasculinized hegemonic models offered during World War II, we will continue to perpetuate narratives of the "good war" passed down by the victory culture. Without a more complicated and embodied account of the war, the cultural memory of World War II will no doubt be wrongly invoked time and again to engender and legitimize other armed conflicts.

LIST OF SURVEY PARTICIPANTS

1.	Fred L. Ritter	31.	Charles Bernstein*
2.	Norman Reitman	32.	Kenneth E. Joel
3.	Albert Handaly	33.	Harold L. Roberts*
4.	Joseph Demasi	34.	Thomas G. Coleman*
5.	Richard Nichols*	35.	Quentin Jacobs*
6.	Theodore Kelly*	36.	Richard J. Mercer
7.	John Hale Conover, Jr.	37.	Samuel Smith*
8.	Kevin Carlton*	38.	John Schroth*
9.	Carol Silverman Levin	39.	Howard F. Canning
10.	Charles Getty	40.	T. R. Rogers
11.	William Benson*	41.	Michael Young*
12.	Samuel I. Errera	42.	Livy Goodman
13.	Peter Arnold*	43.	George Temkin
14.	Nathan Shoehalter	44.	William E. Boes, Jr.
15.	Irwin Peters*	45.	Oliver Roberts*
16.	Robert G. Lauffer	46.	Franklin J. Kneller
17.	Vincent Kerstein*	47.	William W. Kaenzig
18.	Mark Silver*	48.	Joseph G. Lerner
19.	Franklin S. Simon	49.	Alfred Nisnoff
20.	Leslie C. Nelson, Jr.	50.	Walter G. Denise
21.	Anthony R. Ricci	51.	Raymond A. Finley, Jr.
22.	Herbert H. Newton	52.	William G. Halliday
23.	Dennis Mullen*	53.	William S. Gillman
24.	Charles Wiley*	54.	John G. Scherholz
25.	Christopher Maggio	55.	S. Robert Christensen
26.	P. Richard Wexler	56.	John F. Crane
27.	W. Wesley Konrad	57.	Andrew Gordon*
28.	Kurt G. Leuser	58.	David H. Kingston
29.	Charles Johnson*	59.	Frank Richardson*
30.	Brian Walters*	60.	Lawrence Weston*

---

* Indicates that a pseudonym was used

61. Eugene Chesterfield*
62. Samuel Davis*
63. John A. Gausz
64. Thomas Linton
65. Frank Dauster
66. Richard Swales*
67. Solomon Leader
68. George Weston*
69. Bert R. Manhoff
70. Abraham Soltz
71. W. Scott Buist
72. Eric Chilton*
73. Robert C. King
74. Joseph Katz
75. Samuel R. Frankel
76. Joel Stern
77. Jason Rogers*
78. Robert C. Olsen
79. Michael Rollings*
80. Benedict Riley*
81. R. William Reisert
82. Simon Michaels*
83. Ronald Davenport*
84. Alden F. Jacobs
85. Benjamin P. Indeck
86. Roger Brenton*
87. Robert C. Johnson*
88. Harold Goldstein*
89. David Miller
90. Lloyd Kalugim
91. Lyman C. Avery
92. Robert M. Fishkin
93. Carleton Dilatush
94. William Knox
95. Roland A. Winter
96. Bernard Walters*
97. Herbert D. Brown
98. William J. Godfrey, Jr.
99. Nicholas W. Filippone

100. Joseph Thompson*
101. Byron Keller*
102. George H. Elwood
103. William C. Simmons*
104. Roger Mullen*
105. Lewis M. Bloom
106. John J. Dowling, Jr.
107. Adam Bennington*
108. Frank A. Gimpel
109. Samuel E. Blum
110. John Skinner
111. David T. Zimmer*
112. Brendon Sanders*
113. Nathan Alexander*
114. James T. Kenny
115. Louis Javitz*
116. Richard Kennsey*
117. Robert W. Billian
118. Paul R. Van Duren
119. Frank M. Richards*
120. Ronald Jackson*
121. Mark Addison
122. Jack M. Williams
123. Crandon F. Clark
124. Edward C. Piech
125. E. Theodore Stier
126. Howard H. MacDougall
127. Michael Rukeyser*
128. Calvin H. Morton
129. Charles W. McDougall
130. William L. Prout
131. Nelson Greenblatt*
132. James G. Handford
133. Roy W. Brown
134. Christopher W. Keller
135. John W. Berglund
136. Carl Schumaker*
137. James L. Essig
138. John Sommers

LIST OF SURVEY QUESTIONS

1.   Name and Rank (highest attained).

2.   Unit(s) served in.

3.   Length of service (please list beginning and ending dates).

4.   Did you enlist or were you drafted?

5.   Where did you serve? (please list countries, U.S. bases, etc.).

6.   Evaluate your induction medical examination. Did you think the exam a good test of physical and mental fitness? How did you feel during the examination process (i.e., bored, embarrassed, etc.)?

7.   Did you undergo any other preinduction physical examinations? If yes, what did you think of the exam(s)?

8.   Briefly describe and evaluate exercise programs/drills at basic training. Did the programs/drills physically prepare you for your later duties?

9.   Did you notice any improvement in your physical condition during or immediately after basic training? If yes, please describe (weight gain, better cardiovascular condition, etc.).

10. What was your opinion of your military uniform(s)? Did you feel different wearing it (in contrast to civilian clothes)? How were you treated by civilians (on the home front and abroad) when you were in uniform?

11. Did a lot of servicemen in your company smoke cigarettes? Approximately what percentage of men smoked? What brands were most popular?

12. Did you smoke cigarettes while in the service? If yes, why did you smoke (to ease stress, peer acceptance, pleasure, etc.)? Had you smoked prior to joining the military? For what length of time did you smoke?

13. Did many servicemen have or get tattoos? What types of tattoos were popular?

14. What were your attitudes toward combat? Did your peers share these opinions?

15. What did you think of the enemy? Were your views influenced by the American media?

16. Did you engage in combat during the war? If yes, where? Please describe length and nature of combat and any medals received.

17. Were you wounded during the war? (If no, skip to #20). If yes, please describe the type of wound(s) and where/how it occurred.

18. What were (if any) the psychological effects of the wound(s)?

19. Did the wound(s) have any lasting impact on your life? If yes, please describe.

20. Did you ever experience battle fatigue, "shell shock," or post traumatic stress disorder? (If no, skip to 22.) If yes, please describe the nature of it and the conditions under which it occurred.

21. Did you receive any treatment for it? If yes, please describe the treatment and evaluate its effectiveness.

22. Did you become ill or require medical attention while in the service? Please evaluate medical facilities, doctors, and health care.

23. Did you attend any sex hygiene lectures or films? If yes, what was your opinion of them?

24. What was your general opinion of the military's efforts to prevent, control, and treat venereal diseases? Evaluate the appropriateness and effectiveness of the programs.

25. Were there specific fraternization policies addressed to servicemen's interactions with women (abroad, in the U.S., with servicewomen)? Please describe any restrictions or policies.

26. What periodicals or magazines did you read while in the service?

27. What did you think of World War II movies produced shortly after the war?

28. Have you seen *Saving Private Ryan?* If yes, what is your opinion of the film?

29. Did you have any difficulties adjusting to civilian life after the war? Please describe your transition to civilian life.

30. Are there any comments you'd like to add about your wartime service experiences?

NOTES

INTRODUCTION

1. "Dedication of the Marine Corps War Memorial," November 10, 1954, Arlington, Virginia. Available in the Harry Schmidt Collection, Hoover Institution Archives. For more information about the dimensions, construction, various versions, and cultural legacy of the Marine Corps War Memorial, see Karal Ann Marling and John Wetenhall's *Iwo Jima: Monuments, Memories, and the American Hero.*

2. These circulation figures are based on averages of figures in *Magazine Circulation and Rate Trends 1937–1955.*

3. Examples of this scholarship include Bernard Dick's *The Star-Spangled Screen: The American World War II Film,* Jeanine Basinger's *The World War II Combat Film: Anatomy of a Genre,* John Whiteclay Chambers and David Culbert's *World War II, Film, and History,* Thomas Doherty's *Projections of War: Hollywood, American Culture, and World War II,* and Clayton Koppes and Gregory Black's *Hollywood Goes to War: How Politics, Profits, and Propaganda Shaped World War II Movies.*

4. Jennifer Terry and Jacqueline Urla's introduction to *Deviant Bodies: Critical Perspectives on Difference in Science and Popular Culture* provides an excellent overview of Foucault's contributions to the field of body studies as well as an examination of the ways in which medical and social science discourses produce certain "deviant" bodies. To cite only a few of the many fascinating texts that investigate the social construction of bodies, see Susan Bordo's *Unbearable Weight: Feminism, Western Culture, and the Body;* Mike Featherstone, Mike Hepworth, and Bryan S. Turner's *The Body: Social Process and Cultural Theory;* Michel Foucault's *Discipline and Punish: The Birth of the Prison* and *The History of Sexuality, Volume I: An Introduction;* Elizabeth Grosz's *Volatile Bodies: Toward a Corporeal Feminism;* Chris Schilling's *The Body and Social Theory;* and Elaine Scarry's *The Body in Pain: The Making and Unmaking of the World.*

5. As Anne Fausto-Sterling and Suzanne Kessler have shown, even seemingly stable markers of a body's sex such as chromosomes do not necessarily signify whether a body is male or female. See Kessler's "The Medical Construction of Gender" and Fausto-Sterling's "The Five Sexes."

6. See, for example, Londa Schiebinger's discussion of beards as cultural signs of maleness in *Nature's Body: Gender in the Making of Modern Science,* Susan Bordo's analysis of changing contemporary ideals in *The Male Body: A New Look at Men in Public and Private,* and David Gilmore's cross-cultural analysis of masculinity in *Manhood in the Making.*

7. Judith Butler's notion of gender as process constructed through performative "signifying practices" is discussed in her volume *Gender Trouble* and further developed in her 1993 book *Bodies that Matter: On the Discursive Limits of "Sex."*

8. Earlier discussions of how masculinity is constructed in terms of relational hierarchies may be found in Michael Kimmel's introduction to *Changing Men: New Directions in Research on Men and Masculinity* and in R. W. Connell's *Masculinities.*

9. See E. Anthony Rotundo's *American Manhood: Transformations in Masculinity from the Revolution to the Modern Era,* Kristin Hoganson's *Fighting for American Manhood: How Gender Politics Provoked the Spanish-American and Philippine-American Wars,* Gail Bederman's *Manliness and Civilization: A Cultural History of Gender and Race in the United States, 1880–1817,* Susan Jeffords's *The Remasculinization of America: Gender and the Vietnam War* and *Hard Bodies: Hollywood Masculinity in the Reagan Era,* Suzanne Clark's *Cold Warriors: Manliness on Trial in the Rhetoric of the West,* Sally Robinson's *Marked Men: White Masculinity in Crisis,* and Susan Bordo's *The Male Body.*

1—BUILDING THE BODY POLITIC

1. Strong isolationist and antimilitary sentiment in the 1930s also contributed to the lack of preparedness. Disillusioned with the outcome of World War I and the Versailles Treaty and fueled by the findings of the 1934 Nye Committee, which claimed that "the United States had been tricked into World War I by munitions makers" (Nash 111), many Americans in the 1930s were isolationists. A November 1936 Gallup poll, for example, revealed that 95 percent of Americans thought the U.S. should not send troops to aid Britain and France in a war against Italy and Germany, and by April 1939, 84 percent of Americans still favored non-involvement in the same conflict ("War and Peace, 1935–1939," *Life,* April 17, 1939, 15). Although armaments production and wartime preparedness increased sharply after the fall of France in June 1940, the U.S. preparedness program was still largely "piecemeal and experimental" (Nash 120).

2. For studies examining the general symbolic use of muscular, heroic male bodies, see Kenneth Dutton's *The Perfectible Body: The Western Ideal of Male Physical Development* and Nicholas Mirzoeff's *Bodyscape: Art, Modernity and the Ideal Figure.*

3. In terms of unemployment, the United States was particularly hard hit by the worldwide depression of the 1930s. In fact, it had the highest unemployment rate of all industrialized nations. Conversely, between 1941 and 1945 the suicide rate in the U.S. dropped by 40 percent as Americans found a greater sense of purpose with the war (O'Neill, *Democracy* 250).

4. Perhaps one of the most poignant depictions of the crisis in masculinity caused by the depression is contained in a twelve-year-old Chicago boy's letter to F.D.R. In the February 1936 letter, the boy tells Roosevelt that despite visits to relief agency offices, his "father hasn't worked for 5 months," which has resulted in four months unpaid rent and three months of unpaid grocery, electric, and gas bills. The effect on the father and the family is tremendous: "My father he [*sic*] staying home. All the time he's crying because he can't find work. I told him why are you crying daddy, and daddy said why shouldn't I cry when there is nothing in the house. I feel sorry for him. That night I couldn't sleep. The next morning I wrote this letter to you. . . . Please answer right away because we need it. will [*sic*] starve" (qtd. in McElvaine 117).

5. See Tom Pendergast's *Creating the Modern Man: American Magazines and Consumer Culture 1900–1950* and Michael Kimmel's chapter "Muscles, Money, and the M-F Test" in *Manhood in America* for further discussion of these expanded notions of manhood.

6. "The Phrase that Wrecks a MILLION MEN," *Time,* September 10, 1934, 1.

7. "What would happen to us, John, if you lost your job?" *Life,* April 18, 1938, 59. Mid-1930s advertisements for the Union Central Life Insurance Company also preyed upon men's fears about being successful breadwinners and patriarchs; however, instead of focusing on their roles as husbands, these and other insurance ads

emphasized men's identities as fathers. Shamelessly using an image of a dejected young boy and his little sister staring longingly at the display window of a toy store, one December 1935 ad spelled out the repercussions of losing the male breadwinner: "No father . . . *no paychecks* . . . no Christmas." While capitalizing on seasonal worries of depression-era parents to create a happy holiday for their children, the ad specifically exploits men's other concerns as family providers—keeping the family together, paying "the necessary monthly bills," seeing "the children through school," supporting their wives, and providing "other vital kinds of protection" (*Time*, December 14, 1936, 5).

8. Modernism scholars have argued that the impulse to view culture as "feminized" in the early decades of the twentieth century was not restricted to America, but was part of a broader trend during the period as artists and intellectuals critiqued the mass culture industry. According to these critics, since the late nineteenth century the mass culture industry and effects of industrialization had been eroding away "high" masculine culture, leaving Western culture as a whole "feminized." See Andreas Huyssen's *After the Great Divide: Modernism, Mass Culture, Postmodernism,* Suzanne Clark's *Sentimental Modernism: Women Writers and the Revolution of the Word,* and Rita Felski's *The Gender of Modernity.* For a discussion of the "feminization" of American culture during the nineteenth century, see Ann Douglas's *The Feminization of American Culture.*

9. Roy Helton, "The Inner Threat: Our Own Softness," *Harper's Magazine,* September 1940, 337–43.

10. Although certainly part of a broader eugenics movement, Helton's call for a stronger, renewed masculine body politic seems to be specifically linked to turn-of-the-century physical culture programs advocated by people like Theodore Roosevelt and Ernest Thompson Seton, co-founder of the Boy Scouts of America. For further discussion of these movements see Mark Seltzer's chapter "The Love Master" in *Bodies and Machines.*

11. Most deaths from starvation occurred before Roosevelt took office and full-scale federal relief programs were in effect. The areas where starvation- and malnutrition-induced deaths did occur were the already-poor regions like mining towns. In Harlan County, Kentucky, for example, 231 children died because of malnutrition between 1929 and 1931 (Badger 19).

12. It should be noted that the lower rejection rates during the war itself were not necessarily due to a drastic improvement in the health of the American male population. Standards were lowered and often fluctuated during the war as the United States needed more manpower.

13. According to historian Gerald Nash, "a token force of 8,000 young women" did serve in the CCC (77).

14. The original 1933 enrollment restrictions for the CCC specified that only single men between the ages of 18 and 25 could enlist. Later the age restrictions were changed to allow only men between the ages of 17 and 23 to serve. Enrollment criteria varied, however, for the 225,000 veterans and 85,000 Native Americans who ultimately served in separate and independently administered camps (Salmond 37).

15. Please see James McEntee's 1942 "Summary of Certain Phases of the CCC Program" (Merrill 196) for additional statistics on work done by men in CCC camps. For more comprehensive historical studies of the CCC, see John Salmond's *The Civilian Conservation Corps, 1933–1942: A New Deal Case Study,* Perry Merrill's *Roosevelt's Forest Army: A History of the Civilian Conservation Corps, 1932–1942,* and Olen Cole's *The African-American Experience in the Civilian Conservation Corps.*

16. Federal Security Agency, *The CCC at Work: A Story of 2,500,000 Young Men*, Washington, D.C.: Government Printing Office, 1941.

17. See Jeffrey Ryan Suzik's "'Building Better Men': The CCC Boy and the Changing Social Ideal of Manliness."

18. See Salmond's *The Civilian Conservation Corps* and Jennifer Keene's chapter "'The Yanks Are Starving Everywhere': The Bonus March" in *Doughboys, the Great War, and the Remaking of America* for an examination World War I veteran's service in the CCC.

19. Ultimately, the Corps's focus on instilling "proper" work habits did prove to be rather successful. In their volume based on an extensive five-year study of the CCC for the American Youth Commission, Kenneth Holland and Frank Ernest Hill reported that the owners and managers they interviewed remarked that "90 per cent of the considerable number who had been engaged had proved to be good workers" (241). During congressional hearings about the Corps's future, employers from Thompson Products, Marshall Field, the Piper Cub Aircraft Company, and the National Standard Parts Association all "testified to the ability, character, and resourcefulness of former enrollees as workers" (Holland and Hill 241).

20. The task of documenting American life and culture largely fell to artists and scholars working for the Documentary Photography project of the Resettlement Administration (later for the FSA) and the Index of American Design (a branch of the FAP). For a more comprehensive discussion of the various New Deal art programs, their individual goals, and their histories, see Francis O'Connor's *Art for the Millions*, Richard McKinzie's *The New Deal for Artists*, and Bruce Bustard's *A New Deal for the Arts*.

21. The unofficial style of PWAP and Section murals and projects, the "American Scene" featured images of small-town life and specific regional identities while offering "straightforward celebrations of ideals such as community, democracy, and hard work" (Bustard 24).

22. For a more comprehensive discussion of the types of labor presented in New Deal art, see chapter four of Marlene Park and Gerald Markowitz's *Democratic Vistas: Post Offices and Public Art in the New Deal*, as well as Barbara Melosh's *Engendering Culture: Manhood and Womanhood in New Deal Public Art and Theater*.

23. Ben Shahn's "Social Security," "Maurice Glickman's "Construction," William Zorach's "Shoemakers of Stoneham," Michael Lensen's "Mining," Sahl Swarz's "Industry," and William Gropper's "Automobile Industry" offer further examples of heroic male labor.

24. This focus on the human control of labor was not restricted to public artworks. Mid-1930s advertisement campaigns by companies such as Plymouth, T.W.A., National Hotel Management, and Studebaker emphasized the human labor responsible for their products and services. One Studebaker ad appearing in the August 19, 1935, issue of *Time*, in fact, used the headline "It's the HUMAN ELEMENT that means the most in building Studebakers" (11). Featuring a middle-aged worker carefully installing a car window, the ad purposefully omits both images of and reference to the assembly line process. Instead, it highlights the "expert craftsmanship" and "guild-like pride in fine work" of the "over 6,300 skilled artisans" employed in the Studebaker organization" (11). Although it relies on nostalgic notions of the guild rather than on the physical heroism of Studebaker workers, the ad nevertheless addresses cultural concerns about the potential obsolescence of certain types of masculine industrial labor.

25. New Deal art laid the foundation for World War II imaging campaigns in other crucial ways. Not only were 1930s attempts to outline a shared past revamped

in wartime poster campaigns like the "This is America . . . Keep it Free!" series and Frank Capra's *Why We Fight* films, but the technical advances of the Poster Division of the FAP influenced the speed and quality with which wartime posters were produced. Many artists working for the WPA in the late 1930s and early 1940s also worked directly in national defense projects by creating posters, making maps, illustrating military manuals, designing camouflage, taking photographs, and decorating canteens (Harris 150).

26. In employing the term "natural body," I do not mean to suggest that F.D.R.'s body was somehow free from cultural inscription. Instead, I use the term as Kantorowicz and others do to imply that Roosevelt's physical, flesh-and-blood body was distinct, though never wholly separate, from its media representations.

27. Drawing on Theodore Greene's work, Diana Herndl notes in *Figuring Feminine Illness in American Fiction and Culture, 1840–1940* that early twentieth-century American magazines and biographies "equated success, manliness, and health. . . . Almost always in these magazine success stories, ill health for men was a sign of failure or evildoing" (180).

28. "Man of the Year," *Time*, January 7, 1935, 14.

29. Several key events occurred between the summer of 1944 and his death in 1945 that undermined the fiction of F.D.R's healthy body politic. Following his fourth presidential nomination acceptance speech in Chicago, a young editor under a tight deadline accidentally selected a terrible photograph of Roosevelt looking tired and haggard for distribution on the AP wire: "The next day . . . 'all hell broke loose,' as every anti-Roosevelt paper blew the picture up and displayed it prominently" (Goodwin 530).

Though Roosevelt easily won the 1944 election and made an important high-profile trip to Pearl Harbor to meet with his Pacific Command, by March 1945 F.D.R. could not keep up his "splendid deception." Exhausted from his grueling Yalta trip, Roosevelt appeared in front of Congress in his wheelchair on March 1, 1945, to brief members on the Yalta Conference. Joking about his decision to be seated in a soft comfortable chair, Roosevelt offered "the first reference he had ever made to his incapacity, to his impediment" (Frances Perkins qtd. in Goodwin 586). Although his only other public appearances in his wheelchair as president had been to wounded servicemen on his Pacific tour, Roosevelt seemed to have conceded, at last, that there existed a significant gap between his natural and political bodies.

30. An important exception to this, however, is Joseph Leyendecker's famous 1918 poster "Weapons for Liberty," which seemingly combines the figures of Liberty and Columbia. In this poster, Liberty trades her torch and book for sword and shield as she teams up with the Boy Scouts of America to protect her nation.

31. For further discussion of women as national symbols, see George Mosse's *The Image of Man* and Lynn Hunt's *The Family Romance of the French Revolution*.

32. Walton Rawls's *Wake Up, America!: World War I and the American Poster* offers perhaps the best survey and discussion of First World War posters.

33. One of the very few poster appearances of Lady Columbia occurs at the early stage of U.S. involvement in the war in Tom Woodburn's 1942 poster for the army, "Then, Now, Forever." The poster's emphasis is on America's past, as it shows seven generations of soldiers from the Revolutionary War to World War II. A very youthful, pretty, petite Columbia appears above them with laurels in her long, flowing hair and right hand. No longer armed with her sword, this Columbia is much more in keeping with republican female symbols in which women represented chastity and other "female"

virtues. Thus, despite her embodiment of contemporary beauty norms, she is very much tied to the past. This Columbia certainly does not embody America's hope for preserving democracy; that task obviously falls to the soldiers below her.

34. World War I era cartoons such as "A Damper on Opening Day on the Canal" and "Let Him Starve," for example, depicted an Uncle Sam who was not only frail and gaunt, but passive as well. In both cartoons, Sam stands idly by, looking across the ocean at clouds of war in Europe. Even after the U.S. entered the war, Sam largely retained his scarecrow physique and general reserve in political terms. For a survey of Uncle Sam imagery during World War I, see "Great War Cartoons" collection, RG 112, E 322, National Archives and Records Administration (hereafter NARA).

35. In addition to the poster depictions of Uncle Sam, other printed materials such as comic books and propaganda booklets played important roles in refiguring Uncle Sam in the popular American imagination. Steet and Smith's early 1941 comic "Remember Pearl Harbor," which interestingly enough predicted the December attack, provides yet another youthful, well-built Uncle Sam taking part in the war. A perusal of any home front memorabilia book likewise reveals that strong, youthful Sams were pervasive in American popular culture. See, for instance, Robert Heide and John Gilman's *Home Front America: Popular Culture of the World War II Era* and Gary Skoloff et al.'s *To Win the War: Home Front Memorabilia of World War II.*

36. Such studies are found in Dawn Ades et al.'s *Art and Power: Europe Under the Dictators, 1930–45;* J. A. Mangan's *Shaping the Superman: Fascist Body as Political Icon;* Mirzeoff's *Bodyscape;* Mosse's *The Image of Man,* as well as his essay "Beauty without Sensuality/The Exhibition *Entartete Kunst,*" in *"Degenerate Art": The Fate of the Avant-Garde in Nazi Germany;* and Klaus Theweleit's *Male Fantasies, Volume 2: Male Bodies: Psychoanalyzing the White Terror.*

37. Under this policy "sixteen thousand paintings, sculptures, prints, and drawings were removed from public collections" (Barron 6). The most marketable works were sold, others were burned, and some 650 were gathered for the famous Degenerate Art Exhibit *(Entartete Kunst)* that opened along side the Great German Art Exhibition in Munich in 1937. The idea of pairing the shows was to demonstrate that "a spiritually regenerated, nationalist . . . art would triumph over the degeneracy" of Modernism and the racial decay within Germany (Elliot, 271).

38. This idea of lending phallic strength and impenetrability to men's bodies was certainly not restricted to navy recruitment campaigns. In Jes William Schlaijker's 1944 poster "O'er the Ramparts," for example, a young B-17 pilot is shown towering above a formation of planes holding what appears to be a multiple-ton bomb. The bomb, positioned just below the man's waist, has obvious phallic connotations, which seem to lend the subject superhuman strength.

39. This is not to say, however, that America rejected eugenics rhetorics and policies. Between the late-nineteenth century and the early 1930s, in fact, Germany looked to selected state sterilization and marriage restriction laws in the U.S. for inspiration in developing its racial hygiene policies. While concerned with the general health of the country, though, the U.S. as a nation did not adopt Nazi racial hygiene, which linked eugenics with notions of Nordic superiority.

40. I am not suggesting, of course, that the influence between comic book heroes and wartime imagery was one way; clearly the war, 1940s muscle magazines, and changing postwar ideals of masculinity also had an impact on representations of the male body in comic books. For more on the complex relationship between the war and American comic books, see William Savage's *Comic Books and America, 1945–1954.*

41. These changes are very much in keeping with transformations in American bodybuilding. Over the course of the 1920s and 1930s, the instrumental function of the body as evinced in "strong man" figures gave way to a focus on the aesthetics of muscularity (Dutton 130–31).

2—CLASSIFIED BODIES

1. Prior to 1944 there was no system for "classifying the physical capacities of men" (Foster et al. 68) outside of the general categories I-A and I-B. Modeled after the Canadian PULHEMS system, the PULHES method of profiling offered a more detailed classification for rating specific physical and mental qualities. The physical profiling system rated physical capacity or stamina (P), upper extremities (U), lower extremities (L), hearing and ears (H), eyes and vision (E), and psychiatric state (S) individually on a scale from 1 to 4 (1 being the best grade and 4 the worst). Men whose PULHES was 211211 or better were placed in category A, "fit for duty in combat zones and for strenuous work," while those whose profile was between 232231 and 211211 were placed in category B, "fit for close combat support duties." Men making up the final category, C, had profiles between 333231 and 232231 and were deemed "fit for duty in lines of communications, or bases overseas, or in the continental United States" (Foster et al. 71). For more on the physical profiling system, see chapter five of William Foster et al.'s *Physical Standards in World War II.*

2. In December 1943, the classification for general military service changed from I-A to I-A (H), and the classification for limited military service changed from I-B to I-A (L). Also at the time, physically fit conscientious objectors were classified as I-A-O, available for noncombatant duty. Formerly conscientious objectors were IV-Es.

3. Numerical scores on the GCT were grouped into five categories, with Class I containing men of the highest general intelligence and Class V the lowest. These classes were used to determine who would be sent to officer candidate school (Classes I and II only). They were also utilized to ensure that different branches of the army received appropriate proportions of variously classed men. See Robert Palmer, Bell Wiley, and William Keast's *The Procurement and Training of Ground Combat Troops* for further discussion of the GCT and class assignments.

4. The total number of draft infractions was much higher; during the war 13,986 men were convicted and sentenced for violating the Selective Service Act for various reasons such as failing to report for induction, reporting false information, and refusing to comply with civilian work assignments. Please see pages 196–201 of Lewis Hershey's *Selective Service and Victory: The Fourth Report of the Director of the Selective Service* for additional discussion of these violations.

5. Beginning on January 1, 1942, local boards stopped giving full medical examinations and began screening for easily detectable defects, leaving most of the screening to the induction centers. Earlier problems had arisen when men, thinking they were fit for military service, took care of all their personal affairs only to be later rejected by the military at the induction station. Policies on preinduction physicals changed throughout the war; however, the induction physical was always the deciding factor in determining one's entrance into the service. For more on preinduction and induction exam policies see Foster et al.'s *Physical Standards in World War II.*

6. The MR 1-9 were general standards, revised throughout the war, for selecting regular army enlisted men. Despite the fact that the army and navy held joint medical examinations, the navy and marines had similar though separate physical

requirements. Additional Army Regulations 40–100 were also employed to determine physical standards in special situations such as admission to the U.S. Military Academy, ROTC, or flying school.

7. Full lyrics are available on the sound recording *Praise the Lord and Pass the Ammunition: Songs of World War I and World War II.*

8. See page 81 of Edgar Palmer's *G.I. Songs Written, Composed and/or Collected by the Men in the Service* for the song's entire lyrics.

9. Leonard Rowntree, "Physical Fitness for America," *Hygeia,* October 1944, 744–45, 790.

10. "Army's 'Rejection' Ratio Alarms President," *New York Times,* October 3, 1941, 8. Hereafter cited as "Reject."

11. Cabel Phillips, "What the Draft Reveals About Us," *New York Times,* July 13, 1941, 10, 24.

12. For further comparisons of World War II rejection statistics with those from World War I and the Civil War, see Nathan Sinai, "Physical Fitness and the Draft," *Hygeia,* October 1941, 546–52. For other dissenting opinions on the relationship between rejection figures and national fitness, see R. L. Sensenich's "Are We Fit or Not?" *Hygeia,* December 1941, 910–11, and "These Army Rejections," *New York Times,* October 19, 1941, 8.

13. Norman Wetzel, "The Simultaneous Screening and Assessment of School Children," *Journal of Health and Physical Education* 13.10 (1942): 576–77, 622–24.

14. With rejection rates exceeding expectations, in October 1941 the army adopted a policy of physical rehabilitation for "men between the ages of 21 and 28 years of age who had been found at induction to have remediable defects" (Foster et al. 18). At first men's physical defects were corrected prior to induction; however, following Pearl Harbor, men were inducted into the military with easily correctable defects such a poor teeth, impaired vision, hernias, and venereal diseases.

15. Physical Fitness Coaching School's *Lectures Given at the Physical Fitness Coaching School Conducted by the U.S. Naval Pre-Flight School and the University of North Carolina,* hereafter cited as Coaching School.

16. Capturing the general sentiment of many of my World War II survey respondents, Harold Goldstein reported that he noticed a "tremendous difference in strength and stamina." Lt. Colonel Alden Jacobs likewise noted that a combination of basic athletic drills, extensive hikes, marches, and bivouacs made him "lean and mean" as he "weighed in at 175, 6'2", [with] good cardiovascular and muscle tone" (World War II Survey).

17. Committee on Physical Education, Federal Security Agency, " Civilian Physical Fitness," *Journal of Health and Physical Education* 14.10 (1943): 518. Hereafter cited as "CPF."

18. Predating the Committee on Physical Fitness was the Division of Physical Fitness, operating under the jurisdiction of the ODHWS. The move from being a division of the ODHWS to a committee created in its own right represented increased prestige and support.

19. For a fuller discussion of the muscular Christianity movement in England and the United States, see Donald Hall's *Muscular Christianity: Embodying the Victorian Age,* David Macleod's *Building Character in the American Boy: The Boy Scouts, YMCA, and their Forerunners, 1870–1920,* and J. A. Mangan and James Walvin's *Manliness and Morality: Middle-Class Masculinity in Britain and America, 1800–1940.*

20. Rowntree's address was published in the article "Education, Health, and Physical Fitness," *Journal of Health and Physical Education* 14.7 (1943): 370–72, 388–91.

21. John Studebaker, "Our Schools Serve the War Effort," *Journal of Health and Physical Education* 14.9 (1943): 483.

22. Three 1943 *Journal of Physical Education* articles—Warren Arthur's "Physical Education for Young Men in Wartime" (May/June), Lynn Russell's "Wartime Influences on YMCA Physical Education" (Jan./Feb.), and Thomas O'Hare's "Vigor for Victory Program" (Jan./Feb.)—provide additional discussion of military influence on YMCA fitness programs.

23. I am not suggesting that the influence between the military and physical education programs was unidirectional. Since the late nineteenth century, the army and navy had looked to physical education and sports programs for training and recreational activities. For a history of the development of sports programs in the various armed forces, see Wanda Ellen Wakefield's *Playing to Win: Sports and the American Military, 1898–1945*.

24. The address was published later that year in a November *Journal of Health and Physical Education* article. David Brace, "Physical Fitness in Schools and Colleges," *Journal of Health and Physical Education* 15.9 (1944): 488–89.

25. E. B. Degroot, "Is Compulsory Military Training the Answer? Yes!" *Journal of Health and Physical Education* 16.2 (1945): 64.

26. One element of the army's venereal disease control program was the regular inspection of men's genitals for signs of venereal disease. Conducted at the company level under the supervision of a medic and a company officer, these examinations were nicknamed "short arm" inspections by servicemen. Not surprisingly, these inspections were unpopular with the men. As veteran Andrew Gordon explains, "the 'short arm' inspections were demeaning, especially when they were done en masse in open fields. [There was] no privacy whatever." I am indebted to Brian Walters and Andrew Gordon for details concerning these inspections (World War II Survey).

27. Although lesbians were also explicitly banned from the armed forces later in the war, I will be using the term "homosexual" to refer to male homosexuals. For a discussion of wartime military policies toward lesbians, see Leisa Meyer's *Creating G.I. Jane: Sexuality and Power in the Women's Army Corps during World War II* and Allan Bérubé's *Coming Out Under Fire: The History of Gay Men and Women in World War Two*.

28. The September 9, 1942, memorandum to Lt. Col. Julian C. Hyer of the Eighth Service Command, along with other War Department correspondence on the subject written between 1941 and 1944, is contained in the Sodomists file, RG 407, decimal file 250.1, box 992, NARA.

29. These questions were outlined in the School of Military Psychiatry's "Suggestions for the Neuro-psychiatric Screening of Troops," Office of the Surgeon, APO 502, South Pacific Base Command, January 1 to January 31, 1944: 1–3, RG 112, entry 31, box 308, NARA.

30. Dr. Tracy J. Putnam, "Suggested Rearrangements of MR 1-9 (Section XIX and XX) and AR 40-105," RG 215, entry 61, box 5, NARA. Hereafter cited by author.

31. While military doctors conducted their own studies to locate homosexuality in biology, they relied primarily on previous studies that linked homosexuality to constitutional factors. For insights into prewar studies of constitutional factors in homosexuality, see George Henry and Hugh Galbraith's "Constitutional Factors in Homosexuality," *The American Journal of Psychiatry* 91 (May 1934): 1249–70; Joseph Wortis's "A Note on the Body Build of the Male Homosexual," *The American Journal of Psychiatry* 93 (March 1937): 1121–25; and Terry and Urla's *Deviant Bodies*.

32. See, for example, A. C. Cornsweet and M. F. Hayes, "Conditioned Response to Fellatio," *The American Journal of Psychiatry* 103 (July 1946): 76–78; Herbert Greenspan and John Campbell, "The Homosexual as Personality Type," *The American Journal of Psychiatry* 101 (March 1945): 682–89; and B. H. McNeel, "War Psychiatry in Retrospect," *The American Journal of Psychiatry* 102 (January 1946): 500–6. Hereafter articles cited by author. Bérubé provides more in-depth coverage of some of these studies in the chapter "Pioneering Experts" in *Coming Out Under Fire*.

33. Many of these studies sought to find biological or constitutional clues to signal homosexuality. One study worth noting is E. L. Sevringhaus and John Chornyak's examination of the supposed abnormality of homosexual men's sex hormones present in urine samples, "A Study of Homosexual Adult Males," *Psychosomatic Medicine* 7.5 (1934) 302–5. Hoping to use urine tests as a way of screening out homosexuals, Sevringhaus and Chornyak studied urine samples from "overt homosexuals" and from a control group. To their surprise, they were unable to find clear "endocrine disturbance accompanying [homosexual] behavior" (303).

34. Nicolai Gioscia, "The Gag Reflex and Fellatio," *The American Journal of Psychiatry* 107 (November 1950): 380.

35. Brigadier General H. B. Lewis, "Sodomists," Memorandum No. W615-4-43, Adjutant's General Office, Washington, D.C., January 10, 1943, RG 407, Sodomists file 250.1, box 992, NARA. Hereafter cited by author.

36. Although the "true" homosexual was presumed to be the active partner in fellatio, he was supposed to be the passive partner during anal intercourse. Because of assumptions about the male homosexual's "feminine" nature, military psychiatrists generally presumed that "true" homosexuals would not penetrate another male.

37. G. C. Marshall, "Homosexuals," War Department Circular #3, Washington, D.C., January 3, 1944, RG 407, Sodomists file 250.1, box 992, NARA.

38. Reactions to the military's venereal disease programs were mixed. While some servicemen like Theodore Kelly and Kurt Leuser described the films as "simplistic, sophomoric" "Mickey Mouse movies," others found the films' and lectures' graphic depictions of venereal diseases to be "scary," even "gruesome." Richard Mercer, for example, said the films were effective because they "scared the hell out of us." During the most graphic films, John Gausz explains, "many got sick and some had to walk out . . . for fear of getting ill." Quotes are from World War II Survey responses from Theodore Kelly, Kurt Leuser, Richard Mercer, and John Gausz.

39. A number of military venereal disease prevention programs used in World War II originated in the First World War. In addition to closing red-light districts in the United States, the military and other government agencies issued pamphlets, posters, and prophylactics to servicemen in efforts to control VD rates. For further study of World War I programs, see Allan Brandt's *No Magic Bullet: A Social History of Venereal Disease in the United States since 1880*, especially chapters two and three, and Nancy K. Bristow's *Making Men Moral: Social Engineering during the Great War*.

40. Eliot Ness, "The Federal Government's Program in Attacking the Problem of Prostitution," Office of Defense Health and Welfare Services, Washington, D.C.: 1–7, RG 215, entry 37, box 1, NARA. Hereafter cited by author.

41. "The Facts About Social Protection," Office of Community War Services, Social Protection Division, Washington, D.C.: 3, RG 215, entry 37, box 1, NARA. Hereafter cited as "The Facts."

42. "Relationships of the Army and Navy, the U.S. Public Health Service, the Office of Defense Health and Welfare Services, and the American Social Hygiene Association." Reprinted from *The Journal of Social Hygiene* 29.2 (February 1943): 1–6. RG 215, entry 37, box 1, NARA.

43. The pamphlet was part of a larger Social Protection Division educational campaign featuring the theme "She May Look Clean—But." Many posters using this slogan featured images of wholesome-looking, clean-cut white women, who, despite their innocent appearance, presented terrible menaces to the health of servicemen and civilians alike. The posters warned that "pick-ups, 'good time' girls, [and] prostitutes SPREAD SYPHILIS and GONORRHEA." The premise behind the "She May Look Clean" campaign was that all women, not just the more easily identified prostitute, presented potential threats to men's sexual health. Like the pamphlet, the posters ultimately focused on the loss of manpower that resulted from venereal infection, reminding viewers that "you can't beat the Axis if you get VD."

44. These and other World War II military venereal disease prevention posters can be found in the Walter Reed World War II Historical Collection, OHA 355, National Museum of Health and Medicine's Otis Historical Archives.

45. This War Department pamphlet, along with other military brochures on venereal disease, may be found in RG 215, entry 44, box 1, NARA.

46. Unlike military posters and pamphlets that presented servicemen's bodies as special wards to be protected, ASHA posters often depicted civilian men as protectors of home and nation. One New York ASHA poster (#2), for example, focused on a man who "had a blood test and examination to protect his job and family." Whereas the serviceman's ultimate status as a protector of America was unquestioned, perhaps the ASHA felt that it was important to preserve the civilian man's protective role because his lack of military service might raise questions about his manhood.

47. G. C. Marshall, "Venereal Disease," Circular #249, War Department, Washington, D.C., December 5, 1941, RG 215, entry 47, box 1, NARA.

48. "Excerpts from Statements Made at the Joint Army and Navy Conference," Washington, D.C., February 28, 1941, RG 215, entry 37, box 1, NARA.

49. Various mechanical and chemical prophylaxis kits were distributed and sold at post exchanges during the war. Ten-cent kits containing three condoms and lubricating jelly were available at the PX and vending machines. Historian Allan Brandt estimates that "as many as fifty million condoms were sold or freely distributed each month of the war" (164). Other kits, intended for use after intercourse, contained various chemical treatments like sulfathiazole, "calomel, a soap-impregnated cloth, and an instructions sheet" (Hoff, vol. 3: 199). For a more extensive discussion of PRO-KITs and other forms of prophylaxis, see Ebbe Curtis Hoff's *Preventative Medicine in World War II, Volume 3: Personal Health and Immunization*, especially pages 198–204.

50. J. D. Ratcliff, "The War Against Syphilis," *Collier's*, April 10, 1943, 14–16.

51. According to a January 28, 1944, Office of War Information Report, "Changing Views on the Venereal Disease Problem" (#C23), the government considered compulsory blood testing and treatment programs for the general public. The report advised against mandatory testing, offering the following reasons: "because 'compulsory' is a red flag, because some people would feel insulted, because some would fear exposure." It further stated, "that compulsory blood testing and also compulsory treatment are already in effect to some extent; the usual belief, however, is that the public will accept this much and no more" (iii–iv). The report is available in RG 215, entry 37, box 8, NARA.

3—REPRESENTING WOUNDED BODIES

1. Although most scholars agree with this statistic, placing the mortality rate somewhere between 3 and 4 percent, some sources offer slightly higher mortality rates for the army. According to U.S. Bureau of the Census statistics, in the army the rate for wounded who subsequently died from battle injuries was 4.5 percent. The navy and marines boasted a slightly lower combined rate of 3.2 percent. Nevertheless, these figures marked significant advances in the medical treatment of American war wounded; during the Civil War 13.3 percent of the wounded later died of their injuries, while between 8 and 9 percent died of battle wounds in World War I. For further study of war casualty and treatment statistics, see page 1140 of the Census Bureau's *The Statistical History of the United States: From Colonial Times to the Present.* Also see Albert Cowdrey's *Fighting for Life: American Military Medicine in World War II* and Frank Reister's *Medical Statistics in World War II.*

2. As *Powers of Horror* reveals, bodily fluids are only some of the elements that constitute the abject; certain foods, waste, corpses—other entities specifically rendered improper or unclean by a given culture—can be considered abject (Kristeva 2).

3. I am not suggesting, of course, that this was the primary reason for withholding bloody pictures of American war dead; obviously morale and notions of propriety played a key role in the decision.

4. This line comes from Norman Mailer's *The Naked and the Dead.* Red first dispenses this advice to Hennessey before their beach landing at Anopopei, but many of the veteran combat soldiers repeat the phrase throughout the novel.

5. The idea of the wounded part of the body as alien also appears frequently in nonfiction wounding narratives. In *We Are the Wounded*, for example, Keith Wheeler describes the experience of marine Pete Zurlinden: "It twisted away from his body at a grotesque angle that proved it wasn't any part of him. It was a leg but it was a total stranger" (56). Later in the text, Wheeler proceeds to characterize men with traumatic amputations as "living fragments" and men with "shattered bodies" (111).

6. While there is general agreement on the number of U.S. battle deaths, there are inconsistencies in statistics on the number of nonfatal wounded. The U.S. Bureau of the Census gives a figure of 670,846 (1140) while *Defense Almanac 91* (Sept/Oct #47) offers a slightly higher figure of 671,846.

7. Sergeant Roland Winter, for example, recalls that the case of jungle rot he contracted in Leyte did not clear up until 1948—more than two years after his discharge. According to Winter, doctors in the U.S. had little experience treating tropical diseases and thus could offer few cures (WWII Survey). For further discussion of Pacific and other theaters' diseases, see Cowdrey's *Fighting for Life* or the Army Medical Department volumes on communicable diseases.

8. These statistics vary slightly from those given in the army's *Medical Statistics in World War II*, where the number of admissions is purported to be 16,744,724.

9. Albert Groves Hulett, "Malingering," in *War Medicine: A Symposium,* ed. Winfield Scott Pugh (New York: Philosophical Library, 1942), 519–30.

10. 184th General Hospital Interview, Corporal Homer Miller (712th Tank Battalion, 90th Division); 117th General Hospital Interview, Lieutenant Charles R. Crispin (23rd Infantry, 5th Division). All hospital interviews cited in this chapter are from RG407, entry 427, boxes 24240–42, NARA.

11. 184th General Hospital Interview, Corporal Homer Miller (712th Tank Battalion, 90th Division).

12. 192nd General Hospital Interview, Colonel H.V. Lyon (315 Troop Carrier Group); 55th General Hospital Interview, Private Elton Cannon (104th Infantry, 26th Division); 55th General Hospital Interview, Lieutenant William M. Obley (513th Parachute Infantry, 17th Airborne Division).

13. The circumstances surrounding an injury also become important in novels featuring wounded veterans. In works such as *Ward Twenty, The Long Walk,* and *Year One,* the "heroes" or most noble characters are those whose wounds were obtained bravely in battle. In these texts, cowardly, clownish characters receive their wounds in ignominious situations such as running from a brothel while it is bombed, as in the case of *The Long Walk*.

14. See Joanna Bourke's *Dismembering the Male: Men's Bodies, Britain, and the Great War* for a discussion of post–World War I representations of wounded soldiers in Britain. Also see Erin O'Connor's "'Fractions of Men': Engendering Amputation in Victorian Culture" for analysis of post–Civil War constructions in the United States. David Serlin's chapter "The Other Arms Race: The Politics of Prosthetics during the Cold War" provides an excellent overview of recent studies of prosthetics and rehabilitation medicine.

15. Scenes of valorous rescue are present in posters such as Lester Beall's 1943 "Dare You Say or Think You Do Not Feel the Bullet," which shows a Coast Guard captain assisting a sailor with bullet wound in the shoulder; Saul Tepper's 1944 "We Caught Hell," which depicts a soldier carrying a wounded man over his shoulder as he escapes an enemy ambush; and the anonymous "Our Fighters Deserve the Best," which portrays a G.I. helping a wounded man while still holding his rifle high in a bellicose pose.

16. See Susan Hartmann's *The Home Front and Beyond: Women in the 1940s,* David Gerber's "Heroes and Misfits: The Troubled Social Reintegration of Disabled Veterans in *The Best Years of Our Lives,*" and Timothy Shuker-Haines's "Home is the Hunter: Representations of Returning World War II Veterans and the Reconstruction of Masculinity, 1944–1951."

17. Shuker-Haines's study "Home is the Hunter" offers a more in-depth discussion of the multiple models of postwar masculinities. Shuker-Haines contends that there are three constructions of postwar masculinity: domestic masculinity, where "romance and family heal the veteran" (50); reactionary masculinity, where the veteran exists as an isolated individual outside of a corrupt, feminized society (50); and syncretic masculinity, which incorporates both domestic and reactionary masculinity. For further discussion of these models see the introduction and conclusion of "Home is the Hunter."

18. Contemporary periodicals with primarily female readerships also stressed women's roles in restoring wounded veteran's confidence and masculinity. *Collier's,* for example, printed stories such as "They See Without Looking," which detailed the healing powers of visits by junior hostesses to battle casualties in veterans hospitals. Barrie Stavis, "They See Without Looking," *Collier's,* September 8, 1945, 33, 57.

19. Earlier in the novel, George outlines other reasons to reject embodied subjectivity. During a homecoming dinner, George hints at his thoughts on the limitations of the human body, pointing to the lobsters they are about to consume as superior embodied beings. After remarking that lobsters are "smarter in some ways than [humans] are," George explains his reasoning: "Ever hear of a human who lost an arm or a leg growing another exactly like it? That's one thing lobsters can do" (17).

20. *Physical Reconditioning: War Department Technical Manual 8-292,* Washington, D.C.: U.S. Government Printing Office, 1944: 2–3.

21. Not only does the film fail to present marriage as the principal means of rehabilitating the wounded veteran, but also it suggests, at points, that women can hinder veterans' recoveries. The subplot focusing on Norm Butler, for example, involves a serious romantic relationship that ends not with a wedding—as Norm had planned—but with Laverne taking $900 of his money and fleeing to Canada. Far from promising rehabilitation through feminine curative powers, the subplot demonstrates that many wounded veterans must rely on their self-discipline and strenuous physical reconditioning to regain their masculinity and lost social status.

22. The Paralyzed Veterans Association Board at the hospital ultimately helps Ken come to this conclusion by voting to dismiss him from the hospital after considering his drunk driving charges. As Norm explains, however, the board's decision is not meant to be punitive; Norm casts the deciding vote in favor of discharge because he wants Wiloceck to regain his independence and sense of responsibility.

23. A July 1946 *Journal of the American Medical Association (JAMA)* article estimated that by 1946 there were "approximately 23,000 veterans amputees throughout the country" ("Amputees Get Cards" 1009). Other sources, however, offer different statistics. In his article "Artificial Limbs—Today and Tomorrow," for example, F. S. Strong cites a slightly higher number of 27,000. Historian Geoffrey Perrett suggests that the figure was much lower—17,000. While Perrett's figure may refer only to combat-wounded amputees, I cannot account for the divergence in statistics. The figure of 100,000 civilian amputations comes from page 340 of Perrett's *Days of Sadness, Years of Triumph*.

24. "Discussion of Amputations," *JAMA* 124.15 (1944): 1047.

25. "For Neglected Heroes," *Time*, August 27, 1945, 90, 93. Hereafter cited as "Neglected."

26. Qtd. in "Further Requests for Better Artificial Limbs for Wounded Servicemen," *JAMA* 128.15 (1945): 1115.

27. "Army to Establish Committee on Prosthetic Devices," *JAMA* 127.14: 925.

28. According to a March 1944 *JAMA* article, although the United States seemingly conducted little of its own research during this time, limb manufacturers and hospitals did benefit from advances in British prosthetic research. Since the end of the First World War, the Artificial Limb Center in Roehampton had been modernizing artificial limbs, designing models of "light and simple construction." During World War II, American surgeons and doctors trained at Roehampton to learn surgical and limb-fitting advances. These techniques were utilized at overseas military hospitals as well as at the fourteen limb-fitting centers in the United States ("The Artificial Limb Center at Roehampton," *JAMA* 124.12 [1944]: 790).

29. "Arms & the Men," letter, *Time*, September 24, 1945, 7.

30. These figures are taken from "Artificial Limb Production to Be Standardized," *JAMA* 127.8 (1945): 468. For further background on postwar developments in artificial limbs, see the following *JAMA* articles: "Amputees Get Cards Authorizing Free Prosthetic Repairs," 131.12 (1946): 1009; "Army to Establish Committee on Prosthetic Devices," 127.14: 925; "The Artificial Limb Center at Roehampton," 124.12 (1944): 790; "Development of 'Cosmetic' Artificial Hand at Walter Reed," 130.6 (1946): 358; "Development of Improved Artificial Hand by Navy Technicians," 128.16 (1945): 1178; and "Patterson and Bradley Pledge Intensified Research on Artificial Limbs," 131.16 (1946): 1364. Hereafter articles cited by title.

31. "The Price They Paid," *Time*, November 26, 1945, 85–86.

32. The United States soon started sharing its advances in prosthetics with other war-torn nations. Relief agencies established artificial limb programs to aid in

the development and production of prosthetics in the Soviet Union, Greece, Yugoslavia, Ukraine, and Poland. In the Philippines, the army set up its own artificial limb shop to "provide facilities for training Filipino personnel in the manufacture of artificial limbs, in addition to supplying amputees' requirements" ("Army to Set Up Artificial Limb Shop in Philippines," *JAMA* 130.16 [1946]: 1166). For additional information on U.S. efforts to aid foreign artificial limb production, see "Artificial Limb Program in Liberated Countries," *JAMA* 130.11 (1946): 710; and "Artificial Limb Program for Soviet Union," *JAMA* 130.7 (1946): 440.

    33. "New Limbs for Old," *Time,* January 22, 1945, 52. Hereafter cited as "New Limbs."

    34. "McGonegal Showed Them," *Time,* February 14, 1944, 21.

    35. Atha Thomas, "The Permanent Prosthesis," *JAMA* 124.15 (1944): 1044.

    36. "Disabled Veterans to Train for Skilled Jobs, " *JAMA* 130.14 (1946): 942.

4—"WHITE MAN'S WAR?"

    1. "White Man's War?" *Time,* March 2, 1942, 13–14. Although "race" was still frequently used as a scientific category during World War II, I will employ the term as a discursive classification tied to cultural, historical, political, and linguistic contexts. Because this chapter will examine the particular cultural constructions of race in the United States during the war, I will often utilize the terms "white" and "black," in keeping with racial designations of the time. As Susan Bordo has pointed out, "When describing the content of racist ideology, ethnic or national descriptions would be incorrect and misleading" (*Unbearable Weight* 301). For further examination of the term "race," see Elazar Barkan's *The Retreat of Scientific Racism: Changing Concepts of Race in Britain and the United States between the Wars* and Michael Banton's chapter "Race as Designation" in *Racial Theories.*

    2. See bell hook's *Yearning: Race, Gender, and Cultural Politics,* Schiebinger's *Nature's Body,* Homi Bhabha's "The Other Question: Difference, Discrimination and the Discourse of Colonialism," and Anne Cranny-Francis's chapter "Embodying the Other" in *The Body in the Text.*

    3. In *War without Mercy: Race and Power in the Pacific War,* John Dower describes the "hidden Holocaust" as the "conveniently forgotten one—in which the annihilation of the Jews was actively supported by French and Dutch citizens, Poles, Hungarians, Rumanians, Slovaks, Ukrainians, Lithuanians, and Latvians" (4). Dower also connects the "hidden Holocaust" to British and U.S. failures to publicize Nazi genocide practices and to take in Jewish refugees. For further study of the international eugenics movements informing Nazi policies, see Robert Proctor's *Racial Hygiene: Medicine under the Nazis* and Michael Burleigh and Wolfgang Wippermann's *The Racial State: Germany 1933–1945.*

    4. A March 9, 1945, edition of "The Soldier Speaks" in *Yank* captured these differing views of the German and Japanese enemy. Addressing the question "Which was the greater menace to our country and our values, Germany or Japan?" servicemen frequently commented that Germany was "like us," while Japan was "completely foreign." For example, Sergeant Nathan Minkoff noted that "We always thought of Germans as people like ourselves," while Corporal Phil Stearns wrote that Germany was "a nice, agreeable member of the family of nations" (11). Technical Sergeant Jerold Gorby, meanwhile, characterized the Japanese as "a hideous, barbaric race, a race that lives on the misfortune of the illiterate masses" (11).

5. This was the name of John Trevor's quota plan, which served as the basis for 1924 immigration quotas. See Allan Chase's *The Legacy of Malthus: The Social Costs of the New Scientific Racism* for additional discussion of the origins of the 1924 immigration quotas.

6. The original 1882 act was a temporary law that was extended for ten additional years in 1892. For additional discussion of anti-Asian legislation, see Roger Daniel's *Prisoners without Trial: Japanese Americans in World War II* and Daniel et al.'s *Japanese Americans: From Relocation to Redress.*

7. C. Vann Woodward's seminal study *The Strange Career of Jim Crow* provides an excellent overview of the history and particular ordinances of the Jim Crow system in the United States.

8. For further discussion of Hollywood's efforts to depict a pluralistic military and an ethnically diverse American nation, see Dick's *The Star-Spangled Screen* and Koppes and Black's *Hollywood Goes to War.*

9. A number of recent historical texts have been devoted to this topic. For further study, see James et al.'s *Fighting Racism in World War II*, Neil Wynn's *The Afro-American and the Second World War*, Mary Motley's *The Invisible Soldier: The Experience of the Black Soldier, World War II*, and Nat Brandt's *Harlem at War: The Black Experience in World War II.* See also chapters nine through twelve of Bernhard Nalty's *Strength for the Fight: A History of Black Americans in the Military* and chapter six of John Morton Blum's *V Was for Victory: Politics and American Culture during World War II.*

10. In 1943 alone, a Fisk University study reported, there were 242 racial riots in 47 cities (Graham 449).

11. "Portrait of a Japanese," *Time*, January 12, 1942, 17–18; Cecil Brown, "How Japan Wages War," *Life*, May 11, 1942, 98–108. Hereafter *Time* article cited as "Portrait."

12. Paul Williams Thompson et al., *The Jap Army* (Washington, D.C.: Infantry Journal, 1942). The notion of the Japanese enemy as somehow "unknowable" continued throughout the war. Various books and articles such as *Life*'s August 16, 1943, piece "How Strong is Japan?" included disclaimers that the information presented about the Japanese was based on "facts and guesses . . . plucked out of a fog of ignorance and deception" (87). Even during the final year of the war, Otto Tolischus began his study of the enemy *Through Japanese Eyes* with the following lines: "The Japanese are usually considered to be a mysterious, inscrutable, secretive, and uncommunicative people, incomprehensible in their mental processes, unfathomable in their emotional reactions, and unpredictable in their actions" (foreword).

13. "Portrait of Pvt. Moto," *Yank*, July 1, 1942, 14. Hereafter cited as "Moto."

14. This is not to say that the European theater was free from wartime atrocities and the grisly treatment of bodies. Nazi treatment of Holocaust victims was nothing if not ghastly and dehumanizing.

15. Immigrants from the Philippines were originally not included in this restriction because they were citizens of a U.S. territory. A separate 1934 act, however, banned all Filipino immigration after the Philippines was given limited independence as a U.S. commonwealth.

16. Please see Jachinson Chan's *Chinese American Masculinities: From Fu Manchu to Bruce Lee* for a more detailed discussion of the history and respective popular cultural roles of the Fu Manchu and Charlie Chan stereotypes.

17. For further analysis of the events leading to and the significance of the Magnuson Act, see chapter seven of Dower's *War Without Mercy,* chapter one of Lisa Lowe's *Immigrant Acts: On Asian American Cultural Politics,* and chapter six of Ronald Takaki's *Double Victory: A Multicultural History of America during World War II.*

18. Several "Remember Caloocan!" leaflets along with an extensive collection of Japanese propaganda distributed in the Philippines are available in the Lee Telesco collection, accession #47025-8.30, box 1, Hoover Institution Archives.

19. For a more detailed discussion of the film and its history, see chapter nine of Koppes and Black's *Hollywood Goes to War.*

20. This egalitarian treatment is somewhat noteworthy for a World War II combat novel. Niven Busch's 1944 novel *They Dream of Home* is more typical in its narrative treatment of an ethnically diverse cast of characters. Although the group's small number prevents the inclusion of certain stock characters such as the drawling Texan, it does contain an African American, a Native American, a "young Jew with a broken nose" (Busch 3), and two non–ethnically marked Protestant men. In addition to the group's pluralism, the novel, like Uris's *Battle Cry,* makes frequent mention of the characters' supposed racial tolerance and open-mindedness. In one such passage, the narrator explains, "Neither in training nor combat had a man's race been held a subject for comment; whether Slav, Hawaiian, Indian, or Filipino, his status had been determined by his personal qualities" (Busch 241). Nevertheless, despite this apparent pluralism, open-mindedness, and racial tolerance, the novel quickly reveals its privileging of white American manhood. Although the novel purports to detail the experiences of and bonds between all five men, the three racially and religiously marked men are quickly marginalized from a narrative perspective. The two white Protestant characters, Sergeant Earl T. Wastrous (Gunny) and Cliff Harper, and their attempts to solidify their masculinity quickly take center stage.

21. Although several hundred Italian and German residents classified as "enemy aliens" were arrested and questioned following Executive Order 9066, German and Italian Americans were not subject to the same harassment or laws mandating internment that Japanese Americans were. In fact, in October 1942, Roosevelt "lifted the enemy-alien designation from them and established simplified procedures for their rapid naturalization" (Blum 154).

22. I have created the term "pop ethnography" to describe the many nonscientific studies of human culture that appeared in popular American periodicals during the war. In addition to these briefer, less scholarly informed articles, *National Geographic* continued to devote substantial space to studies of the peoples and lands American service personnel were encountering in the Pacific. Articles by British and American servicemen with titles such as "What the Fighting Yanks See" (October 1944), "War Finds its Way to the Gilbert Islands" (January 1943), and "Fiji Patrol on Bougainville" (January 1945) highlight the ways in which the war shaped the content of *National Geographic* during the early and mid-1940s.

23. Other pop ethnographies such as Noel Busch's June 26, 1944, *Life* article "Random Notes on Pacific Life" base their arguments about American superiority on Western technology and approaches to island occupations. Busch explains:

> There are two ways to fight amphibious, hemispheric, explorative warfare. One is to adapt yourself to the terrain, to squirm into the sand or to climb the trees, to cross the land on foot and the water by barge. The other is to adapt the terrain to yourself by building houses and chopping the trees down, constructing roads and crossing the water

in floating airdromes full of planes. The former, well-suited to their character, is the method by which the Japs won their temporary empire. The latter, well-suited to the U.S. character, is the method by which it is being taken from them. (55)

24. E. J. Kahn Jr., "The Army Life: Somewhere in New Guinea," *The New Yorker Book of War Pieces* (New York: Reynal and Hitchcock, 1947) 127–29.

25. These non-fraternization policies were also used to curtail black servicemen's interactions with "native" women. In these instances, it seems that the men's status as American citizens was privileged over their racial identity. Because these non-fraternization policies varied so greatly from place to place, it is difficult to discern the military's official position on this topic.

26. As Beth Bailey and David Farber have noted, in Hawaii most "native" women and "hula girls" were actually not Hawaiian at all: "Hawaiian women, by and large, were big and strong and solid. They did not look the way men from the mainland, schooled by Hollywood, expected them to look. The men preferred their exotic women on the petite side" (212). Thus many of these "native" and "hula" women were Puerto Rican or Filipino.

27. The former three statistics come from Takaki's *Double Victory* (161, 61, 115), while the latter three figures are taken from Hershey's *Selective Service and Victory* (189).

28. See chapter nine of Nalty's *Strength for the Fight* for a more complete discussion of the complex political discussions and actions—especially those related to the 1940 presidential election—that led to the expanded opportunities for African Americans in the military and war defense industries.

29. White officers throughout the armed forces echoed these sentiments. In a December 20, 1944, memo to Assistant Secretary of War John McCloy, Civilian Aide Truman Gibson provided many examples of racist attitudes held by white officers in the army's 92nd Division. Truman reported that Colonel McCaffery claimed that "the Negro is panicky and his environment has not conditioned him to accept responsibilities," while Major Thomas Arnold mentioned that he had "no confidence in the fighting ability of Negro soldiers" (2). The three-page memo, along with other correspondence on the 92nd, is available in the Benjamin O. Davis, Sr. Papers, box T-6, U.S. Military History Institute (USMHI).

30. For example, magazines such as *Time* and *Life* called the black press "sensational," "thin-skinned and irritable," "irresponsible," "excitable," and dissatisfied. See *Life's* "Negroes at War," June 15, 1942, 86, and *Time's* "Unhappy Soldier," July 10, 1944, 65.

31. Ralph Martin, "Negroes in Combat," *Yank*, February 23, 1945, 6–7.

32. Despite efforts to slight the accomplishments of African American soldiers, the government, press, and private organizations "distributed more respectful visual images of blacks than it had in the previous century and a half" (Roeder, *Censored War* 45).

33. Please see the Benjamin O. Davis papers, box T-6, USMHI.

34. Daniel Kryder's *Divided Arsenal: Race and the American State during World War II* provides detailed discussion of the many instances of white military police violence and miscarriages of justice that occurred in military posts throughout the United States during the war.

35. "Scandal at Selfridge," *Time*, May 17, 1943, 65–66; "Colman's Court," *Time*, September 27, 1943, 65–66.

36. "Survey Excerpts from A Study of Negro and White Soldiers' Attitude Toward the Army," Benjamin O. Davis papers, box T-3, USMHI.

37. Truman Gibson, memorandum to Brigadier General B. O. Davis, June 30, 1943, Benjamin O. Davis papers, box T-6, USMHI.

38. These statistics are confirmed and further discussed by Bernard Nalty in chapter eleven of *Strength for the Fight*.

39. Edwin R. Carter, "The Racial Problem in England," Benjamin O. Davis papers, box T-6, USMHI. Hereafter cited by author.

40. Graham Smith's *When Jim Crow Met John Bull* provides a thorough and insightful discussion of the treatment of black U.S. troops in England.

41. After black servicemen protested, the complete ban was downgraded; with special permission, servicemen could keep photographs marked "'For personal use only—not for publication'" (Roeder, *Censored War* 57).

42. Howard Kessinger, "Memorandum for Colonel Berry," War Department General Staff, Personnel Division, Washington, D.C., August 28, 1943, Benjamin O. Davis papers, box T-3, USMHI.

5—(RE)MEMBERING THE DEAD

1. The list of deceased servicemen, "Killed In Action," and the accompanying editorial, "The American Purpose," appeared on pages 15–38 and page 39 respectively in the July 5, 1943, issue of *Life*.

2. With the exception of the Civil War, U.S. battle and overall military deaths from previous wars pale in comparison. According to *Defense Almanac* 91 (Sept/Oct #47), U.S. war deaths in previous conflicts were as follows: Revolutionary War—4,435 (battle related); War of 1812—2,260 (battle related); Mexican War—1,733 (battle related), 11,550 (other causes); Spanish-American War—385 (battle related), 2,061 (other causes); World War I—53,402 (battle related), 63,114 (other causes).

3. Several scholars have examined World War I's impact on modern (and modernist) conceptions of death. Bourke's *Dismembering the Male* examines changes in British funerary practices and customs initiated by the high casualty rates of World War I; Edith Wyschogrod's *Spirit in Ashes* explores the broader impact of twentieth-century man-made mass death and "the death world" from a philosophical perspective; and Alan Friedman's essay "Modernist Attitudes toward Death" in *Death and the Quest for Meaning* analyzes literary and cultural narratives to explore the effects of World War I upon modernist perspectives on death.

4. This statistic comes from the *Arlington National Cemetery Home Page* June 22, 1999, <http://www.arlingtoncemetery.com/unk-vn.htm>.

5. See Kristin Hass's *Carried to the Wall*, George Mosse's *Fallen Soldiers*, and Kurt Piehler's *Remembering War the American Way*.

6. In fact, by August 1943 "only one letter out of some 4,000 received from next of kin of the dead had not requested the return of remains to the homeland" (Steere and Boardman 179). During the last two years of the war, when heavier casualties were sustained (over two-thirds of fatalities occurred during 1944 and 1945), this percentage dropped significantly. The general estimate, though, was that 70 percent of families would favor repatriation.

7. These arguments were raised in Blake Ehrlich's article "Shall We Bring Home the Dead of World War II?" *Saturday Evening Post*, May 31, 1947, 25, 127–28, 130.

8. An additional 78,956 missing are commemorated in various U.S. memorials

at home and abroad. Plane crashes, burials at sea, and burials in remote locations and inhospitable climates account for a good portion of these unrecovered remains (Nishiura 7). Presumably the 63,000 military personnel not accounted for in these statistics were in the United States at the time of their deaths.

9. As George Roeder observes in *The Censored War,* the U.S. military and government were especially careful to censor war information in the six months following Pearl Harbor. The lack of any U.S. offensive or victories caused them to worry that "the public might become demoralized or impatient for peace" (8). A mid-1942 opinion poll, in fact, revealed that "'three out of every ten Americans would view favorably a negotiated peace with the German army leaders'" (Roeder, *Censored War* 8).

10. Quentin Reynolds, "They're Coming Home," *Collier's,* August 11, 1945, 19, 34.

11. The notion of dead servicemen's bodies transforming overseas cemeteries into American soil surfaces as a recurring theme in two June 1957 *National Geographic* articles, General George Marshall's "Our War Memorials Abroad: A Faith Kept" and Howell Walker's "Here Rests in Honored Glory. . . ." For further discussion of creation of the World War II's overseas cemeteries and the ABMC's maintenance of them, see Elizabeth Nishiura's *American Battle Monuments* and Dean Holt's *American Military Cemeteries.*

12. "War Memorials that Further Practical Democracy," *The American City,* October 1944, 72.

13. Edith Stern, "Legacy to the Living," Commission for Community War Memorials for Physical Fitness brochure, Washington, D.C., 1945, RG215, entry 22, box 2, NARA.

14. For arguments opposing living memorials, see Margaret Cresson's "Memorials Symbolic of the Spirit of Man," *New York Times Magazine,* July 22, 1945, 14–15, 38–39, and Lewis Mumford's "Monuments and Memorials," *Good Housekeeping,* January 1945, 17, 106.

15. Marling and Wetenhall's *Iwo Jima: Monuments, Memories, and the American Hero* provides additional discussion of the various Iwo Jima memorials that were built during the immediate postwar and cold war period. Their study also provides insightful analysis of the desires for traditional heroism that gave rise to these and other war monuments.

16. These initial plans changed slightly over the next few years. Between 1948 and 1950, it was decided that the selection ceremony would take place at Independence Hall in Philadelphia and that a Medal of Honor winner would make the selection instead of the president. Additionally, planners decided to add a sixth candidate from the Alaska Command. For additional background on early plans for interring World War II's Unknown Soldier, see B. C. Mossman and M. W. Stark's *The Last Salute: Civil and Military Funerals, 1921–1969* and the Defense Department's *The Unknowns of World War II and Korea.* The latter source is available in RG 92, entry 1898D, box 2, NARA.

17. While the selection and burial of America's first Unknown Soldier did much to unite a nation that had not entirely backed the First World War, the ceremonies also strengthened America's international relations and commitments to world peace. The selection ceremonies at Chalons-sur-Marne incorporated French military leaders and top officials, and the final funeral services at Arlington Cemetery involved numerous foreign dignitaries. During the ceremonies, the Unknown Soldier was not only awarded the U.S. Medal of Honor but also received Belgium's Croix de Guerre, England's Victoria Cross, France's Medaille Militaire, Romania's Virutea Militara, Italy's Medal of Valor, Czechoslovakia's War Cross, and Poland's Virtuti Militari. Since many of these awards had never been presented to a foreigner,

the ceremonies confirmed America's status as a world power and her growing international esteem. Moreover, as Kurt Piehler has noted, the final burial ceremonies strategically "coincided with a major international conference on disarmament in Washington" (121). Harding's address, which made a plea for peace, further associated the First Unknown Soldier with pacifism.

18. In an attempt to reassure the American people that the U.S. had not fallen behind in the space race, the December 6, 1957, launch of the Vanguard missile was televised. When it rose only two feet and crashed, the press stepped up its criticisms of America's space and weapons programs, calling the missile "Flopnik" and "Stayputnik" (Patterson 418).

19. The ceremony for selecting the Korean and TransPacific Unknown was a joint ceremony. Medal of Honor winner Ned Lyle selected the Korean Unknown from four possible candidates.

20. Defense Department's *The Unknowns of World War II and Korea* hereafter cited as *Unknowns*. The U.S. Atlantic Fleet's "Narrative Report of World War II and Korean Conflict Unknown Ceremonies" provides additional details about the selection ceremonies (RG 92, entry E1898D, box 1, NARA).

21. All quotations from Eisenhower's address to the Medal of Honor winners are taken from "Text of President's Remarks to Heroes," *New York Times,* May 31, 1958, 4.

22. As Irwin Peters explained in his survey response, "11% of my graduating class were killed. This is what I cannot forget" (WWII Survey). Peters's comments were echoed by other survey participants who found the loss of friends during the war to be the hardest part of readjustment.

23. "Commission of Fine Arts Approves National WWII Memorial Preliminary Design," *National World War II Memorial Home Page* June 22, 1999, <http://www.wwiimemorial.com/news/CFA%20approval%20May%2099.htm>.

24. "Design Concept," *National World War II Memorial Home Page* June 22, 1999, <http://www.wwiimemorial.com/news/Concept.htm>.

25. "Memorial Design," *National World War II Memorial Home Page* February 13, 2003, <http://www.wwiimemorial.com/default.asp?page=design.asp&subpage=memorialdesign>.

26. One trend in Holocaust memorialization is displaying the personal belongings (i.e., eyeglasses, shoes, coats, etc.) or hair of victims in museum exhibits. Because "there is still something of the subject bound up with them," these bodily and personal remains evoke the Holocaust's corporeal destruction in a different way than a list of names does (Grosz 81). While she does not discuss Holocaust memorialization practices, Elizabeth Grosz offers an interesting discussion of the psychically invested qualities of "detachable" body parts in *Volatile Bodies,* especially on pages 80–82. For additional study of Holocaust museums and memorials, see James Young's *The Art of Memory.*

CONCLUSION

1. While Jeffords was the first scholar to use the term "remasculinization" in her analysis of American cultural narratives about the Vietnam War, historian Erin O'Connor convincingly demonstrates that an earlier process of remasculinization took place after the Civil War in popular writings and discourses about prosthetics. See Jeffords's *The Remasculinization of America* and O'Connor's "'Fractions of Men': Engendering Amputation in Victorian Culture."

2. Phillips, "What the Draft Reveals About Us," 10, 24.

3. Merle Miller, "Separation," *Yank,* December 28, 1945, 16–17.

4. These proposals came from individual health educators rather than government offices. Fearing that servicemen "now passing through separation centers [would] revert back to physical lassitude," health enthusiasts such as Arthur Byrnes called for a "nationwide, highly publicized and scientifically accurate physical education program" to "maintain what the services have started for us" (193). For further discussion of Byrnes's plan, see his article "Physical Fitness, Health and the Returning Servicemen," *Hygeia,* March 1946, 192–93, 216. While Byrnes's proposal was principally aimed at improving the general "well being" of most Americans, other discussions of postwar fitness programs focused on preparedness. Boy Scouts public relations director E. B. Degroot, for instance, advocated formal physical education programs along with compulsory military training for America's young men in order to give "a dynamic meaning to our national defense" (64). As he explained, "Never again must America be caught unready to go to war at the drop of a hat" (64).

5. David Serlin explores this idea in his chapter "The Other Arms Race."

6. For further discussion of U.S. postwar victory culture and its legacy, see Tom Engelhardt's *The End of Victory Culture.*

7. See George Herring's *America's Longest War* and Nixon's public papers for additional background on these quotes and speeches.

8. I examine these revisions in my essay "The Vietnamization of World War II in *Slaughterhouse-Five* and *Gravity's Rainbow.*"

SELECTED BIBLIOGRAPHY

NOTE ON PERIODICAL SOURCES

Because I was primarily interested in analyzing the ways in which servicemen's bodies and masculinity were represented in the popular imagination, I chose to focus my study of magazines on those with high wartime circulation rates aimed at broad audiences. After determining from my survey findings which periodicals servicemen often read, I examined the entire series of *Yank, the Army Weekly* (June 1942 to December 1945) and virtually every issue of *Life, Time,* and *Newsweek* from mid-1940 through December 1946. For the latter three sources, I studied clusters of issues throughout the 1930s as well. Reading more selectively and sampling fewer issues from America's wartime years, I analyzed articles, editorials, and advertisements from *Collier's, National Geographic, Atlantic Monthly, Harper's Magazine,* and select runs of *Stars and Stripes.* Although news, general interest, and military weeklies made up the majority of the large-circulation periodicals I surveyed, issues of *Good Housekeeping, Ladies Home Journal,* and *House Beautiful* from the late wartime and early postwar period also offered insights into how gender identities and memorialization practices were specifically presented to female readers.

To complement my study of popular periodicals, I investigated a range of specialized, largely noncommercial journals from the fields of medicine and physical education. Offering a more explicit focus on the human body and notions of health and fitness, these journals provided more in-depth discussions of the training, wounds, and medical treatment servicemen received during the war. Concentrating on the later years of the war and postwar period, when large numbers of physically and psychologically wounded servicemen were being rehabilitated, I examined articles on veterans' treatments in the *Journal of the American Medical Association, American Journal of Psychiatry, American Journal of Public Health,* and *Psychiatric Quarterly.* Issues of the *Journal of Health and Physical Education* and *Hygeia,* meanwhile, were surveyed for the entire wartime period.

Although no systematic study of any newspapers was undertaken, I frequently examined the *Washington Post's* and *New York Times'* coverage of key events such as the attack at Pearl Harbor, the release of Selective Service statistics, and the burial of the World War II Unknown.

All citations for the aforementioned periodical sources appear in the notes section.

BOOKS AND ARTICLES

Ades, Dawn, et al., comp. *Art and Power: Europe Under the Dictators, 1930–45.* London: Thames & Hudson, 1996.

Ambrose, Stephen. *Citizen Soldiers: The U.S. Army from the Normandy Beaches to the Bulge to the Surrender of Germany, June 7, 1944–May 7, 1945.* New York: Simon & Schuster, 1997.

American Commission for Living War Memorials. *More About Memorials That Live.* Columbus, Ohio: American Commission for Living War Memorials, 1945.

Anderson, Patricia, ed. *All of Us: Americans Talk about the Meaning of Death.* New York: Delacorte Press, 1996.

Ariès, Phillippe. *Western Attitudes Toward Death: From the Middle Ages to the Present.* Baltimore: Johns Hopkins University Press, 1974.

Armstrong, Tim. *Modernism, Technology, and the Body: A Cultural Study.* Cambridge: Cambridge University Press, 1998.

Association of National Advertisers. *Magazine Circulation and Rate Trends, 1937–1955.* New York: Association of National Advertisers, 1956.

Atleson, James B. *Labor and the Wartime State: Labor Relations and Law during World War II.* Urbana: University of Illinois Press, 1998.

Axtell, James. *The European and the Indian: Essays in the Ethnohistory of Colonial North America.* New York: Oxford University Press, 1981.

Badger, Anthony. *The New Deal: The Depression Years, 1933–40.* New York: Noonday Press, 1989.

Bailey, Beth, and David Farber. *The First Strange Place: The Alchemy of Race and Sex in World War II Hawaii.* New York: Free Press, 1992.

Banton, Michael. *Racial Theories.* 2nd ed. Cambridge: Cambridge University Press, 1998.

Barkan, Elazar. *The Retreat of Scientific Racism: Changing Concepts of Race in Britain and the United States between the World Wars.* New York: Cambridge University Press, 1992.

Barker, Francis, Peter Hulme, and Margaret Iversen, eds. *Colonial Discourse/Postcolonial Theory.* New York: Manchester University Press, 1994.

Barron, Stephanie. *"Degenerate Art": The Fate of the Avant-Garde in Nazi Germany.* New York: H. N. Abrams, 1991.

Barton, Betsy. *The Long Walk.* New York: Duell, Sloan & Pearce, 1948.

Basinger, Jeanine. *The World War II Combat Film: Anatomy of a Genre.* New York: Columbia University Press, 1986.

Bataan. Directed by Tay Garnett. MGM Home Entertainment, 1943.

Battle of China. Directed by Frank Capra and Anatole Litvak. War Department, Signal Corps, Army Service Forces for the Morale Services Division, 1944.

Bauman, Zygmunt. *Modernity and the Holocaust.* Ithaca: Cornell University Press, 1989.

Bederman, Gail. *Manliness and Civilization: A Cultural History of Gender and Race in the United States, 1880–1917.* Chicago: University of Chicago Press, 1995.

Beebe, Gilbert, and Michael E. DeBakey. *Battle Casualties: Incidence, Mortality, and Logistic Considerations.* Springfield, Ill.: Charles C. Thomas, 1952.

Behling, Laura. *The Masculine Woman in America, 1890–1935.* Urbana: University of Illinois Press, 2001.

Bellah, James Warner. *Ward Twenty.* New York: Doubleday, 1946.

Berger, Maurice, Brian Wallis, and Simon Watson, eds. *Constructing Masculinity.* New York: Routledge, 1995.

Bèrubè, Allan. *Coming Out Under Fire: The History of Gay Men and Women in World War Two.* New York: Free Press, 1990.

The Best from Yank, the Army Weekly. Ed. *Yank.* New York: E. P. Dutton, 1945.

Beverly-Giddings, A. R. *Broad Margin.* New York: William Morrow, 1945.

Bhabha, Homi K., ed. *Nation and Narration.* New York: Routledge, 1990.

————. "The Other Question: Difference, Discrimination and the Discourse of Colonialism." In *Out There: Marginalization and Contemporary Cultures*, ed. Russell Ferguson et al. Cambridge: MIT Press, 1990. 71–88.

Bird, Caroline. *The Invisible Scar.* New York: David McKay, 1966.

Bird, William, and Harry Rubenstein. *Design for Victory: World War II Posters on the American Home Front.* Princeton: Princeton Architectural Press, 1998.

Bischof, Günter, and Robert Dupont, eds. *The Pacific War Revisited.* Baton Rouge: Louisiana State University Press, 1997.

Blanchot, Maurice. *The Space of Literature.* Lincoln: University of Nebraska Press, 1982.

Blum, John Morton. *V Was For Victory: Politics and American Culture during World War II.* New York: First Harvest, 1976.

Bodnar, John. *Remaking America: Public Memory, Commemoration, and Patriotism in the Twentieth Century.* Princeton: Princeton University Press, 1992.

Bonney, Betty. "He's 1-A in the Army and A-1 in My Heart." *Praise the Lord and Pass the Ammunition: Songs of World War I and II.* New World Records, 1977.

Bordo, Susan. *The Male Body: A New Look at Men in Public and Private.* New York: Farrar, Straus & Giroux, 1999.

————. "Reading the Male Body." *Michigan Quarterly Review* 32.4 (Fall 1993): 696–737.

————. *Unbearable Weight: Feminism, Western Culture, and the Body.* Berkeley: University of California Press, 1993.

Bourke, Joanna. *Dismembering the Male: Men's Bodies, Britain, and the Great War.* Chicago: University of Chicago Press, 1996.

————. *An Intimate History of Killing: Face to Face Killing in 20th Century Warfare.* New York: Basic Books, 1999.

Brandt, Allan M. *No Magic Bullet: A Social History of Venereal Disease in the United States since 1880.* New York: Oxford University Press, 1985.

Brandt, Nat. *Harlem at War: The Black Experience in World War II.* Syracuse: Syracuse University Press, 1996.

Braverman, Jordan. *To Hasten the Homecoming: How Americans Fought World War II Through the Media.* New York: Madison Books, 1996.

Brinkley, Alan. "The New Political Paradigm." In *The War in American Culture: Society and Consciousness during World War II*, ed. Lewis Erenberg and Susan Hirsch. Chicago: University of Chicago Press, 1996. 313–30.

Brinkley, David. *Washington Goes to War.* New York: A. A. Knopf, 1988.

Bristow, Nancy K. *Making Men Moral: Social Engineering during the Great War.* New York: New York University Press, 1996.

Buchanan, Russell A. *Black Americans in World War II.* Santa Barbara: Clio Books, 1977.

Budd, Michael Anton. *The Sculpture Machine: Physical Culture and Body Politics in the Age of Empire.* New York: New York University Press, 1997.

Burg, David. *The Great Depression: An Eyewitness History.* New York: Facts on File, 1996.

Burleigh, Michael, and Wolfgang Wippermann. *The Racial State: Germany 1933–1945.* New York: Cambridge University Press, 1991.

Burns, James MacGregor. *Roosevelt: The Lion and the Fox.* New York: Harcourt Brace Jovanovich, 1984.

————. *Roosevelt: The Soldier of Freedom.* New York: Harcourt Brace Jovanovich, 1970.

Busch, Niven. *They Dream of Home.* New York: D. Appleton-Century, 1944.

Bustard, Bruce. *A New Deal for the Arts.* Washington, D.C.: National Archives and Records Administration, 1997.

Butler, Judith. *Bodies that Matter: On the Discursive Limits of "Sex."* New York: Routledge, 1993.

———. *Gender Trouble: Feminism and the Subversion of Identity.* New York: Routledge, 1990.

Butler, Ovid, ed. *Youth Rebuilds: Stories from the C.C.C.* Washington, D.C.: American Forestry Association, 1934.

Byas, Hugh. *The Japanese Enemy: His Power and His Vulnerability.* New York: A. A. Knopf, 1942.

Byrd, Rudolph P., and Beverly Guy-Sheftall. *Traps: African American Men on Gender and Sexuality.* Bloomington: Indiana University Press, 2001.

Capra, Frank, supervisor. *War Comes to America.* War Department, Army Pictorial Service for the Office of Information and Education Division, 1945.

Carroll, Peter. *It Seemed Like Nothing Happened: The Tragedy and Promise of America in the 1970s.* New York: Holt, Rinehart and Winstom, 1982.

Cartwright, Lisa. *Screening the Body: Tracing Medicine's Visual Culture.* Minneapolis: University of Minnesota Press, 1995.

Chan, Jachinson. *Chinese American Masculinities: From Fu Manchu to Bruce Lee.* New York: Routledge, 2001.

Chapman, Mary, and Glenn Hendler, eds. *Sentimental Men: Masculinity and the Politics of Affect in American Culture.* Berkeley: University of California Press, 1999.

Chase, Allan. *The Legacy of Malthus: The Social Costs of the New Scientific Racism.* Urbana: University of Illinois Press, 1980.

Clark, David, ed. *The Sociology of Death: Theory, Culture, Practice.* Cambridge: Blackwell Publishers, 1993.

Clark, Suzanne. *Cold Warriors: Manliness on Trial in the Rhetoric of the West.* Carbondale: Southern Illinois University Press, 2000.

———. *Sentimental Modernism: Women Writers and the Revolution of the Word.* Bloomington: Indiana University Press, 1991.

Coben, Stanley. "The First Years of Modern America: 1918–1933." In *The Unfinished Century: America since 1900,* ed. William E. Leuchtenburg. Boston: Little, Brown, 1973. 255–353.

Cole, Olen, Jr. *The African-American Experience in the Civilian Conservation Corps.* Gainesville: University of Florida Press, 1999.

Collins, Lawrence. *The 56th Evac. Hospital: Letters of a WWII Army Doctor.* Denton: University of North Texas Press, 1995.

Connell, R. W. *Masculinities.* Berkeley: University of California Press, 1995.

———. *The Men and the Boys.* Berkeley: University of California Press, 2000.

Connery, Sam. "One Thousand and One Ways of Saying Uncle." *Smithsonian* (July 1995): 70–73.

Cooper, Helen M., Adrienne Auslander Munich, and Susan Merrill Squier, eds. *Arms and the Woman: War, Gender, and Literary Representation.* Chapel Hill: University of North Carolina Press, 1989.

Corber, Robert J. *Homosexuality in Cold War America: Resistance and the Crisis of Masculinity.* Durham: Duke University Press, 1997.

Costello, John. *Virtue Under Fire: How World War II Changed Our Social and Sexual Attitudes.* Boston: Little, Brown, 1985.

Cowdrey, Albert. *Fighting for Life: American Military Medicine in World War II.* New York: Free Press, 1994.

Craig, David, and Michael Egan. *Extreme Situations: Literature and Crisis from the Great War to the Atom Bomb.* Totawa, N.J.: Barnes & Noble Books, 1979.

Crampton, C. Ward. *Fighting Fitness: A Premilitary Training Guide.* New York: McGraw-Hill, 1944.

Cranny-Francis, Anne. *The Body in the Text.* Carlton South, Victoria: Melbourne University Press, 1995.

Crawford, Anthony, ed. *Posters of World War I and World War II in the George C. Marshall Research Foundation.* Charlottesville: University Press of Virginia, 1979.

Crispell, Kenneth R., and Carlos F. Gomez. *Hidden Illness in the White House.* Durham: Duke University Press, 1988.

Dahir, James. *Community Centers as Living Memorials: A Select Bibliography with Interpretative Comments.* New York: Russell Sage Foundation, 1946.

Damousi, Joy, and Marilyn Lake, eds. *Gender and War: Australians at War in the Twentieth Century.* Cambridge: Cambridge University Press, 1995.

Daniels, Roger. *Prisoners without Trial: Japanese Americans in World War II.* New York: Hill & Wang, 1993.

Daniels, Roger, Sandra Taylor, and Harry H. L. Kitano, eds. *Japanese Americans: From Relocation to Redress.* Salt Lake City: University of Utah Press, 1986.

Davies, John. "War Memorials." In *The Sociology of Death: Theory, Culture, Practice,* ed. David Clark. Cambridge: Blackwell Publishers, 1993. 112–28.

Dean, Robert. *Imperial Brotherhood: Gender and the Making of Cold War Foreign Policy.* Amherst: University of Massachusetts Press, 2001.

Dear, I. C. B., ed. *The Oxford Companion to World War II.* New York and Oxford: Oxford University Press, 1995.

Delehanty, Elizabeth. *Year One.* New York: E. P. Dutton, 1946.

D'Eliscu, Francois. *How to Prepare for Military Fitness.* New York: W. W. Norton, 1943.

DeNoon, Christopher. *Posters of the W.P.A.* Los Angeles: Wheatley Press, 1987.

Deutsch, James. "Coming Home From 'The Good War': World War II Veterans as Depicted in American Film and Fiction." Ph.D. diss., George Washington University, 1991.

Dick, Bernard F. *The Star-Spangled Screen: The American World War II Film.* Lexington: University of Kentucky Press, 1985.

Doherty, Thomas Patrick. *Projections of War: Hollywood, American Culture, and World War II.* New York: Columbia University Press, 1993.

Doherty, William Brown, and Dagobert D. Runes, eds. *Rehabilitation of the War Injured.* New York: Philosophical Library, 1943.

Douglas, Ann. *The Feminization of American Culture.* New York: Doubleday, 1988.

Dower, John. "The Challenge of Race and Resistance to Change Race, Language, and War in Two Cultures: World War II in Asia." In *The War in American Culture: Society and Consciousness during World War II,* ed. Lewis Erenberg and Susan Hirsch. Chicago: University of Chicago Press, 1996. 169–201.

———. *War without Mercy: Race and Power in the Pacific War.* New York: Pantheon Books, 1986.

Dutton, Kenneth R. *The Perfectible Body: The Western Ideal of Male Physical Development.* New York: Continuum, 1995.

Elliot, David. "A Life-and-Death Struggle." In *Art and Power: Europe under the Dictators, 1930–45,* comp. Dawn Ades et al. London: Thames & Hudson, 1996. 270–76.

Eng, David L., *Racial Castration: Managing Masculinity in Asian America.* Durham: Duke University Press, 2001.

Engelhardt, Tom. *The End of Victory Culture: Cold War America and the Disillusioning of a Generation.* New York: Basic Books, 1995.

Erenberg, Lewis, and Susan Hirsch. Introduction to *The War in American Culture: Society and Consciousness during World War II*, ed. Lewis Erenberg and Susan Hirsch. Chicago: University of Chicago Press, 1996. 1–13.

Evans, Martin, and Ken Lunn, eds. *War and Memory in the Twentieth Century*. New York: Berg, 1997.

This Fabulous Century: 1940–1950. Vol. 1. Ed. Time-Life Books. New York: Time-Life, 1969.

Faludi, Susan. *Stiffed: The Betrayal of the American Man*. New York: William Morrow, 1999.

Fanon, Franz. *Black Skin, White Masks*. New York: Grove Press, 1967.

Farrell, James. *Inventing the American Way of Death, 1830–1920*. Philadelphia: Temple University Press, 1980.

Fausto-Sterling, Anne. "The Five Sexes: Why Male and Female Are Not Enough." *The Sciences* (March/April 1993): 20–25.

Featherstone, Mike, Mike Hepworth, and Bryan S. Turner, eds. *The Body: Social Process and Cultural Theory*. London: Sage, 1991.

Felski, Rita. *The Gender of Modernity*. Cambridge: Harvard University Press, 1995.

Fleisher, Wilfrid. *Our Enemy Japan*. New York: Doubleday, Doran, 1942.

Foster, William, et al. *Physical Standards in World War II*. Ed. Charles Wiltse. Washington, D.C.: Office of the Surgeon General, Department of the Army, 1967.

Foucault, Michel. *Discipline and Punish: The Birth of the Prison*. New York: Vintage, 1979.

———. *The History of Sexuality, Volume I: An Introduction*. New York: Vintage, 1990.

———. "Nietzsche, Genealogy, History." In *Language, Counter-Memory, Practice: Selected Essays and Interviews*, ed. Donald F. Bouchard. Ithaca: Cornell University Press, 1977. 139–64.

Fox, Stephen. *The Unknown Internment: An Oral History of Italian Americans during World War II*. Boston: Twayne Publishers, 1990.

French, Ralph. "Physical Aspects of the Missile Casualty." Washington, D.C.: Army Medical Center, 1947.

Friedman, Alan Warren. *Fictional Death and the Modernist Enterprise*. Cambridge: Cambridge University Press, 1995.

———. "Modernist Attitudes toward Death." In *Death and the Quest for Meaning: Essays in Honor of Herman Feifel*, ed. Stephen Strack. Northvale, N.J.: Aronson, 1997. 109–33.

From Pearl Harbor into Tokyo. New York: Columbia Broadcasting System, 1945.

Fussell, Paul. *The Great War and Modern Memory*. New York: Oxford University Press, 1975.

———. *Wartime: Understanding and Behavior in the Second World War*. New York: Oxford University Press, 1989.

Gerber, David. "Heroes and Misfits: The Troubled Social Reintegration of Disabled Veterans in *The Best Years of Our Lives*." *American Quarterly* 46.4 (1994): 545–74.

Gibbs, Marilyn, and Claudius Griffin. "Physical Fitness." In *Handbook of American Popular Culture*, ed. M. Thomas Inge. Vol. 2. 2nd ed. New York: Greenwood Press, 1989. 931–55.

Giddens, Anthony. *Modernity and Self-Identity: Self and Society in the Late Modern Age*. Stanford: Stanford University Press, 1991.

Gillis, John R., ed. *Commemorations: The Politics of National Identity*. Princeton: Princeton University Press, 1994.

Gilman, Sander. *Disease and Representation: Images of Illness from Madness to AIDS.* Ithaca: Cornell University Press, 1988.

Gilmore, David. *Manhood in the Making: Cultural Concepts of Masculinity.* New Haven: Yale University Press, 1990.

Glass, Albert, ed. *Neuropsychiatry in World War II.* Washington, D.C.: Office of the Surgeon General, Department of the Army, 1973.

Glass, Albert, and Robert Bernucci, eds. *Neuropsychiatry in World War II, vol. 1 (Zone of Interior).* Washington, D.C.: Office of the Surgeon General, Department of the Army, 1966.

Goldstein, Joshua. *War and Gender: How Gender Shapes the War System and Vice Versa.* Cambridge: Cambridge University Press, 2001.

Goldstein, Laurence. Introduction to *The Male Body: Features, Destinies, Exposures,* ed. Laurence Goldstein. Ann Arbor: University of Michigan Press, 1994. vii–xiv.

Goodwin, Doris Kearns. *No Ordinary Time: Franklin and Eleanor Roosevelt: The Home Front in World War II.* New York: Simon & Schuster, 1994.

Graebner, William. *The Age of Doubt: American Thought and Culture in the 1940s.* 1991. Reprint, Prospect Heights, Ill.: Waveland Press, 1998.

Graham, Otis L. "Years of Crisis: America in Depression and War, 1933–1945." In *The Unfinished Century: America since 1900,* ed. William E. Leuchtenburg. Boston: Little, Brown, 1973. 357–459.

"The Grandest Job in the World," *FDR,* part 2. Written and directed by David Grubin. Public Broadcasting Service, 1994, videocassette.

Gregory, G. H., ed. *Posters of World War II.* New York: Gramercy Books, 1993.

Grosz, Elizabeth. *Volatile Bodies: Toward a Corporeal Feminism.* Bloomington: Indiana University Press, 1994.

Hall, Donald E., ed. *Muscular Christianity: Embodying the Victorian Age.* Cambridge: Cambridge University Press, 1994.

Halsey, Margaret. *Color Blind: A White Woman Looks at the Negro.* New York: Simon & Schuster, 1946.

Harris, Jonathan. *Federal Art and National Culture: The Politics of Identity in New Deal America.* Cambridge: Cambridge University Press, 1995.

Hartmann, Susan M. *The Home Front and Beyond: Women in the 1940s.* Boston: Twayne Publishers, 1982.

Hass, Kristin Ann. *Carried to the Wall: American Memory and the Vietnam Veterans Memorial.* Berkeley: University of California Press, 1998.

Heide, Robert, and John Gilman. *Home Front America: Popular Culture of the World War II Era.* San Francisco: Chronicle Books, 1995.

Heller, Joseph. *Catch-22.* 1961. Reprint, New York: Dell, 1985.

Herman, Jan. *Battle Station Sickbay: Navy Medicine in World War II.* Annapolis: Naval Institute Press, 1997.

Herndl, Diana Price. *Figuring Feminine Illness in American Fiction and Culture, 1840–1940.* Chapel Hill: University of North Carolina Press, 1993.

Herring, George. *America's Longest War: The United States and Vietnam, 1950–1975.* 2nd ed. New York: A. A. Knopf, 1986.

Hersey, John. *Hiroshima.* New York: A. A. Knopf, 1946.

Hershey, Lewis. *Selective Service and Victory: The Fourth Report of the Director of the Selective Service.* Vol. 4. Washington, D.C.: Government Printing Office, 1948.

———. *Selective Service as the Tide of War Turns: The Third Report of the Director of Selective Service.* Vol. 3. Washington, D.C.: Government Printing Office, 1945.

————. *Selective Service in Peacetime: First Report of the Director of Selective Service, 1940–41.* Washington, D.C.: Government Printing Office, 1942.

————. *Selective Service in Wartime: Second Report of the Director of Selective Service, 1941–42.* Vol. 2. Washington, D.C.: Government Printing Office, 1943.

Herzlich, Claudine, and Janine Pierret. *Illness and Self in Society.* Trans. Elborg Forster. Baltimore: Johns Hopkins University Press, 1987.

Higonnet, Margaret Randolph, Jane Jenson, Sonya Michel, and Margaret Collins Weitz, eds. *Behind the Lines: Gender and the Two World Wars.* New Haven: Yale University Press, 1987.

Hill, Frank Ernest. *The School in the Camps: The Educational Program of the Civilian Conservation Corps.* New York: American Association for Adult Education, 1935.

Hill, Robert A., ed. *The FBI's RACON: Racial Conditions in the United States during World War II.* Boston: Northeastern University Press, 1995.

Hoff, Ebbe Curtis, ed. *Preventive Medicine in World War II, Volume 3: Personal Health Measures and Immunization.* Washington, D.C.: Office of the Surgeon General, Department of the Army, 1955.

————. *Preventive Medicine in World War II, Volume 5: Communicable Diseases Transmitted through Contact or by Unknown Means.* Washington, D.C.: Office of the Surgeon General, Department of the Army, 1960.

Hoffman, Frederick. *Army Anthropometry and Medical Rejection Statistics.* Newark, N.J.: Prudential Press, 1918.

Hoganson, Kristin. *Fighting for American Manhood: How Gender Politics Provoked the Spanish-American and Philippine-American Wars.* New Haven: Yale University Press, 1998.

Holland, Kenneth, and Frank Ernest Hill. *Youth in the CCC.* Washington, D.C.: American Council on Education, 1942

Holsinger, Paul M., and Mary Anne Schofield, eds. *Visions of War: World War II in Popular Literature and Culture.* Bowling Green, Ohio: Bowling Green State University Popular Press, 1992.

Holt, Dean W. *American Military Cemeteries: A Comprehensive Illustrated Guide to the Hallowed Grounds of the United States Including Cemeteries Overseas.* Jefferson, N.C.: McFarland, 1992.

hooks, bell. *Yearning: Race, Gender, and Cultural Politics.* Boston: South End Press, 1990.

Horowitz, Roger, ed. *Boys and Their Toys? Masculinity, Technology, and Class in America.* New York: Routledge, 2001.

Horsman, Reginald. *Race and Manifest Destiny: The Origins of American Racial Anglo-Saxonism.* Cambridge: Harvard University Press, 1981.

Hulett, Albert Groves. "Malingering." In *War Medicine: A Symposium,* ed. Winfield Scott Pugh. New York: Philosophical Library, 1942. 519–30.

Hunt, Lynn, ed. *Eroticism and the Body Politic.* Baltimore: Johns Hopkins University Press, 1991.

————. *The Family Romance of the French Revolution.* Berkeley: University of California Press, 1992.

Huyssen, Andreas. *After the Great Divide: Modernism, Mass Culture, Postmodernism.* Bloomington: Indiana University Press, 1986.

Illich, Ivan. "A Plea for Body History." *Michigan Quarterly Review* 26.2 (1987): 342–48.

Isaacs, Arnold. *Vietnam Shadows: The War, Its Ghosts, and Its Legacy.* Baltimore: Johns Hopkins University Press, 1997.

Iserson, Kenneth. *Death to Dust: What Happens to Dead Bodies?* Tucson, Ariz.: Galen Press, 1994.

James, Clayton D., and Anne Sharpe Wells. *From Pearl Harbor to V-J Day: The American Armed Forces in World War II.* Ed. Fred Stanton. Chicago: I.R. Dee, 1995.

James, Cyril Lionel Robert, et al. *Fighting Racism in World War II.* Ed. Fred Stanton. New York: Monad Press, 1980.

Jarvis, Christina. "The Vietnamization of World War II in *Slaughterhouse-Five* and *Gravity's Rainbow.*" *War, Literature, and the Arts: An International Journal of the Humanities* 15 (forthcoming).

Jeffords, Susan. *Hard Bodies: Hollywood Masculinity in the Reagan Era.* New Brunswick, N.J.: Rutgers University Press, 1994.

———. *The Remasculinizaton of America: Gender and the Vietnam War.* Bloomington: Indiana University Press, 1989.

Jeffords, Susan, and Lauren Rabinovitz, eds. *Seeing Through the Media: The Persian Gulf War.* New Brunswick, N.J.: Rutgers University Press, 1994.

Jones, James. *From Here to Eternity.* 1951. Reprint, New York: Signet Books, 1953.

———. *The Thin Red Line.* 1962. Reprint, New York: Bantam Doubleday Dell Publishing Group, 1998.

Judd, Denis. *Posters of World War Two.* London: Wayland Publishers, 1972.

Kantorowicz, Ernst. *The King's Two Bodies: A Study in Medieval Political Theology.* Princeton: Princeton University Press, 1957.

Kasson, John. *Houdini, Tarzan, and the Perfect Man: The White Male Body and the Challenge of Modernity in America.* New York: Hill & Wang, 2001.

Keene, Jennifer D. *Doughboys, the Great War, and the Remaking of America.* Baltimore: Johns Hopkins University Press, 2001.

Kessler, Suzanne. "The Medical Construction of Gender: Case Management of Inter-sexed Infants." *Signs: Journal of Women in Culture and Society* 16 (1990): 3–26.

Kevles, Bettyann Holtzmann. *Naked to the Bone: Medical Imaging in the Twentieth Century.* New Brunswick, N.J.: Rutgers University Press, 1997.

Kimmel, Michael. "Consuming Manhood: The Feminization of American Culture and the Recreation of the Male Body." In *The Male Body: Features, Destinies, Exposures,* ed. Laurence Goldstein. Ann Arbor: University of Michigan Press, 1994. 12–41.

———. *Manhood in America: A Cultural History.* New York: Free Press, 1996.

Kimmel, Michael, and Michael Messner, eds. *Men's Lives.* New York: Macmillan, 1989.

Kinsey, Alfred. *Sexual Behavior in the Human Male.* Philadelphia: W. B. Saunders, 1948.

Klopsteg, Paul E., and Philip Wilson. *Human Limbs and Their Substitutes.* New York: McGraw-Hill, 1954.

Koppes, Clayton, and Gregory Black. *Hollywood Goes to War: How Politics, Profits, and Propaganda Shaped World War II Movies.* New York: Free Press, 1987.

Kristeva, Julia. *Powers of Horror: An Essay on Abjection.* Trans. Leon S. Roudiez. New York: Columbia University Press, 1982.

Kryder, Daniel. *Divided Arsenal: Race and the American State during World War II.* Cambridge: Cambridge University Press, 2000.

Krutnik, Frank. *In a Lonely Street: Film Noir, Genre, Masculinity.* New York: Routledge, 1991.

Landau, Ellen. *Artists for Victory: An Exhibition Catalog.* Washington, D.C.: Library of Congress, 1983.

Lee, Ulysses. *The Employment of Negro Troops*. Washington, D.C.: U.S. Government Printing Office, 1994.

Lehman, Peter. *Running Scared: Masculinity and the Representation of the Male Body*. Philadelphia: Temple University Press, 1993.

Leuchtenburg, William E. *Franklin D. Roosevelt and the New Deal*. New York: Harper & Row, 1963.

———, ed. *The Unfinished Century: America since 1900*. Boston: Little, Brown, 1973.

Lewis, Warfield, ed. *Fighting Words: Stories and Cartoons by Members of the Armed Forces of America*. New York: J. B. Lippincott, 1944.

Limon, John. *Writing after War: American War Fiction from Realism to Postmodernism*. New York: Oxford University Press, 1994.

Linderman, Gerald F. *The World within War: America's Combat Experience in World War II*. New York: Free Press, 1997.

Lindley, Betty, and Ernest K. *A New Deal for Youth: The Story of the National Youth Administration*. New York: Viking Press, 1938.

Lingeman, Richard R. *Don't You Know There's A War On? The American Home Front, 1941–1945*. New York: Putnam, 1976.

Lipsitz, George. *Time Passages: Collective Memory and American Popular Culture*. Minneapolis: University of Minnesota Press, 1990.

Lipsky, Regina, ed. *WPA/FAP Graphics*. Washington, D.C.: Smithsonian Institute Press, 1976.

Liso, Donald J. "A Blunder Becomes a Catastrophe: Hoover, the Legion, and the Bonus Army." In *The Dissonance of Change, 1929 to the Present*, ed. Paul Glad. New York: Random House, 1970. 25–43.

Looker, Earle. "Is Franklin D. Roosevelt Physically Fit To Be President?" In *The Liberty Years 1924–1950: An Anthology*, ed. Allen Churchill. Englewood Cliffs, N.J.: Prentice Hall, 1969. 142–46.

Lorant, Stefan. *FDR: A Pictorial Biography*. New York: Simon & Schuster, 1950.

Lowe, Lisa. *Immigrant Acts: On Asian American Cultural Politics*. Durham: Duke University Press, 1996.

Luciano, Lynne. *Looking Good: Male Body Image in Modern America*. New York: Hill & Wang, 2001.

Macleod, David I. *Building Character in the American Boy: The Boy Scouts, YMCA, and Their Forerunners, 1870–1920*. Madison: University of Wisconsin Press, 1983.

Mailer, Norman. *The Naked and the Dead*. 1948. Reprint, New York: Signet, 1972.

Maisel, Albert Q. *Miracles of Military Medicine*. New York: Duell, Sloan & Pearce, 1943.

Mangan, J. A., ed. *Shaping the Superman: Fascist Body as Political Icon*. Portland, Oreg.: Frank Cass, 1999.

Mangan, J. A., and James Walvin, eds. *Manliness and Morality: Middle-Class Masculinity in Britain and America, 1800–1940*. New York: St. Martin's Press, 1987.

Marling, Karal Ann, and John Wetenhall. *Iwo Jima: Monuments, Memories, and the American Hero*. Cambridge: Harvard University Press, 1991.

Martin, Emily. *Flexible Bodies: Tracking Immunity in American Culture—From the Days of Polio to the Age of AIDS*. Boston: Beacon Press, 1994.

Martin, Ralph. *The GI War, 1941–1945*. Boston: Little, Brown, 1967.

May, Larry, Robert Strikwerda, and Patrick D. Hopkins, eds. *Rethinking Masculinity: Philosophical Explorations in Light of Feminism*. 2nd ed. New York: Rowman & Littlefield Publishers, 1996.

Mayo, James. *War Memorials as Political Landscape: The American Experience and Beyond*. New York: Praeger, 1988.

McElvaine, Robert, ed. *Down and Out in the Great Depression: Letters from the Forgotten Man.* Chapel Hill: University of North Carolina Press, 1983.

McEntee, James J. *Now They Are Men: The Story of the CCC.* Washington, D.C.: National Home Library Foundation, 1940.

McKinzie, Richard. *The New Deal for Artists.* Princeton: Princeton University Press, 1973.

McMinn, John, and Max Levin. *Personnel in World War II.* Ed. Charles Wiltse. Washington, D.C. Office of the Surgeon General, Department of the Army, 1963.

Mellor, Phillip. "Death in High Modernity: The Contemporary Presence and Absence of Death." In *The Sociology of Death: Theory, Culture, Practice,* ed. David Clark. Cambridge: Blackwell Publishers, 1993. 11–30.

Melosh, Barbara. *Engendering Culture: Manhood and Womanhood in New Deal Public Art and Theater.* Washington, D.C.: Smithsonian Institution Press, 1991.

The Men. Directed by Fred Zinnemann. United Artists, 1950.

Menninger, William. *Psychiatry in a Troubled World: Yesterday's War and Today's Challenge.* New York: Macmillan, 1948.

Merrill, Perry H. *Roosevelt's Forest Army: A History of the Civilian Conservation Corps, 1933–1942.* Montpelier, Vt.: Perry H. Merrill, 1981.

Meyer, Leisa D. *Creating G.I. Jane: Sexuality and Power in the Women's Army Corps during World War II.* New York: Columbia University Press, 1996.

Meyer, Stephen. "Work, Play, and Power: Masculine Culture on the Automotive Shop Floor, 1930–1960." In *Boys and Their Toys? Masculinity, Technology, and Class in America,* ed. Roger Horowitz. New York: Routledge, 2001. 13–32.

Miller, Carol. "Native Sons and the Good War: Retelling the Myth of American Indian Assimilation." In *The War in American Culture: Society and Consciousness during World War II,* ed. Lewis Erenberg and Susan Hirsch. Chicago: University of Chicago Press, 1996. 217–37.

Milton, Sybil. *In Fitting Memory: The Art and Politics of Holocaust Memorials.* Detroit: Wayne State University Press, 1991.

Mirzoeff, Nicholas. *Bodyscape: Art, Modernity and the Ideal Figure.* New York: Routledge, 1995.

Mitford, Jessica. *The American Way of Death Revisited.* New York: A. A. Knopf, 1998.

Morris, Ernst, and David Loth. *American Sexual Behavior and the Kinsey Report.* New York: Greystone Press, 1948.

Mosse, George L. "Beauty without Sensuality/The Exhibition *Entartete Kunst.*" In *"Degenerate Art": The Fate of the Avant-Garde in Nazi Germany,* ed. Stephanie Barron. New York: H. N. Abrams, 1991. 25–31.

———. *Fallen Soldiers: Reshaping the Memory of the World Wars.* Oxford: Oxford University Press, 1990.

———. *The Image of Man: The Creation of Modern Masculinity.* New York: Oxford University Press, 1996

Mossman, B. C., and M. W. Stark. *The Last Salute: Civil and Military Funerals, 1921–1969.* Washington, D.C.: Government Printing Office, 1971.

Motley, Mary Penick, ed. *The Invisible Soldier: The Experience of the Black Soldier, World War II.* Detroit: Wayne State University Press, 1975.

Murphy, Peter. "The Body Politic." In *Troubled Bodies: Critical Perspectives on Postmodernism, Medical Ethics, and the Body,* ed. Paul A. Komesaroff. Durham: Duke University Press, 1995. 103–24.

Nadel, Alan. *Containment Culture: American Narratives, Postmodernism, and the Atomic Age.* Durham: Duke University Press, 1995.

Nalty, Bernard. *Strength for the Fight: A History of Black Americans in the Military.* New York: Free Press, 1986.

Nash, Gerald. *The Crucial Era: The Great Depression and World War II, 1929–1945,* 2nd ed. New York: St. Martin's Press, 1992.

National Archives and Records Administration. *Records Relating to Personal Participation in World War II: American Military Casualties and Burials.* Comp. Benjamin DeWhitt. Washington, D.C.: National Archives and Records Administration, 1993.

National Recreation Association. *Community Recreation Buildings as War Memorials.* New York: National Recreation Association, 1944.

Nicolai, Bernd. "Tectonic Sculpture: Autonomous and Political Sculpture." In *Art and Power: Europe Under the Dictators, 1930–45,* comp. Dawn Ades et al. London: Thames & Hudson, 1996. 334–37.

Nicholas, Lynn. *The Rape of Europa: The Fate of Europe's Treasures in the Third Reich and the Second World War.* New York: Vintage Books, 1995.

Nishiura, Elizabeth, ed. *American Battle Monuments: A Guide to Military Cemeteries and Monuments Maintained by the American Battle Monuments Commission.* Detroit: Omnigraphics, 1989.

Nye, Robert A. *Masculinity and Male Codes of Honor in Modern France.* New York: Oxford University Press, 1993.

Oakley, J. Ronald. *God's Country: America in the Fifties.* New York: Dembner Books, 1990.

O'Brien, Kenneth Paul, and Lynn Hudson Parsons, eds. *The Home Front War: World War II and American Society.* Westport, Conn.: Greenwood Press, 1995.

O'Connor, Erin. "'Fractions of Men': Engendering Amputation in Victorian Culture." *Comparative Studies in Society and History* 39.4 (1997): 742–77.

O'Connor, Francis, ed. *Art for the Millions: Essays from the 1930s by Artists and Administrators of the WPA Federal Art Project.* Greenwich: New York Graphic Society, 1973.

———. *The New Deal Art Projects: An Anthology of Memoirs.* Washington, D.C.: Smithsonian Institution Press, 1972.

Okihiro, Gary, and Joan Meyers. *Whispered Silences: Japanese Americans and World War II.* Seattle: University of Washington Press, 1996.

O'Neill, William L. *American High: The Years of Confidence, 1945–1960.* New York: Free Press, 1986.

———. *A Democracy at War: America's Fight at Home and Abroad in World War II.* New York: Free Press, 1993.

Osur, Alan. *Blacks in the Army Air Forces during World War II.* Washington, D.C.: Government Printing Office, 1977.

Overy, Richard. "Total War II: The Second World War." In *The Oxford Illustrated History of Modern War,* ed. Charles Townshend. New York: Oxford University Press, 1997. 120–37.

Palmer, Edgar A. [Eric Posselt], ed. *G.I. Songs Written, Composed and/or Collected by the Men in the Service.* New York: Sheridan House, 1944.

Palmer, Robert, Bell Wiley, and William R. Keast. *The Procurement and Training of Ground Combat Troops.* Vol. 1. Washington, D.C.: Historical Division, Department of the Army, 1948.

Park, Marlene and Gerald Markowitz. *Democratic Vistas: Post Offices and Public Art in the New Deal.* Philadelphia: Temple University Press, 1984.

————. *New Deal for Art.* Hamilton, N.Y.: Gallery Association of New York State, 1977.

Parks, Robert. *Medical Training in World War II.* Washington, D.C.: Office of the Surgeon General, Department of the Army, 1974.

Parran, Thomas. *Shadow on the Land: Syphilis.* New York: Reynal & Hitchcock, 1937.

Parran, Thomas, and R. A. Vonderlehr. *Plain Words About Venereal Disease.* New York: Reynal & Hitchcock, 1941.

Patterson, James. *Grand Expectations: The United States, 1945–1974.* New York: Oxford University Press, 1996.

Pendergast, Tom. *Creating the Modern Man: American Magazines and Consumer Culture 1900–1950.* Columbia: University of Missouri Press, 2000.

Perrett, Geoffrey. *Days of Sadness, Years of Triumph: The American People, 1939–1945.* 1973. Reprint, Madison: University of Wisconsin Press, 1985.

Physical Fitness Coaching School. *Lectures Given at the Physical Fitness Coaching School Conducted by the U.S. Naval Pre-Flight School and the University of North Carolina.* Durham, N.C.: 1942.

Piehler, Kurt G. *Remembering War the American Way.* Washington, D.C.: Smithsonian Institution Press, 1995.

Polson, C. J., R. P. Brittain, and T. K. Marshall. *The Disposal of the Dead.* Ed. C. J. Polson. Springfield, Ill.: Charles C. Thomas, 1962.

Praise the Lord and Pass the Ammunition: Songs of World War I and World War II. Program notes by C. H. Steele. New World Records, 1977. 1–6.

Prevratil, Rudolf, and Karel Richter, eds. *Witnesses of the Great Victory: World War II in Reports, Epics, Memoirs.* Prague: International Organization of Journalists, 1985.

Proctor, Robert. *Racial Hygiene: Medicine under the Nazis.* Cambridge: Harvard University Press, 1988.

Pugh, Winfield Scott, ed. *War Medicine: A Symposium.* New York: Philosophical Library, 1942.

Pynchon, Thomas. *Gravity's Rainbow.* 1973. Reprint, New York: Penguin, 1995.

Quigley, Christine. *The Corpse: A History.* Jefferson, N.C.: McFarland, 1996.

Rabinbach, Anson. *The Human Motor: Energy, Fatigue, and the Origins of Modernity.* New York: Basic Books, 1990.

Randall, Francis, and Melvyn Baer. "Survey of Body Size of Army Personnel, Methodology." Washington, D.C.: Office of the Quartermaster General, 1947.

Rawls, Walton. *Wake Up, America! World War I and the American Poster.* New York: Abbeville Press, 1988.

Reiman, Richard A. *The New Deal & American Youth: Ideas & Ideals in a Depression Decade.* Athens: University of Georgia Press, 1992.

Reister, Frank A. *Medical Statistics in World War II.* Ed. John Lada. Washington, D.C.: Government Printing Office, 1975.

Rhodes, Charles Harker, comp. *Soldiering for Uncle Sam.* Chicago: Reilly and Lee, 1942.

Rickards, Maurice. *Posters of the First World War.* New York: Walker, 1968.

Riegel, O. W. Introduction to *Posters of World War I and World War II in the George C. Marshall Research Foundation,* ed. Anthony Crawford. Charlottesville: University Press of Virginia, 1979. 1–15.

Robbins, Trina. *From Girls to Grrrlz: A History of Comics from Teens to Zines.* San Francisco: Chronicle Books, 1999.

Robinson, Sally. *Marked Men: White Masculinity in Crisis.* New York: Columbia University Press, 2000.

Roeder, George, Jr. *The Censored War: American Visual Experience during World War Two.* New Haven: Yale University Press, 1993.

———. "Censoring Disorder: American Visual Imagery of World War II." In *The War in American Culture: Society and Consciousness during World War II,* ed. Lewis Erenberg and Susan Hirsch. Chicago: University of Chicago Press, 1996. 46–70.

Rotundo, Anthony. *American Manhood: Transformations in Masculinity from the Revolution to the Modern Era.* New York: Basic Books, 1993.

Salmond, John A. *The Civilian Conservation Corps, 1933–1942: A New Deal Case Study.* Durham: Duke University Press, 1967.

Samuel, Lawrence. *Pledging Allegiance: American Identity and the Bond Drive of World War II.* Washington, D.C.: Smithsonian Institute Press, 1997.

Savage, William W. *Comic Books and America, 1945–1954.* Norman: University of Oklahoma Press, 1990.

Savran, David. *Taking it Like a Man: White Masculinity, Masochism, and Contemporary American Culture.* Princeton: Princeton University Press, 1998.

Scarry, Elaine. *The Body in Pain: The Making and Unmaking of the World.* New York: Oxford University Press, 1985.

Schiebinger, Londa. *The Mind Has No Sex? Women in the Origins of Modern Science.* Cambridge: Harvard University Press, 1989.

———. *Nature's Body: Gender in the Making of Modern Science.* Boston: Beacon Press, 1993.

Schilling, Chris. *The Body and Social Theory.* London: Sage, 1993.

Seltzer, Mark. *Bodies and Machines.* New York: Routledge, 1992.

Serlin, David. "Built for Living: Imagining the American Body Through Medical Science, 1945–1965." Ph.D. diss., New York University, 1999.

Sherry, Michael S. *In the Shadow of War: The United States since the 1930s.* New Haven: Yale University Press, 1995.

Shuker-Haines, Timothy. "Home is the Hunter: Representations of Returning World War II Veterans and the Reconstruction of Masculinity, 1944–1951." Ph.D. diss., University of Michigan, 1994.

Silverman, Kaja. *Male Subjectivity at the Margins.* New York: Routledge, 1992.

Skoloff, Gary, et al. *To Win the War: Home Front Memorabilia of World War II.* Missoula, Mont.: Pictorial Histories Publishing, 1995.

Smith, Graham. *When Jim Crow Met John Bull: Black American Soldiers in World War II Britain.* New York: St. Martin's Press, 1987.

Sohn, Monte. *The Flesh and Mary Duncan.* New York: Dodd, Mead, 1948.

Solomon-Godeau, Abigail. *Male Trouble: A Crisis in Representation.* London: Thames & Hudson, 1997.

Spiller, Roger. "The Real War: An Interview with Paul Fussell." *American Heritage,* November 1989. 126, 130–38.

Stannard, David, ed. *Death in America.* Philadelphia: University of Pennsylvania Press, 1975.

Steere, Edward. *The Graves Registration Service in World War II.* Q.M.C. Historical Studies 21. Washington, D.C.: Office of the Quartermaster General, 1951.

Steere, Edward, and Thayer Boardman. *Final Disposition of World War II Dead, 1945–51.* Q.M.C. Historical Studies Series 2, no. 4. Washington, D.C.: Office of the Quartermaster General, 1957.

Sternberg, Thomas H., et al. "Venereal Diseases." In *Preventive Medicine in World War II, Volume 5: Communicable Diseases Transmitted through Contact or by Unknown*

Means, ed. Ebbe Curtis Hoff. Washington, D.C.: Office of the Surgeon General, Department of the Army, 1960. 139–332.

Strong, F. S. "Artificial Limbs—Today and Tomorrow." *Selected Articles from "Artificial Limbs," January 1954–Spring 1966*. Huntington, N.Y.: Robert E. Krieger Publishing, 1970. 1–3.

Suleiman, Susan Rubin, ed. *The Female Body in Western Culture*. Cambridge: Harvard University Press, 1986.

Suzik, Jeffrey Ryan. "'Building Better Men': The CCC Boy and the Changing Social Ideal of Manliness." *Men and Masculinities* 2.2 (Oct. 1999): 152–79.

Sweeney, Michael. *Secrets of Victory: The Office of Censorship and the American Press and Radio in World War II*. Chapel Hill: University of North Carolina Press, 2001.

Takaki, Ronald. *Double Victory: A Multicultural History of America in World War II*. New York: Little, Brown, 2000.

Terkel, Studs. *"The Good War": An Oral History of World War Two*. New York: Pantheon Books, 1984.

———. *Hard Times: An Oral History of the Great Depression*. New York: Pantheon Books, 1970.

Terry, Jennifer, and Jacqueline Urla, eds. *Deviant Bodies: Critical Perspectives on Difference in Science and Popular Culture*. Bloomington: University of Indiana Press, 1995.

Theweleit, Klaus. *Male Fantasies, Volume 1: Women, Floods, Bodies, History*. Trans. Stephen Conway. Minneapolis: University of Minnesota Press, 1987.

———. *Male Fantasies, Volume 2: Male Bodies: Psychoanalyzing the White Terror*. Trans. Erica Carter and Chris Turner. Minneapolis: University of Minnesota Press, 1989.

Thompson, Morton. *How to Be a Civilian*. Garden City, New York: Doubleday, 1946.

Thompson, Paul Williams, et al. *The Jap Army*. Washington, D.C.: Infantry Journal, 1942.

Tolischus, Otto. *Through Japanese Eyes*. New York: Reynal & Hitchcok, 1945.

Tregaskis, Richard. *Guadalcanal Diary*. New York: Random House, 1943.

Tuana, Nancy, et al., eds. *Revealing Male Bodies*. Indianapolis: Indiana University Press, 2002.

Ueda, Reed. "The Changing Path to Citizenship: Ethnicity and Naturalization during World War II." In *The War in American Culture: Society and Consciousness during World War II*, ed. Lewis Erenberg and Susan Hirsch. Chicago: University of Chicago Press, 1996. 202–16.

Uris, Leon. *Battle Cry*. 1953. Reprint, New York: Bantam, 1962.

U.S. Atlantic Fleet. "Narrative Report of World War II and Korean Conflict Unknown Ceremonies." Norfolk, Va.: U.S. Atlantic Fleet, 1958.

U.S. Bureau of the Census. *The Statistical History of the United States: From Colonial Times to the Present*. Prepared by the United States Bureau of the Census. New York: Basic Books, 1976.

U.S. Congress. House. Committee on Military Affairs. *National Cemeteries and Evacuation and Repatriation of Remains of Persons Buried Outside Continental Limits of United States: Hearings before the Committee on Military Affairs on S524, H.R. 3650, and H.R. 3936*. 79th Congress. 1st sess., October 15 and 22, 1945.

U.S. Department of Defense. *The Unknowns of World War II and Korea*. Washington, D.C.: Government Printing Office, 1959.

U.S. Department of War. *Plan for the Repatriation of the Dead of World War II and Establishment of Permanent United States Military Cemeteries at Home and Abroad.* Washington, D.C.: Quartermaster General, War Department, 1945.

U.S. Federal Security Agency. *The CCC at Work: A Story of 2,500,000 Young Men.* Washington, D.C.: Government Printing Office, 1941.

Van Houten, John G. "The Interment of the Unknowns World War II and Korea." Washington, D.C.: Office of the Commanding General, 1958.

Vonnegut, Kurt. *Slaughterhouse-Five, or the Children's Crusade.* 1969. Reprint, New York: Bantam Doubleday Dell Publishing Group, 1991.

Wakefield, Wanda Ellen. *Playing to Win: Sports and the American Military, 1898–1945.* Albany: State University of New York Press, 1997.

Walker, Helen M. *The CCC Through the Eyes of 272 Boys: A summary of a group study of the reactions of 272 Cleveland boys to their experience in the Civilian Conservation Corps.* Cleveland: Western Reserve University Press, 1938.

Wallechinsky, David, ed. *The People's Almanac Presents the 20th Century.* New York: Little, Brown, 1995.

Warner, Rex. *Return of the Traveler.* New York: J. B. Lippincott, 1944.

Weingartner, James. "Trophies of War: U.S. Troops and the Mutilation of Japanese War Dead, 1941–1945." *Pacific Historical Review* 41 (1992): 53–67.

Weithas, Art, ed. *Close to Glory: The Untold Stories of WWII by the GIs Who Saw and Reported the War.* Austin, Tex.: Eakin Press, 1991.

Wheeler, Keith. *We Are the Wounded.* New York: E. P. Dutton, 1945.

Willett, John, comp. and trans. "Peroration of Speech at the Great German Art Exhibition, 1937." In *Art and Power: Europe Under the Dictators, 1930–45,* comp. Dawn Ades et al. London: Thames & Hudson, 1996. 338–39.

Williams, Patrick, and Laura Chrisman, eds. *Colonial Discourse and Post-Colonial Theory: A Reader.* New York: Columbia University Press, 1994.

Winter, Thomas. *Making Men, Making Class: The YMCA and Workingmen, 1877–1920.* Chicago: University of Chicago Press, 2002.

Wood, Edward, Jr. *On Being Wounded.* Golden, Colo.: Fulcrum Publishing, 1991.

Wooden, Howard. *American Art of the Great Depression: Two Sides of the Coin.* Wichita, Kans.: Wichita Art Museum, 1985.

Woodward, C. Vann. *The Strange Career of Jim Crow.* 3rd rev. ed. New York: Oxford University Press, 1974.

Wynn, Neil A. *The Afro-American and the Second World War.* Rev. ed. New York: Holmes & Meier, 1993.

Wyschogrod, Edith. *Spirit in Ashes: Hegel, Heidegger, and Man-made Mass Death.* New Haven: Yale University Press, 1985.

Young, James, ed. *The Art of Memory: Holocaust Memorials in History.* New York: Prestel, 1994.

Zeman, Zbynek. *Selling the War: Art and Propaganda in World War II.* New York: Exeter Books, 1978.

INDEX

Graham, F. W., 162
graves, registered, 159, 162
Gravity's Rainbow. See Pynchon, Thomas
Great Depression, 4, 10, 15–20, 186; effects on families, 198n4; labor movements during, 26; starvation during, 199n11; suicide during, 16; working women in, 18
Greenspan, Herbert, and John Campbell, 76
Grey, Frank, 136
Gropper, K. William, 26–28
Grosz, Elizabeth, 7, 89, 217n26
Guadalcanal, 44, 48, 128, 140, 164–65, 169
Guam, 125, 141
Gulf War, 189

Halsey, Margaret, 152; *Color Blind*, 144
Halstead, Francis, 35
Harper's, 18, 142
Hartmann, Susan, 102
Hass, Kristen, 159
health, nation's: and children's, 64, 67; during Great Depression, 19
Heller, Joseph, 190
Helton, Roy, 18–19
Henry, John, 50, 52
Hersey, John, 128–29
Hershey, Lewis, 60
Hickam Air Force Base, 181
Hill, Frank Ernest, 24
Hiroshima, bombing of, 128, 158
Hirsch, Susan, 121, 123
Hitler, Adolph, 19, 45–46, 80, 128, 149, 190
Holland, Kenneth, 24
Hollywood's War Activities Committee, 97
Holocaust, 121, 158; "hidden," 211n3; museums, 183, 217n26
homosexuality: banning in military, 73–74; clinical studies, 75; dishonorable discharge for, 77; screening for, 58, 73–75
hooks, bell, 120, 128
Hoover, Herbert, 32
Horsman, Reginald, 121
Howe, Louie, 30
Hudnut, Joseph, 156, 177

immigration: anti-Asian, 121; Chinese Exclusion Law, 122, 124; John-Reed Immigration Act, 122, 131, 137
impotence, 105–6
inductees: after basic training, 65–66; screening, 58–59
induction statistics, by race, 146
injuries. *See* wounds
Interment, Reports of, 161
internment of Japanese Americans, 84, 121, 123
interracial cooperation, 50
isolationism, 198n1
Iwo Jima: flag-raising, 3, 177–78

Janesch, Albert, 47
Japanese enemy, 8, 120, 121, 132–33, 140, 211n4, 212n12; changing representations of, 124–31; dehumanized, 128; and hunt metaphor, 129–30
Jeffords, Susan, 185, 217n1
Jews, social barriers to, 137
Jim Crow military, 5, 120, 146–55; dismantling of, 154
Jim Crow system, 122, 138, 149, 212n7; US attempt to export, 154
Johnson, Lyndon B., 189
Johnson-Reed Immigration Act (1924), 122, 131, 137
Jones, James, 96, 119, 130; *From Here to Eternity*, 72–73, 119; *Thin Red Line*, 96, 119–20, 130, 163, 164, 169, 172
Journal of Health and Physical Education, 64, 71
Journal of the American Medical Association (JAMA), 112

Kai-shek, Chiang, 134
Kantorowicz, Ernst, 29
Kimmel, Michael, 10, 16, 144
Knox, William, 149, 150, 152
Korean War, 179, 189
Kristeva, Julia, 88–89, 163–64
Ku Klux Klan, 122, 137

Lady Columbia, 35, 36 (illus.); feminine virtues, 201n33; history of, 37–38, 186
Lady Liberty, 35, 37 (illus.), 186; feminine virtues of, 38